SOUTHERN ARCHITECTURE

SOUTHERN ARCHITECTURE

350 Years of
Distinctive American Buildings

KENNETH SEVERENS

E. P. DUTTON   NEW YORK

Published in the United States by
Elsevier-Dutton Publishing Co., Inc.,
2 Park Avenue, New York, N.Y. 10016

Library of Congress Cataloging in Publication Data

Severens, Kenneth.
Southern architecture.

Includes bibliographical references.
1. Architecture—Southern States. I. Title.
NA720.S48 1981   720'.975   80-24727

ISBN: 0-525-20692-2

Published simultaneously in Canada by
Clarke, Irwin & Company Limited, Toronto and Vancouver

Designed by Mary Gale Moyes

10 9 8 7 6 5 4 3 2 1

First Edition

For Martha Severens

CONTENTS

LIST OF ILLUSTRATIONS

ACKNOWLEDGMENTS

For the buildings that still remain in private hands, I am grateful to the owners who have enthusiastically welcomed me. For those maintained by various organizations, I have great admiration for the dedicated individuals who open the buildings to the public and interpret the past through its material culture. Exceptionally helpful have been the staffs of three Charleston institutions—the Robert Scott Small Library at the College of Charleston, the Charleston Library Society, and the South Carolina Historical Society—as well as other libraries and archives throughout the South. To William Westfall I am especially indebted for his sensitive criticism of the manuscript, and to John Macrae, III, who first suggested this book and supported it throughout its revisions.

Charleston, South Carolina   KENNETH W. SEVERENS
January 1981

SOUTHERN ARCHITECTURE

CHAPTER ONE

THE DISTINCTNESS OF THE SOUTH AND ITS ARCHITECTURE

The South as a region of the United States has historical roots beginning with the first English settlements. Virginia was the name originally given by Sir Walter Raleigh to all that part of North America destined to become the thirteen colonies. In 1606, however, James I chartered two different joint-stock companies to promote, finance, and profit from the overseas venture; the Virginia Company of Plymouth was granted land between the thirty-eighth and forty-fifth parallels, while the Virginia Company of London received land farther south between the thirty-fourth and forty-first parallels. Although the boundaries were subsequently redrawn and royal governance replaced the joint-stock organization, the basis of geographical sectionalism had been established.

In the seventeenth century the differences between the northern colonies of New England and those of the South, despite the religious dissimilarity of Pilgrims and Puritans in the former and Anglicans in the latter, were mainly climatic and topographical. Whereas New England was hilly, rocky, and capable of sustaining only small farms, the area from the Chesapeake Bay to Spanish Florida contained broad expanses of land along wide, slow-moving rivers. Here the long growing season was well suited to large-scale agriculture, on land which contemporary observers occasionally described as a Garden of Eden. Gradually the South developed its distinctive plantations based on extensive landholdings, one-crop agriculture, and unfree labor. During the struggle for independence from England, however, the attitudes of the North and South were not rigidly fixed, nor did they prevail over the inexorable nationalism of all the states. Once peace was made with England in 1783, many Americans expected that confederacies would arise among the New England, middle, and southern states respectively. But the Constitutional Convention of 1787 established the basis for strong federal government. And the location in 1790 of the new national capital on the Potomac River was a compromise between North and South, the site being near the geographical center of the country.

The nineteenth century saw the evolution of a distinctively southern ideology based on the plantation system. To the traditional staple crops—tobacco, rice, and indigo—cotton was profitably added following the invention of the cotton gin in 1793. Seemingly unlimited possibilities for expansion and a worldwide market for cotton gave the southern planter the same sense of optimism which the yeoman farmer had with the opening of the Northwest Territory in 1785. By the denial of Spanish claims to parts of Alabama and Mississippi, the purchase of Louisiana from France in 1803, and the cession of Florida in 1819, the Deep South became part of the United States. But at the very moment when the future of the South appeared so promising, an irresolvable problem emerged. In Europe slavery was under attack as economically unsound and morally reprehensible. The South, requiring labor to work the new lands, embraced slavery as its "peculiar institution." Slavery as the central theme in antebellum history has been, and still is, controversial, but two conclusions are incontestable: it engendered in the North an impassioned attack on the South, and forced the South to defend slavery with equal fervor as a positive good. The collision of antislavery and proslavery apologists signified unequivocally that the South was a distinct section of the United States.

The Civil War can be interpreted as the ultimate test of southern uniqueness, and its outcome confirmed that the South was once more a part of the total American experience. But the sense that the Old South had disappeared enhanced the idea of southern distinctiveness, and in the process of romanticizing its culture a mythical society was described more often than the real one—a glamorized agrarianism presided over by chivalrous gentlemen and gracious ladies descended from the English nobility. However, in *The Mind of the South*, Wilbur Cash has argued cogently against this so-called Cavalier thesis. Most planters were simply successful farmers who through energy, acumen, and good fortune had surpassed their middle-class peers. The enormous expanse of land from the Chesapeake Bay to the Mississippi River offered genuine opportunities for the enterprising yeoman farmer to rise within the social structure. An ever-present phenomenon was the frontier—the area between civilization and wilderness—which produced planters in Tidewater Virginia and Low Country Carolina during the colonial period, and in the Deep South during the antebellum years. The legendary aristocratic planters were often just a generation removed from the frontier. In architecture the consequence of all this was the erection of plantation houses that expressed the sudden rise of an individual to the ranks of the landed gentry.

The plantation ideology itself tended to deny the uncertainties of frontier agriculture in favor of establishment and stability based on Old World models. Whereas the pioneers were adventurers, the planters were conservatives. Whereas the frontier respected only hard work and ingenuity, the plantation virtually freed the planter from physical labor.

Plantations were dispersed throughout the countryside, usually at great distances from each other. But the way of life they cultivated emphasized gregarious social arts more often associated with urban centers. The cities of the South were intimately related to the plantations as commercial ports through which the agricultural staples could be shipped and as cultural centers from which current fashions radiated to the interior.

Another manifestation of the tendency to romanticize the antebellum South is the belief that plantations yielded abundant wealth. In fact, planters led an economically tenuous existence. Dependence on staple crops was riskier than diversified agriculture, and rapid exhaustion of the soil, particularly by the growing of tobacco, often reversed a planter's fortune. Planters frequently needed loans between harvests, and they often used the crops growing in their fields as collateral. Consequently, very little hard cash was ever available. Even in Virginia, where colonial planters amassed landholdings of more than 100,000 acres, wealth was more fabulous than real. William Byrd II of Westover had debts throughout his life. By the time of the American Revolution, the Lees of Stratford Hall had shifted from tobacco cultivation to wheat and corn, which were grown increasingly by tenant farmers on their lands. George Washington left only a modest inheritance when he died in 1799, and in 1815 financial difficulties forced Thomas Jefferson to sell much of his prized library, despite his wish to give it to the University of Virginia. The wealth of South Carolina decreased in the nineteenth century as tariffs were raised; and the price of cotton fluctuated on the world market, adding economic uncertainty to the inherent risks of agriculture.

The construction of a great plantation house was not an inevitable development, but rather an act of will, whose aim was the establishment of a sense of place, conforming to the broad ideology of the plantation but at the same time staunchly individualistic. C. Vann Woodward, in *The Burden of Southern History*, speaks of Thornton Wilder's generalization of American temperament as tending toward abstraction, an emphasis on physical mobility, and an "indifference or . . . superiority to place, to locality, to environment," and goes on to say that it does not apply to the South. Rather, in the words of Robert Penn Warren, among southerners "the fear of abstraction" threatens the "massiveness of experience [and] the concreteness of life." Woodward concludes by quoting the Mississippi author Eudora Welty: "I am myself touched off by place. The place where I am and the place I know . . . are what set me to writing my stories." Southern plantations are "stories" about specific places, beginning with the history of the site and of the individual who transformed it from the natural state to profitable cultivation, and ultimately to the realm of art.

Sense of place is a dominant architectural characteristic of a remarkable number of great southern houses. Although patronage also led to the erection of churches and civic buildings, plantation houses as ancestral seats are the preeminent contributions of the South to American architecture. The distinguished houses in the North were often parsonages or the residences of prominent merchants. The former by definition could not be inherited, and the latter were subject to the vicissitudes of commercial affairs. Plantations, on the other hand, were meant to be passed down through the generations, and almost always were given distinctive names which emphasized their uniqueness as places. Furthermore, the natural siting in a rural environment allowed a plantation to become a world unto itself, rather than part of an ever-encroaching townscape— the situation in the North.

Although plantations occasionally existed in groups—along the James River in Virginia, in the Carolina Low Country, and on the lower Mississippi River—they generally were separated by great distances. Diversity was further encouraged by the states'-rights theory of government, which increasingly prevailed in the South. Yet, remarkable connections are to be found among widespread examples of plantation architecture. The monumental colonnaded porch of Mount Vernon became the hallmark of antebellum houses from Virginia to Louisiana. Thomas Jefferson offered advice and actual designs for about ten houses from Williamsburg to Louisville. Andrew Jackson's Hermitage responded to influences as disparate as Natchez and Mount Vernon. Plantation architecture bridged not only geography but also time, as a consequence of the relatively stable and enduring ideology that prevailed until the Civil War.

In *Gone with the Wind*, Margaret Mitchell vividly describes two plantations. The O'Haras' Tara "was built by slave labor, a clumsy sprawling building that crowned the rise of ground overlooking the green incline of pasture running down to the river. The old oaks, which had seen Indians pass under their limbs, hugged the house closely with their great trunks and towered their branches over the roof in dense shade. . . . The house had been built according to no architectural plan whatever, with extra rooms added where and when it seemed convenient." In contrast to Tara's organic and almost accidental quality was Twelve Oaks, the home of the Wilkes family. "The white house reared its perfect symmetry before her, tall of columns, wide of verandas, flat of roof, beautiful as a woman is beautiful who is so sure of her charm that she can be generous and gracious to all."

Few plantation houses were actually like Twelve Oaks. Most of them had the additive character and impure style of Tara, and were surrounded by a clutter of outbuildings. Between plantations, for miles, the buildings were ordinary and the scenery monotonous. Small subsistence farming was the overwhelming rule in the antebellum South. The proportion of white southerners belonging to "planter" families is estimated at no more than from 5 to 7 percent. Of all those who owned slaves, moreover, half had fewer than five. Only occasionally did a yeoman farmer build a house with architectural significance—a fact borne out by numerous travelers' descriptions and by such comments as those of Frederick Law Olmsted, the great American landscape architect, who wrote in 1856 that "hardly a poor woman's cow on [Cape Cod was] not better housed and more carefully provided for than a majority of the white people in Georgia."

The very small minority of planters who built elegant mansions exerted an inordinate influence on southern culture. High-style architecture generally expresses the established ideals which transcend simple, functional building. The conservatism implicit in the plantation ideology, calling as it did for stable conditions and fixed values amid a world of change, led to the preference for conventional forms, particularly those of classical architecture. As exemplary of almost the entire course of Western civilization, excepting only the Middle Ages, the classical styles conveyed a sense of timelessness, of being beyond specific historic circumstances. The historical definition of "southernness" is associated with the political issues of states' rights, nullification, secession, and Reconstruction; yet southern architecture in no way reflects these issues. Nor did the classical styles offer precise solutions to the problem of building in a subtropical climate. In their disregard of these apparent contradictions, planters indulged in their own kind of romanticism.

A recurring paradox in southern architecture is, then, the interrelation of classical forms and romantic meaning. Notwithstanding the South's early identity as a region, classicism and romanticism combined to impede the development of a truly indigenous architecture. Of those colonial plantation houses that achieved high style, nearly all have an ambience of self-conscious Englishness, or Frenchness in the case of Louisiana. After the United States became independent, however, classical architecture was favored as expressing the virtues of Roman republicanism and Greek democracy.

Southern buildings differ from those of the rest of the United States not so much because of style as because of that ambience most clearly evident in plantation houses. It is also apparent in the architecture of churches and colleges. Southern colonial churches, except for the French-speaking parts of the Deep South, were primarily Anglican and were accordingly built in emulation of English models, whose high style expressed the continuity of a state religion authorized and supported by the monarchy. The Anglican liturgy, performed in a traditional church building with conventional ecclesiastical furnishings, reinforced cultural roots. After the country became independent, religious diversity increased in the South, but because of the region's inherent conservatism, the established styles in church buildings were perpetuated. Southern colleges also manifest a cultural idealism, and, as a result of their location in a country setting or their landscaping, have escaped destruction through subsequent development. Of the ten colleges designated as National Historic Landmarks, seven are in the South, and no section of the country has been more influential than the South in campus planning.

Although the plantation ideology dominated southern culture, the South also produced distinguished cities, envisioned as works of art transcending utilitarian needs. In those of the North, with the exception of Philadelphia, growth was largely unplanned and often even unexpected. In contrast, Charleston, Annapolis, Williamsburg, New Orleans, and Savannah were both conceived and laid out in advance as commercial, political, and cultural centers. Once established, they became the places where elegant townhouses as well as vernacular architecture flourished. Today, historic southern cities retain the appearance of their past far more abundantly than their counterparts in the North, and they serve as exemplars of the currently growing conviction that humane urban environments are fundamental to American society.

Because of the geographical expanse of the South and the traditionalism of its culture, a strictly chronological survey of buildings is neither possible nor desirable. Stylistic periods, such as Georgian, Federal, Greek Revival, and Victorian, frequently overlap, and within any given period a number of freely designed regional adaptations, rather than pure examples of a particular style, are to be found. Throughout the colonial and antebellum periods, what was fashionable along the older coastal settlements usually appeared in the upcountry or trans-Appalachian area a generation later. Accordingly, it becomes appropriate to approach southern architecture by way of the major categories of building—cities, plantations, churches, and colleges. Chronological order within each category has been observed, so as to set forth the evolving nature of southern society. Even more significant, however, are the dominant themes which transcend time and space. The early chapters of this book will trace the development of cities, plantations, and churches from their colonial origins to the outbreak of the Civil War. The middle section will take up more specific themes of the postrevolutionary and antebellum periods, when southern distinctiveness became undeniable. The final chapters treat the architecture of the New South and the preservation of the South's great architectural heritage.

Whenever possible, the buildings will be presented through the descriptions of contemporary observers and illustrated with early views. Today, southern architecture is all too frequently encountered in the form either of historic houses set aside as museums or of restored residential neighborhoods. The tendencies of the former to suspend living processes at a particular moment in time, and of the latter to give the impression of living in the past, both need to be tempered by the reality of each building's original circumstances, and of each builder's aspirations. A southern building can be fully understood only when its unique story is re-created, including how it survived to the present.

The persistent sectional strife during the antebellum period and the calamitous defeat in the Civil War subjected the South to a confrontation with history whose directness is unparalleled elsewhere in America. Hardly any public event was independent of the defense of the "peculiar institution," or the reorganization of society during and after Reconstruction. The compelling force of history led naturally to the emergence in the South of many of the initial efforts to commemorate historic places.

The preservation of sites associated with southern history, and particularly its leaders, followed inevitably from the southern experience itself. In the *Charleston Mercury* for December 2, 1853, Ann Pamela Cunningham addressed the "Ladies of the South" with a rationale for saving Mount Vernon from deterioration and desecration: "A descendant of Virginia, and now a daughter of Carolina, moved by feelings of reverence for departed greatness and goodness, by patriotism and a sense of national, and above all, of Southern honor, ventures to appeal to you in behalf of the 'home and grave' of Washington." Toward the end of this decidedly sectional appeal, the specter of the approaching Civil War is evoked: "And should there ever be again 'times to try men's souls,' there will be found among and of you, as of old, heroines, superior to fear and selfish consideration, acting for country and its honor." The movement to preserve Mount Vernon, consummated in 1858 with the founding of the Mount Vernon Ladies' Association, linked the future of Mount Vernon with the inviolate honor and virtue of the South.

Not all such efforts were successful. After Henry Clay died in 1852, his son James B. Clay purchased Ashland, the family home on the outskirts of Lexington, Kentucky, and rebuilt it in a thoroughly Victorian manner. Newspapers across the country castigated the "young gentleman who tore down the old mansion of his immortal father, instead of leaving it to be resorted to and gazed on with emotions of reverential awe by the men of future generations." Andrew Jackson was more perspicacious; he willed the Hermitage to his adopted son with the understanding that if the property ever had to be sold, it should be offered first to the state of Tennessee. That in fact occurred in 1856, and the state legislature authorized the purchase, proclaiming that government should "inculcate sentiments of veneration for those departed heroes who have rendered important services to their country." It was proposed that the Hermitage and its 500 acres be developed as a southern branch of the United States Military Academy. The late 1850s were not propitious years for the federal government to establish a military school in the South, however, and consequently the Hermitage was not really preserved for the public until 1889, when the Ladies' Hermitage Association was organized.

Robert E. Lee's home, Arlington, is the epitome of the historic house affected by sectional strife. Situated across the Potomac River from the city of Washington, it was seized by federal troops in 1861. According to a persistent rumor, Secretary of War Edwin Stanton was determined not to allow the Lees to return. To ensure that they did not, a National Cemetery was established on the property in 1864, incorporating a few graves so near the house as to be distasteful to the Lees. Not until 1883 did the federal government acquire undisputed title to the property, and up until 1925 continuing bitterness prevented the restoration of the house to the way it had been when the Lees lived in it.

As the early preservation efforts show, the consciousness of southern distinctiveness that culminated in the Civil War had an influence on the survival of southern architecture. Although the warfare itself caused more destruction than any other single factor, southern buildings survived in considerable numbers after the Civil War because economic stagnation precluded the development of highly urbanized and industrialized metropolises like those of the Northeast and Midwest. The association of architecture with sectional strife gave such buildings the character of a legacy for the twentieth century, when preservation projects often assumed the zeal of crusades. Following World War I, when prosperity increasingly brought visitors to the South from other sections of the country, it became all too easy to acquire for a collector, or even a museum, the paneling of a Georgian house. Throughout the South this threat was vigorously countered by the work of preservation societies, and by the establishment of protected historic districts through zoning ordinances.

Individual buildings were saved as well as whole neighborhoods restored—Ansonborough in Charleston, the Lower Garden District in New Orleans, and the Victorian District in Savannah. The desire to maintain relatively homogeneous residential areas has nurtured the continuity of living, albeit in environments where modern technology is superimposed on traditional patterns. Preserved and restored houses offer sublime opportunities to root contemporary life in place and time. Southern buildings were erected to ennoble ideals, men, and sites; and they still serve the purposes that emanate from their historic origins.

CHAPTER TWO

FROM FRONTIER SETTLEMENTS TO URBANE CITIES

Southern cities were often designed as such from the start, whereas northern settlements evolved into cities with less conscious planning. Most Massachusetts Bay towns were primarily agricultural; Boston, identified early as a port, developed organically rather than according to a formal plan. New Haven, the most regular of New England towns, consisted of a square grid divided into nine identical blocks, whose large size gave them a rural rather than an urban flavor. New York began as a small fortified garrison whose function was to protect Dutch fur trading interests in the Hudson River valley. Even Philadelphia, which came rapidly to manifest truly urban aspirations, was originally envisioned by William Penn as a "greene country towne," where traditional rural values were to be sustained by communal organization.

JAMESTOWN, VIRGINIA

The first permanent English settlement in the western hemisphere was not urban in plan, nor did it grow into a city. In 1607 one hundred settlers reached the Virginia coast and chose a site 30 miles inland on the James River. The Virginia Company of London, which promoted the venture, instructed the colonists to build first a storehouse and then an orderly town: "It shall be advisably done to set your houses even and by a line, that your streets may have a good breadth, and be carried square about your market place."[1] By 1610, according to a surviving description, the settlers had built a triangular palisade, enclosing a central area that contained a marketplace, storehouse, guardhouse, and chapel. The houses were "as yet in no great uniformity, either for the fashion, or beauty of

9

the street." Jamestown four years later, when the settlement began to gain a sound footing, progressed to "a handsome form [with] two fair rows of houses, all of framed timber, two stories, . . . besides three large and substantial storehouses, . . . [and outside the palisade] some very pleasant and beautiful houses, two block houses . . . and certain other farm houses."

Optimism about the emergence of a significant town was, however, short-lived, since the course of Virginia's development was set in 1612 when tobacco cultivation was introduced. Within a decade, what had begun as a group of adventurers in search of mineral wealth was on its way to becoming a plantation economy based on large landholdings. As a port for the shipment of tobacco to England, Jamestown was no better situated than any of several other towns that had sprung up along the James River. The Virginia Company still directed that "houses and buildings be so contrived together, as may make if not handsome towns, yet compact and orderly villages." But Jamestown in 1617 had tobacco growing in its streets and open spaces. Two years later the first shipload of Negroes arrived, and the distribution of land in large parcels began soon afterward. Following the initial instructions on establishing a town, there were several attempts at expanding outside the triangular palisade, as well as efforts to make house lots available at modest costs. But Jamestown simply did not grow. It remained the colonial capital until 1699, a stagnating, architecturally undistinguished village of about one hundred inhabitants. Today the site of the original settlement cannot even be seen, having long ago been obliterated by erosion along the banks of the James River.

CHARLESTON, SOUTH CAROLINA

Carolina was established in 1663, when Charles II granted to eight noblemen the territory south of Virginia and north of Spanish Florida. The colony was based on a quasi-feudal constitution which John Locke wrote in collaboration with Lord Ashley-Cooper, one of the primary proprietors. Plantations similar to those of Barbados in the British Indies, as well as those which were developing in Virginia, were envisioned, to be served by a "great port town." In 1670 the first settlers arrived at Albemarle Point, just across from the peninsula formed by the Ashley and Cooper rivers, which together form one of the finest natural harbors on the Atlantic coast, with landing places for oceangoing ships, favorable locations for shipbuilding, and opportunities for developing a fishing industry. Because of marshy ground, the initial location of the settlement proved to be unhealthful, as well as unsuited to the development of a

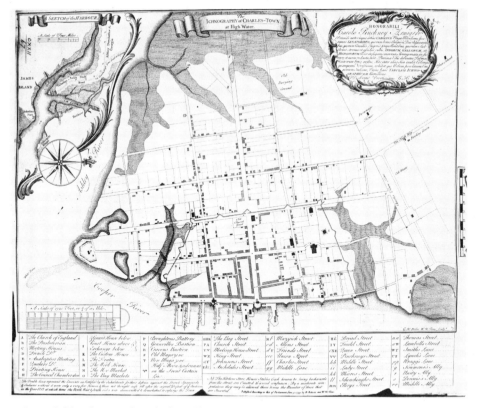

Plan of Charleston, South Carolina: 1739. By 1739 the city had expanded outside the original fortifications, and conforming to the proprietors' initial instructions, two major streets intersected at a central civic square. (Library of Congress.)

large town, and within a year a new site was being sought. The proprietors, none of whom ever came to Carolina, oversaw the undertaking from England and from Barbados, frequently giving such instructions as these: "When the place for the town is chosen, the surveyor shall lay out streets according to the model herewith sent as near as the particular situation of the place will admit."[2] Lord Ashley-Cooper himself offered more specific advice:

> It is necessary that you lay out the *great port town* [italics mine] into regular streets for be the buildings never so mean and thin at first yet as the town increases in riches and people the void spaces will be filled up and the buildings will grow more beautiful. If you design six score squares of 300 foot each to be divided one from the other by streets and alleys it will be a good proportion of a town. . . . Your great street cannot be less than one hundred or six score broad, your lesser streets none under sixty, your alleys eight or ten foot. A palisade round the town with a small ditch is a sufficient fortification against the Indians. . . . We desire you would use your endeavor to

have the streets laid out as large, orderly, and convenient as possible, and when that is done the houses which shall hereafter be built on each side those designed streets, will grow in beauty with the trade and riches of the town. To prevent the like inconvenience hereafter I desire you would be early enough in choosing a place and laying out the model of an exact regular town. . . . Charles Towne we intend for the port town where we will oblige all ships to unload all their goods and to take in all their loading.

When Charleston was actually platted in 1680, these instructions were generally heeded, although the size of the town and the width of the streets were both somewhat reduced. Four streets, 60 feet wide, converged at a square covering two acres, and a public wharf, also 60 feet wide, was laid out along the Cooper River. The layout on a grid with a central square appears to have drawn on, in simplified form, several of the plans for rebuilding London after the great fire of 1666, and was similar as well to the plan of Londonderry in northern Ireland, a town platted by the English as a colonial outpost in the early seventeenth cen-

"Single Houses" on Church Street, Charleston, South Carolina: c. 1760 and 1807. Charleston's remarkably homogeneous streetscapes are to a considerable degree the result of "single houses," built to interrelate with each other as well as to respond to the subtropical climate.

tury. A plan of Charleston in 1704 shows that the grid was imposed on the peninsula with little regard for the topography of creeks and marshes, with eight somewhat irregular blocks enclosed within a system of fortifications. Development was most dense along the harbor street on the Cooper River, and two blocks had by then been subdivided by alleys. By 1739, when another plan was made, the fortifications had been dismantled and the streets extended southward, westward, and northward. The intersection of the two main streets still revealed the original intention of building around a public square, but already a market building encroached upon the space, and public buildings were erected in each of its corners by the end of the century.

Further manifesting the urban character of Charleston is the "single house," the city's most distinctive contribution to American domestic architecture. It is rectangular in plan, with the short side fronting directly on the street. A central hallway/stairway divides the interior into two rooms, to give, in the typical three-story elevation, a house of six rooms. In the eighteenth century the entrance might be either on the street façade or on the long side; some houses had both. By the time of the American Revolution, piazzas had been added, providing the final feature of the "single house." A door on the street led onto the piazza and down the long side to a central doorway through which the house was entered.

As an example of vernacular architecture with analogies to buildings in the West Indies, the "single house" was a creative response to indigenous factors. As the demand for houses increased, lots were subdivided; and since the blocks were so large, these new lots tended to be rectangular, with minimal frontage on the street and considerable depth into the block. This circumstance, coupled with the practice of taxing a property owner on the street width of his structure, reinforced the advantages of the "single house" plan. One room wide, the house grew tall in proportion, allowing the most formal entertaining room to be located on the second floor where it could be effectively ventilated by breezes. The piazza on the south or west was oriented to the prevailing summer breeze, and eighteenth-century visitors were most impressed by this feature:

Most of the houses are of brick, three stories high, some of them elegant, and all neat habitations; within they are genteely [sic] furnished, and without exposed as much as possible to the refreshing breezes from the sea. Many of them are indeed encumbered with balconies and piazzas, but these are found convenient and even necessary during the hot season.[3]

Everything peculiar to the buildings of this place is formed to moderate the excessive heats; the windows are open, the doors pass through both sides of the houses. Every endeavor is used to refresh the apartments within with fresh air. Large galleries are formed to shelter the upper part of the house from the force of the sun's rays. . . . In Charleston persons vie with one another, not who shall have the finest, but who the coolest house.[4]

The "single house" is a curious architectural phenomenon created by anonymous master builders rather than architects. Gaunt in its verticality and eccentric in its asymmetry, it is meaningful only *in situ.* Depending on the orientation of the street, the north or east wall was placed near the lot line and had few window openings; the chimneys were usually part of this wall, and the close proximity to the neighboring house led to a virtually unbroken surface to provide privacy from house to house. In contrast, the south or west wall was open with windows, piazzas, and gardens. A "single house" in isolation on a spacious lot would be a peculiar anomaly, but in context it is a remarkably sensitive adaptation to historical and environmental circumstances. One of the strongest arguments for preservation in Charleston has been the integrity of streetscapes, which resulted in part from continuous building of "single houses" into the twentieth century. Various styles, such as Georgian, Federal, Greek Revival, and Victorian, can be distinguished in the treatment of the classical orders of the piazzas and the interior ornamentation. But the "single house" as a vernacular type has transcended the vicissitudes of climate, taste, and prosperity.

ANNAPOLIS, MARYLAND

In 1694, soon after Francis Nicholson became governor of Maryland, Arundel Towne was founded at the mouth of the Severn River on Chesapeake Bay. Later that year the town was designated the capital of Maryland, and its name was changed to Annapolis.[5] Nicholson had just returned from London, where he apparently had become familiar with the various plans for rebuilding after the fire of 1666. The plan of Annapolis features a "Public Circle," more than 520 feet in diameter; a "Church Circle" over 300 feet across; "Bloomsbury Square," 350 feet on a side; and a "Market Place," 125 feet per side. In addition to a rectangular grid of streets, diagonal avenues radiate from the circle in an ostentatious manner belying the modest size of the area that was actually platted. Less conservative than Charleston, Annapolis reflected the bolder London plans of Christopher Wren and John Evelyn, both of whom Nicholson may have known. The Baroque planning principles of Wren and Evelyn were a formal yet complicated fusion of distinct elements: a regular grid, radial avenues from varied and imposing open spaces, and the placement of major buildings to terminate street vistas. At Annapolis these principles appear not to have been fully understood, since the radiating avenues do not emanate from the centers of the circles—though the anomaly may have come from adjusting the plan to an uneven terrain. Also, the four urban spaces seem overly pretentious for the realities of a colonial capital. Nevertheless, Annapolis was based on the Baroque notion of an entire city as a unified work of art.

Unlike the "great port town" of Charleston, Annapolis grew slowly into a political and cultural center, rather than an economic metropolis. It became a place where planters enjoyed an increasingly aristocratic society, as an English visitor observed in 1769:

> At present, this city has more the appearance of an agreeable village, than the metropolis of an opulent province. . . . But in a few years, it will probably be one of the best built cities in America. . . . It is the seat of government; the public offices are here established; and as many of the principal families have chosen this place for their residence, there are few towns of the same size in any part of the British dominions, that can boast a more polished society.[6]

Because it remained the capital even though commercial development largely passed it by, Annapolis has retained its historic ambience of large houses with landscaped gardens interspersed among more modest row houses. Three successive statehouses were built on the larger circle, and the present structure of 1772–1779 is the oldest state capitol still used for its original purpose. Its dome is the most prominent feature of the townscape, relating in shape to the circle and crowning the highest site. Like the overall plan, it reveals colonial aspirations rather than English sophistication in its pretentious attempt at monumentality (based ultimately on Wren's Baroque masterpiece, St. Paul's Cathedral in London). Three churches of St. Anne were erected on the smaller circle, the present one dating from the mid-nineteenth century. Bloomsbury Square never really developed as the intended residential quarter for artisans, nor did the Market Place, which was arbitrarily located too far from the commercial activity of the harbor.

WILLIAMSBURG, VIRGINIA

The will and talents of Francis Nicholson, one of the ablest of colonial administrators, showed themselves as well in the planning of Williamsburg, begun in the early 1690s with the establishment of the College of William and Mary. As envisioned by its promoters—notably the Reverend James Blair, the commissary of the Bishop of London in Virginia, along with Nicholson, who was then lieutenant governor of the colony—this multipurpose institution was to include a seminary to train Anglican

1. Front View of the State-House &c. *at* ANNAPOLIS *the Capital of* MARYLAND.

*View of the Statehouse, Annapolis, Maryland: 1789. The "Public Circle" of
the Annapolis plan was sited on a promontory with a commanding view,
leading to an ambitious provincial version of English Baroque for the
statehouse.* (Columbian Magazine, *1789, Library of Congress*)

ministers, a college for the liberal arts, a grammar school for the teaching
of Latin and Greek, and an Indian school. In 1693 the English monarchs,
William and Mary, granted it a charter, specifying that support for the
college was to come from quitrents, taxes on exported tobacco, fees from
the surveyor-general's office, and an outright gift of 20,000 acres of land.
The general assembly of Virginia chose Middle Plantation (halfway between the James and the York rivers) as the site and stipulated that the
college should be built as near Bruton Parish Church as convenient.
Since the colonial capital remained at Jamestown, the college at this stage
was somewhat analogous to Oxford and Cambridge in its rural location,
away from an urban or governmental center.

In 1698, after his tenure as governor of Maryland, Nicholson returned to Virginia as governor and immediately began to make Middle
Plantation the colonial capital. Jamestown simply had not grown into a
town of elegance sufficient for a royal governor from England who had
just planned Annapolis with an ambitious Baroque design. Moreover, the
planters who composed the assembly, and who were devoting increasing
attention to the social arts, envisioned a more aristocratic setting where
they could congregate as members of the landed gentry. Twenty years
before, Jamestown had been badly damaged during Bacon's Rebellion,
and the assembly had met for a time at Middle Plantation, which offered
higher, and hence healthier, ground, and whose population was exceeded
only by that of Jamestown. It was, however, the College of William and

Mary that argued most persuasively for the shift of location. During the debate over the move, a student, undoubtedly influenced by the faculty, contended that the college should not remain in rural isolation, but instead should be surrounded by worldly affairs:

> Every one knows it would be a great assistance to the College, if we had the conveniency of a good market, whereby either the College itself might be enabled to keep houses, or the neighbors about this place might be better supplied with all things necessary for our good lodging and diet. . . . Another great benefit to the students at this place, would be the conveniency of good company and conversation; for in such a retired corner of the world, far from business, and action, if we make scholars, they are in danger of proving mere scholars, which make a very ridiculous figure: made up of pedantry, disputatiousness, positiveness, and a great many other ill qualities which render them not so fit for action and conversation. . . . Now there is one way of procuring for us both these conveniencies, that is by contriving a good town at this place, and filling it with all the selectest and best company that is to be had within the government. Providence has put into your hands a way of compassing this, . . . namely the building of the statehouse, which alone will be attended with the seat of government, offices, markets, good company, and all the rest. . . . The College will help to make the town. . . . There is one thing perhaps worthy of our consideration, that is, that by this method we have an opportunity not only of making a town, but such a town as may equal if not outdo Boston, New York, Philadelphia, Charleston, and Annapolis; and consequently such a town as may retrieve the reputation of our country, which has suffered by nothing so much as by neglecting a seat of trade, wealth, and learning.[7]

Thus the legislation enacted in 1699 to move the capital to Middle Plantation (whose name was changed in that year to Williamsburg) had as its underlying rationale an urban ideal in this least likely of American colonies.[8] The plantation system had led to a dispersal of population. The market for tobacco had made these plantations prosperous, but many features of English civilization had been sacrificed—namely, military protection, communal religion, and cultural endeavors. Although throughout the seventeenth century efforts had been directed toward the establishment of towns, even in the most populous, Jamestown, no commercial activity had emerged to stimulate its growth. But whereas the economic reasons for town life were not compelling, the cultural ones were, given the planters' increasing wealth and leisure.

Williamsburg was an idealistic attempt at founding a fountainhead of civilization amid the sparsely populated agrarian countryside. The legislation that established the new provincial capital called for "a healthy, proper, and commodious place, suitable for the reception of a considerable number and concourse of people, that of necessity must resort to the place where the general assemblies will be convened, and where the council and supreme court of justice for his majesty's colony and dominion will be held and kept."[9] The major street, to be named for the Duke of Gloucester, was to be 99 feet wide (considerably wider than the main streets of Charleston), and to run three-quarters of a mile from the College of William and Mary to the Capitol itself. Bruton Parish Church and a market square were located near the midpoint of the street, and next to the church a secondary axis at right angles to Duke of Gloucester Street led to the Governor's Palace. The plan thus envisioned three dominant institutions—the seat of royal government, the provincial capitol, and the college—as its extremities. No other colonial capital was planned so specifically to link and at the same time maintain the separateness of the bodies of political authority. That the ascendancy of Virginia in the foundation of the United States may indeed owe something to the setting of its capital appears likely; clearly, in the planning of the federal capital at Washington, the placement of the White House and the Capitol followed that of the Governor's Palace and the Capitol at Williamsburg.

Two early descriptions mention that Nicholson laid out Williamsburg "in the form of a cipher, made of W and M," representing the initials of William and Mary. Since the earliest plans have not survived, it is now difficult to locate either initial in the actual design; it has been suggested, however, that the ciphers of the original plan occurred at the Capitol and the market square respectively.[10] The mention of the cipher indicates that Williamsburg was conceived as a work of art, in which the ceremonial context was as important as the actual urban functions. Furthermore, the plan reveals a subtle but effective zoning: Bruton Parish Church is the center of the residential quarter, with the governmental sector with its shops, taverns, and inns lying to the east of the market square. The effect of Duke of Gloucester Street, three-quarters of a mile of buildings set close together and at a uniform distance back from the street, was emphatically urban. On the other hand, its great width and that of the treelined Palace Green, more than 200 feet across, gave a parklike ambience to the primary and secondary axes. Williamsburg was a city in theory, style, and manners, but the setting amid the natural and cultivated landscape gave its architecture the look of stage scenery.

The urban aspirations of the plan are best seen in the major structures, which were the first colonial buildings to be compared favorably by anyone with those of the mother country. According to Hugh Jones, rector of the church in Jamestown and also professor of mathematics at the College of William and Mary from 1716 to 1721, Williamsburg was a "delightful, healthful, and thriving city" where people "live in the same neat manner, dress after the same modes, and behave themselves exactly as the gentry in London," and whose buildings were "justly reputed the best in all the English America, and are exceeded by few of their kind in England."[11] Jones attributed to Christopher Wren the original idea for the main college building, which was then "adapted to the nature of the country by the gentlemen there." As surveyor-general of the King's

Works, Wren might indeed have contributed to the project, the college being a royal foundation. The first design, whatever its source, was nevertheless revised by the trustees in Virginia. Jones also noted that the building, begun in 1695, had been destroyed by fire ten years later, and that the second building (erected between 1709 and 1716) was architecturally more ambitious. In fact, its plan was similar to the old one, since the original foundations were reused. The addition of a projecting and pedimented central bay may account for Jones's assertion that the renovated structure was "not altogether unlike Chelsea Hospital," one of Wren's major commissions. By attributing a colonial building to the greatest English architect of the time and by identifying a specific London parallel, Jones recognized that high-style architecture accompanied the planning of Williamsburg.

Jones was no less enthusiastic about the other buildings. The Capitol was "noble, beautiful, and . . . the best and most commodious pile of its kind that I have seen or heard of." The Governor's Palace was "a magnificent structure . . . finished and beautiful with gates, fine gardens,

Views of the major buildings of Williamsburg, Virginia: c. 1737. The upper register shows the College of William and Mary with the Brafferton School for Indians and the President's House on either side of the "Wren" Building. Below from left to right are the Capitol, the back of the "Wren" Building, and the Governor's Palace. ("Bodleian Plate," formerly in the Bodleian Library at Oxford and now part of the collections of the Colonial Williamsburg Foundation. Library of Congress.)

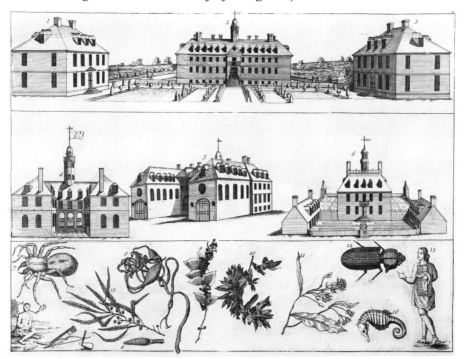

offices, walks, a fine canal, orchards, etc." Bruton Parish Church was "a large strong piece of brickwork in the form of a cross, nicely regular and convenient, and adorned as the best churches in London." The Williamsburg style of architecture featured symmetrical brick façades, crisply articulated and relatively unornamented door and window openings, and steep integrating roofs surmounted by lanterns and cupolas. Most of the details became hallmarks of colonial Georgian—America's first consciously homogeneous architecture.

Williamsburg remained the epitome of urbanity throughout the colonial period. Virginia, a failure in establishing towns, had paradoxically succeeded in conceptualizing a city, albeit one with a very special purpose. However, the economic development that might have transformed Williamsburg from a symbolic image into an urban reality never took place, and in 1779 the General Assembly approved the moving of the capital to Richmond. Thus the life of the most unusual of colonial capitals quietly came to an end, and Williamsburg slumbered for 150 years, to be resurrected in the 1920s as America's most ambitious and influential restoration project.

SAVANNAH, GEORGIA

Whereas Annapolis and Williamsburg were attempts at high-style urbanity, neither of which grew into a city in the economic sense, Savannah began as the center of the least sophisticated of the English colonies and later developed into a major city. Georgia, as the southern part of the territory controlled by the Carolina proprietors until 1720 when South Carolina became a royal colony, was conveyed by George II to a group led by James Oglethorpe in 1732. The colony was envisioned as serving several ends: besides affording defense to the English colonies against Spanish Florida, it was to be a humanitarian refuge for debtors and others who had little chance for advancement in England, a haven for Continental Protestants, a missionary post from which to Christianize the Indians, a moral utopia based on a republican model, and a mercantile enterprise for the appointed trustees.

In 1733, Oglethorpe brought his 114 settlers to Georgia and chose a bluff above the Savannah River, 10 miles inland, as the site for the provincial capital. The town that was platted, as shown in an engraving of 1734, had the regularity and uniformity of a military outpost. Based on a modular square unit consisting of town lots measuring 60 by 90 feet for individual residences, with trustee lots measuring 60 by 180 feet for public buildings, and open space in the center, the plan reflected a system of land tenure which integrated city and country.[12] Each settler received a town lot and, outside the fortifications, a garden lot of 5 acres and a farm of 44 acres—allotments resembling those practices of a New England town. The regulations prevented a colonist from either acquiring more land or subdividing his share. Even the trustees were not permitted to amass large landholdings, and slavery was prohibited. Thus Georgia, despite topography and climate very similar to South Carolina across the Savannah River, was decidedly antiplantation in theory.

But Savannah was no less ambitious in its planning than Annapolis and Williamsburg. As a military outpost, it was fortified like the English settlements in northern Ireland (and as Charleston had been in its early years). The quadrangular module also had affinities with a Roman military camp. Of equal importance, however, were the development of London squares and the plans of Richard Newcourt and Robert Hooke for the rebuilding of London. Moreover, since the surrounding land was controlled by the trustees rather than held in private ownership, the Savannah plan could be easily extended—as it was in the second half of the eighteenth century when the mission of the colony was redefined.

The engraving of 1734 shows four wards (or modules) on which about ninety town lots contained uniformly built one-story houses, whose simplicity and austerity reflected the virtues of yeoman farming in a communal environment. On three of the trustee lots were buildings identified as, respectively, a public mill, an inn for strangers, and a storehouse. The fourth lot in the same ward was designated as the location for a church. The squares were to be used for markets, as drill fields for the militia, and as places of public assembly. However, by 1750, when the initial charter had nearly run its twenty-one-year course, Georgia had begun to change from the distinctive colony conceived by the trustees to one that was more "southern." The prohibition against slavery had ended, and large plantations were emerging; Georgia was becoming similar to South Carolina.

Nevertheless, the Savannah plan remained viable even though its initial purpose had been superseded. Oglethorpe had chosen an advantageous site, which naturally zoned the riverfront from the residential quarter on top of the bluff. Prosperity after the American Revolution encouraged architectural aspirations: dignified three-story row houses were built on the town lots, and elegant mansions rose on the empty trustee lots. The scale and artistic pretensions had changed, but the overall plan was respected. The open spaces were landscaped to offer natural beauty and shade, a decided improvement over the newly cleared land shown in 1734. The contrast between that view and one of 1855 records how Savannah had evolved from an agricultural and military outpost to a picturesque cityscape for the affluent. The great landscape architect Frederick Law Olmsted wrote in 1856 of Savannah's special quality:

Savannah has a curiously rural and modest aspect, for a place of its population and commerce. A very large proportion of the buildings stand detached from each other, and are surrounded by gardens, or courts, shaded by trees, or occupied by shrubbery. There are a great number of small public squares, and some of the streets are double with rows of trees in the center.[13]

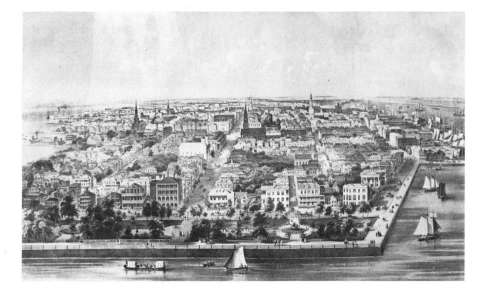

*View of Charleston, South Carolina: 1851. Mid-nineteenth-century
Charleston displayed a masterful integration of extensive port facilities along
the Cooper River, street-oriented houses with private gardens at the side or
rear, and numerous churches interspersed throughout the cityscape. (Drawn
by J. W. Hill, lithography by Smith & Smith: 1851. Carolina Art
Association.)*

Savannah, just 100 miles south of Charleston, has no "single
houses," despite urban density and climatic conditions that might have
recommended a similar structure. That Savannah's domestic architecture
was not so well adapted to the climate as Charleston's was the conclusion,
at least, of several nineteenth-century visitors; but no one can question its
sensitive relationship to the overall plan. This is the true meaning of vernacular architecture: a blending of historical, environmental, and cultural
factors to produce an urban ambience no less distinctive than that of the
outlying plantations.

As port cities, Charleston and Savannah have both retained their
distinctiveness. Charleston is less modular, and its open spaces are largely
restricted to private gardens on the sides of "single houses" and the backs
of larger houses. The result is a prevailing sense of tranquillity, even
though many of the residential streets are very near those devoted to
business and the professions. The gardens of Savannah have a more public character, since they are located in the squares, and a typical block
tends to combine institutions such as churches with row houses and freestanding mansions. The organization is more formal, with the characteristic squares regularly repeated over the entire area of the antebellum
city.

The colonial cities of the South, far more than those in any other
section of the country, have retained their historic character. As compared to the integrity of the cityscape at Annapolis, Williamsburg,

View of Savannah, Georgia: 1856. The squares platted by Oglethorpe developed into public gardens surrounded by residences, with churches and civic buildings on the trustee lots. (Drawn by J. W. Hill, lithograph by Endicott & Company: 1856. Georgia Historical Society.)

Charleston, and Savannah, in such northern cities as Boston, New Haven, New York, and Philadelphia, the surviving structures from the colonial period and the early nineteenth century are a small proportion of the whole, widely scattered, or juxtaposed to more modern buildings often of an unsympathetic character and scale. Southern urbanism thus reveals a twofold anomaly: the emergence of cities in the geographical area where the plantation system was dominant, and the distinctiveness of each city from the other. Annapolis and Williamsburg emerged from a like desire to establish a political and cultural seat, but the plans were significantly different. By the nineteenth century Charleston and Savannah functioned similarly as port cities for the shipment of the staple crops of rice and cotton respectively. Few in number but grand in aspirations, these southern cities were conceived as works of art, designed to serve the plantation economy but also to remedy the cultural deprivations implicit in that system. Hence they looked ambitiously to London, rather than to one another, for ideological sources. With the exception of Savannah, whose initial settlers were humble Englishmen, Jamestown, Charleston, Annapolis, and Williamsburg are all named for English monarchs (as are most of the southern colonies as well). To a considerable extent the self-consciousness and pretension that aimed at establishing New World but thoroughly English seats explain the uniqueness of southern cities.

SPANISH FLORIDA
AND FRENCH LOUISIANA

English colonialism had no part in developing the territory from Florida to Louisiana. In 1565 five Spanish ships with 500 soldiers, 200 sailors, and 100 noncombatants arrived at a site that was named for St. Augustine, with the primary objective of safeguarding the passage of treasure ships and of preventing the French from gaining a foothold in Florida.[14] A fortress was erected to command the entrance to the harbor, but the location was not particularly advantageous for defense, for missionary activity with the Indians, or for a thriving permanent settlement. St. Augustine survived largely because the Spanish had neither the initiative nor the money to move to a more promising site, but also no desire to give up their only real settlement on the Atlantic coast of North America. By 1770, after two hundred years of slow growth, St. Augustine in typical Spanish fashion revolved about a plaza where the church, guardhouse, and governor's house stood. Two-story houses whose lower walls were of coquina limestone, with wood-frame construction above, fronted directly on the streets and had spacious gardens to the rear. Shutters on windows, projecting balconies, and brightly colored surfaces gave a Mediterranean ambience whose counterpart may be found in British West Indian architecture.

Although France colonized Canada mainly with forts and trading posts, establishing relatively few permanent settlements, her territorial ambitions were extravagant. Fort Louis, founded on Mobile Bay in 1702, was intended to guard the entrance to the Mississippi River, to be the commercial meeting place with the Indians south of the Great Lakes, and to at least restrict the English colonies to the Atlantic seaboard, if not drive them from North America altogether. Fort Louis, which served as the capital of Louisiana, was inundated by a flood in 1710, and the following year the French relocated their settlement at the mouth of the Mobile River. The plan featured a fortification with governor's house, storehouse, and guardhouse, a central *place d'armes*, or parade ground, and a residential sector with a regular grid of square blocks. The shift of the capital to New Orleans hampered Mobile's growth, and when France ceded the territory in 1763 the town consisted of 131 buildings outside the fort and an estimated population of three hundred. But as at Savannah, the ambitious plan that had been platted was eventually realized in the nineteenth century, when cotton transformed Mobile into a thriving port.

New Orleans was another non-English settlement that grew into a southern city. The French arrived in 1718 and three years later platted a city whose general plan was almost identical to that of Mobile: forty-four square blocks, as shown in a plan of 1764, whose regularity reveals the penchant of the French colonial bureaucracy toward order and formal planning. Of the several vernacular house types that emerged, relatively few survived a series of devastating fires in the late eighteenth century. The Creole house was essentially a single story in height, although a half-story garret often was added under the pitched roof. The house fronted directly on the street with business rooms, with the family quarters in the rear, usually opening onto an enclosed courtyard. The roof slope frequently projected over the sidewalk to provide shade from the sun and shelter from the rain. The walls were half-timber infilled with a soft brick which required a stucco covering. Modest and without architectural pretensions, these houses were sensitively adapted to the subtropical climate and may be rated with the Charleston "single houses" as a notable example of indigenous architecture.

The *place d'armes*, which evolved into Jackson Square, is an instance of the progressive planning that sets aside a significant site for development over a period of time. Open on one side to the Mississippi River, it in fact resembled the Place de la Concorde in Paris, which was not begun until 1753, and it did indeed become the center of the French Quarter. On its north side, three major buildings dating from the period of Spanish rule (1763–1801) provided an architectural backdrop: in the

Plan of New Orleans, Louisiana: 1764. Eighteenth-century New Orleans consisted of forty-four square blocks, the central one along the Mississippi River reserved as the place d'armes, *a multipurpose public space typical of French colonial planning. (From Bellin.* Le Petit Atlas Maritime, *1764. Library of Congress.)*

View of Jackson Square, New Orleans, Louisiana: 1855. In the nineteenth century the place d'armes became an integrated urban space defined on the north by monumental buildings—the Cabildo, the Cathedral St. Louis, and the Presbytère—and on the sides by the more vernacular Pontalba Buildings. (Drawn by J. Dürler, lithograph by Pessou and Simon: 1855. Historic New Orleans Collection.)

middle was St. Louis Cathedral, built with a classical horizontality that matched the style of the flanking Cabildo and Presbytère—respectively the seats of political and religious authority. In the mid-nineteenth century the cathedral was rebuilt in a more picturesque and vertical manner, and mansard roofs were added to the Cabildo and Presbytère. At that time the row houses known as the Pontalba Buildings were erected on the east and west sides of the square. Unified by the warm red brick and the iron galleries, they completed an elegant enclosure which ranks among the finest urban spaces in America. The placement in 1856 of an equestrian statue of Andrew Jackson (the hero of the Battle of New Orleans in 1815) and the renaming of the *place d'armes* manifests how a historic site can simultaneously respect the past and signal a new era, which began for New Orleans when it became part of the United States in 1803.

As colonial powers, Spain and France both regarded the western hemisphere as a place to work out global strategies of hegemony. The Spanish and French colonies of the South were conceived primarily as centers for military administration, trading, and missionary activity rather than as permanent settlements. By comparison, the English colonies often seemed naïve because of their contradictory objectives and haphazard organization. But the latter thrived, mainly because having been allowed a larger measure of self-government, each colony was in a better position to respond to the specific realities of the New World. Spanish and French colonies were less capable of discovering, for instance, how the South's topography and climate lent itself to the plantation system. France could plan grandiose cities such as Mobile and New Orleans; but Charleston, their English equivalent, was far more successful in every respect, and it likewise remained for the English to conceive of Annapolis and Williamsburg as centers of culture growing out of the peculiar conditions of life in Maryland and Virginia.

CHAPTER THREE

PLANTATIONS: THE ROOTS OF SOUTHERN LIFE

Officially the name for Jamestown was "London's Plantation in the Southern Part of Virginia." William Bradford used the same word in the title of his epic chronicle, *Of Plymouth Plantation.* In both instances, "plantation" meant little more than a settlement. The later concept of the plantation came into being only after the realization that in the South there were unparalleled opportunities for cultivating agricultural staples and shipping them to the mother country. In Virginia, where the staple crop was tobacco, enterprising individuals began to assemble large tracts of land as private property within a decade after the colony was founded, and its initial purpose as a military trading post was gradually forgotten. The establishment of proprietary colonies—Maryland in 1632 and Carolina in 1663—furthered the amassing of large and dispersed landholdings, and by the end of the century, these holdings dominated the coastal South.

ADAM THOROUGHGOOD HOUSE, VIRGINIA BEACH, VIRGINIA (1636–1640)

The evolutionary process at work is evident in the life of Adam Thoroughgood, whose house is the earliest surviving domestic structure in the South. Thoroughgood, who had come to Virginia in 1621 as an indentured servant, worked off his bond and returned to England, bringing back to America with him his wife, his son, and thirty-eight servants. The introduction of settlers into the colony entitled him to land, and by

1636 he owned 5,350 acres on Lynnhaven Bay in Princess Anne County. This early planter was essentially a yeoman farmer who through energy and good fortune came into possession of considerable property.

The house he willed to his wife when he died in 1640 further manifests his middle-class origins.[1] Small and simply planned, it has thick walls expressing a concern for security. The roof is steeply pitched, and there are two massive chimneys for cooking and heating. The use of available materials, such as brick and shingles, was lavish; the use, on the other hand, of glass, which had to be imported, was limited to small diamond-shaped panes set in leaded and hinged casement windows. Up until a central stairway hall was added in 1740, the interior consisted of two main rooms: a hall which was a general-purpose area for cooking, eating, and living; and a slightly smaller parlor which served more formal purposes as well as functioning as a guest room. These rooms are physically distinguished by the treatment of the end chimneys: the one in the hall is external to reduce the heat of cooking, whereas the one in the parlor is internal so as to retain a maximum of heat. Under the gable roof overhead were two sleeping chambers.

Although ornamentation, traditionally one of the elements which raises a building to the status of architecture, is almost entirely absent, both outside and inside, the Thoroughgood House is not without artful craftsmanship. The brickwork is masterful: English bond below the water table and on three sides, and Flemish bond with glazed headers (the small ends of the brick) on the land front—a distinction indicating that Thoroughgood wanted his house to appear as elegant as his means

Adam Thoroughgood House, Virginia Beach, Virginia: 1636–1640. Clearly stated function, sturdy and enduring structure, and simple masterful craftsmanship combined to make the house an established seat for an Englishman in the New World. (Sandak, Inc.)

allowed. Segmental arches articulate the windows, and corbeled brick-work provides a sensitive transition from the end walls to the overhanging eaves. The kitchen chimney is an impressively conceived mass, tapering from the breadth of the cooking hearth to the small fireplace on the second story. The exterior looks symmetrical, although the door is not centered because of the different sizes of the rooms. The overall character suggests that Thoroughgood envisioned the house as a way of rooting his destiny in the New World. The two massive chimneys of earth-oriented brick "plant" the house on the site and transform its utilitarian purpose into a substantial and permanent seat. This same quality is quintessential to the plantation house, and its existence before the plantation ideology had fully developed is prophetic.

MIDDLEBURG,
BERKELEY COUNTY, SOUTH CAROLINA
(c. 1699)

In Carolina the first plantations were laid out along the banks of the Ashley and Cooper rivers, which joined at the "great port town" of Charleston. Mainly because they came later, they differed from those of Virginia in being more conscious and deliberate. The proprietors' expected source of income consisted of quitrents and duties to be imposed on those settlers they granted land. Moreover, the Fundamental Constitution of Carolina, attributed to John Locke, established gradations of rank based on the amount of land an individual held. On the other hand, an extremely liberal policy concerning worship made the colony attractive to settlers in search of religious freedom.

Even though the original semifeudal practice of landholding had been generally abandoned in Carolina by the beginning of the eighteenth century, the manorial ideal inevitably led to the establishment of plantations. The first planters were not aristocrats, but a relatively humble mixture of Barbadian farmers, English Dissenters, and French Huguenots, of whom the latter especially thrived in Carolina. In a colony designed in part to grow subtropical staples, the incoming Huguenots undertook the cultivation of vineyards, olives, and silkworms. All of these crops proved difficult to grow, but rice proved successful because of the Low Country topography of streams and swamps. By 1700 it was recognized as the money crop that would enable the colony to prosper. Rice plantations were closely interrelated to the "great port town" of Charleston—an attractive place, unlike the low-lying, marshy ground—a breeding place for debilitating diseases—on which the plantations were located. Accustomed to an urban life as the Huguenots and many of the English were, upon achieving affluence many of these planters built

*Middleburg, Berkeley County, South Carolina: c. 1699. Except for the
addition about 1800 of a room on the north side (corresponding to the two
windows on the right) and new chimneypiece moldings, Middleburg
remained a simple farmhouse despite the affluence of the nineteenth century,
when it was the center of rice cultivation for the entire east branch of the
Cooper River.*

townhouses in Charleston and lived there during the steamy summers.

Middleburg on the Cooper River exemplifies the simple Low Country plantation house that was erected throughout the eighteenth century.[2] The builder, Benjamin Simons, was a Huguenot who named his
plantation after the Dutch town in Zeeland through which he had passed
on his way to the New World. Dating from the 1690s, it is the oldest
surviving wood-frame and weatherboarded structure in South Carolina.
The main floor originally consisted of two rooms of unequal size, on
either side of an interior chimney. This arrangement facilitated opening
the rooms to breezes through windows and doors; in addition, there were
one-story porches, or piazzas, to shelter each side from the sun. These
features were often present in West Indian domestic architecture, and
were also reflected in the Charleston "single houses." Wood, a plentiful
material that adds to the vernacular character of the house, was used also
because it was thought to be cooler than masonry.

Carolina offered a fresh opportunity to the displaced Huguenot, and
he expressed his true character by building a house whose simplicity, directness, and integrity are an implicit repudiation of the Baroque architecture of Louis XIV. Nevertheless, Middleburg dominated its site, and
in time alleys of live oaks and a formal garden were added to enhance the
special quality of the place. In the nineteenth century a mill was installed
on the banks of the river, making the plantation the center of rice cultivation for all the land watered by the east branch of the Cooper River. But

affluence did not lead Simons's descendants to build a more elegant family seat; rather, the original farmhouse was reverentially preserved, and to this day remains in the possession of descendants of the builder. Though the last rice crop was grown there in the early twentieth century, aside from the natural growth of trees and gardens the property has changed very little since then—successfully preserving a monument to the history of Carolina rice culture.

MULBERRY,
BERKELEY COUNTY, SOUTH CAROLINA
(c. 1714)

With increasing prosperity came a new phase of plantation architecture, of which Mulberry is typical. Built sometime before 1714 by Thomas Broughton, a prominent Indian trader, soldier, politician, and planter, the house commands a bluff overlooking the Cooper River.[3] The site had been an Indian settlement, centered about the mulberry tree that gave the plantation its name, and legend has it that the land was originally reserved for the primary proprietor, Lord Ashley-Cooper. Hence the req-

Mulberry, Berkeley County, South Carolina: c. 1714. Although Mulberry is a large house dominating a bluff above the Cooper River, the proliferation of projecting corner rooms, windows, and dormers gives it a domestic scale and conveys the impression that it grows out of the site.

uisites for virtually every plantation were present: a place deeply rooted in the past, where new life could be cultivated for generations to come.

Mulberry is distinguished by its unusual plan: four almost free-standing pavilions at the external corners of the main rooms. These pavilions have been imaginatively identified as defensive fortifications against the Indians during the Yemassee War, which occurred while the house was being built. They are, however, decidedly domestic in appearance, and more probably reflect a stage in the evolution of the English house, which perpetuated the corner turrets of castles without their military implication. They are, moreover, a masterful way of providing additional rooms for informal purposes without interfering with the ventilation of the central rooms. As important is the way the pavilions extend the house out into its environment. Whereas a simple geometrical shape tends to appear independent of a natural site, the softening of contours and edges integrates Mulberry with the landscape. An unusual picturesqueness results from the breaking up of larger elements—the pavilions with their curvilinear roof slopes, the entry portico and dormer windows, and the gambrel roof with jerkin-head ends. Earth-oriented brick also relates the house comfortably to its site. Carved on the pediment of the portico is a mulberry branch with gigantic ripened fruit encircled by a horseshoe, a naïve but fitting emblem of the origins of the place and the planter's hopes for establishing a silk culture in Carolina.

STRATFORD HALL, WESTMORELAND COUNTY, VIRGINIA (c. 1725–1730)

Virginia plantation houses built after Williamsburg rank among the most impressive buildings in America. Relatively uniform in style, they reflect Virginia's position as the largest, most populated, and most influential colony. In the mid-eighteenth century the province was commonly thought of as stretching westward from the Atlantic to the Pacific, and the destiny of whose inhabitants it was to survey, sell, and settle the entire territory. South Carolina could have made a similar claim; in reality, however, rice cultivation limited a plantation's size to its access to a river or creek, and until the American Revolution the major expansion occurred along the coast rather than inland.

Stratford Hall is typical of the Virginia plantation house based on the vastness of land. Of the large tracts acquired by Thomas Lee, a third-generation colonist, about 4,000 acres in the Northern Neck (between the Potomac and Rappahannock rivers) became the site of Stratford Hall.[4] Lee also was politically prominent; he became a member of the House of Burgesses in 1726 and six years later he sat on the Gover-

Stratford Hall, Westmoreland County, Virginia: c. 1725–1730. The simple geometry and the austere wall surfaces give Stratford Hall a more monumental appearance than Mulberry; yet because of its elevation—a high basement with only one story above—and its clustered chimneys, it is also "planted." (Wayne Andrews.)

nor's Council. He erected Stratford Hall from plans which may be as early as 1725, although actual construction was prompted by a fire which in 1729 destroyed the house he then occupied. Little is known about Lee's architectural taste; he had traveled to England in 1716, but whether the purpose of that trip was to obtain plans is unknown.

Lee chose for his house a high bluff above the Potomac River, a mile away from the site. Aside from such practical considerations as healthful ground, drainage, and a supply of fresh water, the commanding view must have impressed him with its monumental possibilities. H-shaped in plan, the house is a dominating mass domesticated by the warm color of the brick, by the horizontality of the roof, and by its lateral extensions into the landscape. Each wing is a geometrical unit integrated with the subtle means of a hipped roof and four clustered chimneys. Placed diagonally off the corners, four dependency buildings of similar material but reduced scale reinforce an overall effect of austere rectilinearity. Even the name of Stratford Hall was derived from the Lees' ancestral home in England; and the appearance of formal rootedness corresponded not only to Lee's position in colonial Virginia but also to his desire to provide a seat for future generations.

The central section is approached by a stairway of imported Portland stone, an incongruity against the stark walls of indigenous brick, but designed to give ostentatious entry to the most elegant room—a great hall paneled and articulated with Corinthian pilasters and a full entablature. The extravagant entertaining that took place here was in striking contrast to the popular level of culture in so sparsely populated a region, which in

1732 was described as "remote from the seat of government where the common people are generally of a more turbulent and unruly disposition than anywhere else."[5] The high style of Stratford Hall is also notable for its functional deficiencies. Since the chimney clusters are part of the wings, the great hall has no source of heat. The location of the chimney stacks also complicated the planning of the smaller rooms, none of which is symmetrical. Moreover, the main rooms of the *piano nobile* proved to be so awkwardly interconnected that the interior walls were moved within fifty years after the house was finished. There appears to have been no circulation between the floors except by way of exterior stairways on the sides. Impressive formality, concentrated on the exterior and in the great hall, transcended practical considerations at the cost of no little inconvenience.

At the time of his death in 1750, Thomas Lee was acting governor and commander in chief, and his manner of living was patterned after that of the English landed gentry. A Virginia plantation often was the seat of a significant political figure; Stratford Hall sired a dynasty. Two of Thomas Lee's sons, Richard Henry and Francis Lightfoot, were signers of the Declaration of Independence. A son-in-law, "Light Horse Harry" Lee, figured prominently in the Revolutionary War, and it was his son, Robert E. Lee, who added further distinction to the family during the Civil War. Even the preservation of the house reflects the cult of family personalities; in 1929, when the Robert E. Lee Memorial Foundation purchased the plantation, the rooms were restored to emphasize famous family members—the great hall of Thomas Lee, the parlor of "Light Horse Harry" Lee, and the birth chamber of Robert E. Lee.

WESTOVER,
CHARLES CITY COUNTY, VIRGINIA
(c. 1730–1734)

William Byrd II perceived the economic opportunities of the New World, but throughout his life remained more English than American. He inherited a large estate, to which he went on adding; eventually his Virginia holdings totaled 179,440 acres. He was a member of the House of Burgesses, sat for thirty-seven years on the Governor's Council, and served three times as the colony's London agent. Altogether he spent thirty of his seventy years in England, where he received an education and was admitted to the bar.

Westover, the seat from which Byrd managed his plantations, was a vicarious substitute for the social pleasures of London.[6] Built in the early 1730s on a site 25 miles west of Williamsburg, it had the largest library in colonial Virginia (3,625 volumes, including many of the standard architectural handbooks), along with a collection of oil paintings, mainly portraits of Byrd's English friends. It was the setting for such pastimes as the regular reading of Hebrew, Greek, and Latin, in addition to Byrd's more gregarious diversions such as hunting, horseback riding, and dancing. In keeping with the site along the north side of the James River, the house, a simple, freestanding block, was the center of a linear plan, emphasized by flanking dependencies. The kitchen on the west is older than the house, and its chimney stacks may be surviving fragments of the wood-frame house of William Byrd I, who had come to Virginia in the 1670s. The east flanker, which housed the library, was destroyed during the Civil War. The vista onto the river revealed the destiny of the Byrds: downstream to the Atlantic and ultimately England whence they had come, and upstream to Petersburg and Richmond, which William Byrd II surveyed and founded. Wharves near the plantation house provided facilities for loading the tobacco to be exported and for unloading the English goods that made Westover the most stylish house of its time.

The house, with its balance between horizontality and verticality, was derived from an English type, although the Governor's Palace at Williamsburg served as an intermediary. A wrought-iron entrance gate on the land side was dictated by English fashion, a luxury for a plantation

Westover, Charles City County, Virginia: c. 1730–1734. By paralleling the James River immediately in front, Westover relates to its site, which was picturesquely enhanced in the nineteenth century by the growth of shade trees. (Wayne Andrews.)

more often approached by water. The design incorporated Byrd's mono-gram along with two eagles, a reference to his name. The north and south entrances, made of imported Portland stone, were patterned after plates in William Salmon's *Palladio Londinensis* (1734). The mantelpieces were carved in London, and the plaster that ornamented the ceilings was probably cast there also.

Despite Byrd's efforts to build a thoroughly English house, West-over also is "southern" in its strong sense of place and the warm organic quality of the brick. Furthermore, the interior planning is not nearly as symmetrical as the exterior elevations, offering the advantages of variety in the sizes of the rooms but the disadvantages that they are somewhat awkwardly shaped: in several rooms, chimneypieces and windows are inharmoniously juxtaposed, and the sophistication of the London mantels is jarred occasionally by clumsiness in the paneling, presumably the work of local craftsmen. Such anomalies were inevitable, however, once Byrd had decided to build in high style in a province without fully developed building trades.

The tulip poplars that now shade the lawn between the house and the river were planted in the nineteenth century. In Byrd's day the vista would have been unobstructed, so that he could watch the coming and going of ships laden with Virginia produce and English merchandise along the river. Travelers on the river, in turn, would have had a clear view of this powerful testimony to Byrd's aristocratic aspirations.

DRAYTON HALL,
CHARLESTON COUNTY, SOUTH CAROLINA
(1738–1742)

In colonial America, Williamsburg and Charleston were both regarded by their residents as closer to London than to each other. Southern to-pography mandated settlements along navigable rivers, which made land travel very difficult. Colonial governments were legally separate, and the exclusive economic tie between each of the colonies and England pre-cluded intercolonial commerce. Moreover, Carolina had strong ties with the British West Indies which Virginia shared to a considerably lesser extent. Cultural life likewise evolved independently; a Carolina son would far more likely be educated at Oxford or Cambridge than at William and Mary. Correspondingly, the typical Virginia plantation house, of which Westover is the most sumptuous example, had almost no influence in Carolina.

Drayton Hall was built by John Drayton, a third-generation Carolinian who served on the King's Council, and whose family had devel-

Drayton Hall, Charleston County, South Carolina: 1738–1742. The cubical format, the formal geometry, and the two-story portico are more specifically Palladian than many of the English buildings that may have served as intermediaries between the Italian sixteenth-century architect and colonial America.

oped extensive plantation holdings on the Ashley River.[7] Drayton himself was described by a descendant as "a man of indifferent education, of a confined mind, proud, and stingy." Nevertheless, in the late 1730s he built a house based on English Palladian models, whose style was of more recent date than that of Westover. How Drayton came to be influenced by the new architectural ideas of the 1720s is unknown; he never went to England himself. He could have imported an architect or used the recently published handbooks of Colen Campbell, *Vitruvius Britannicus* (1715, 1717, and 1725), and William Salmon, *Palladio Londinensis* (1734). At any rate, Drayton Hall's most distinctive feature, the two-story portico, was derived directly from Palladio, whose *Four Books of Architecture* were translated into English during this period. According to local lore, the Carolina rice planters may actually have realized their affinities with the farmer-aristocrats of the Veneto who built Palladian villas in the sixteenth century.

Conceived mainly as a family seat rather than as a working plantation, Drayton Hall is Palladian in its cubical massing and crisp geometry, and emphasizes formal entertainment rather than the functions of day-to-day living. The double stairway inside the riverfront entrance, ascending through a two-story space, is the first example of its kind in America. In all the rooms there is a striving for pure form based on symmetry, geometrical regularity, and similarity of sizes and shapes. A redundance in the purpose of the main rooms is obvious, and to this day they are described in general terms, as halls and drawing rooms. It is difficult even to identify the dining room definitively. The first-floor room in the northeast corner has been suggested, largely because of a service stairway to the basement, where a kitchen and servants' hall are located. However, the room's very simple ornamentation seems appropriate for no more than family dining. Formal banquets must have taken place in one or more of the rooms now identified as halls and drawing rooms, despite their relative inconvenience.

The elaborate ornamentation in the main rooms might logically be supposed to have come from England, like the mantelpieces and plaster work at Westover. One material that did in fact was the Portland stone for the columns of the two-story portico. On the other hand, the wood of the chimneypieces, pilasters, and cornices is an indigenous yellow poplar, which in several rooms is embellished by West Indian mahogany. Since it would hardly have been sent to England to be carved and then brought back to South Carolina, the quality of the work attests to the level of craftsmanship that a town like Charleston could support. The chimneypiece in the first-floor hall, based on a plate in William Kent, *Designs of Inigo Jones* (1727), is further indicative of direct access to high-style sources.

Drayton Hall, chimneypiece in great hall. The chimneypiece, particularly the overmantel, was derived from plate LXIV in William Kent, Designs of Inigo Jones (*1727*).

Like most plantations, Drayton Hall was anything but the result of a fleeting and whimsical infatuation with passing fashion. Throughout subsequent generations, the house remained virtually unaltered, except for some minor changes about 1800 after a hurricane (most notably the window sashes), the replacement of several mantelpieces, and the addition of a mid-nineteenth-century ceiling in the first-floor hall. Not even plumbing and electricity had been installed. It remained the Draytons' possession until the early 1970s, having survived the ravages of the Civil War, when many Ashley River plantations were destroyed by contingents of Sherman's army—because, according to legend, someone shrewdly reported that Drayton Hall was being used as a hospital for smallpox victims, with the result that the Union troops passed it by. Today, Drayton Hall is a property of the National Trust for Historic Preservation, and purely in terms of architecture—since it is presented to the public without interior furnishings—it has become the South's most significant house museum. In the words of one writer, Drayton Hall gives "the feeling that the Draytons have just gone, leaving nothing to come between the present and the past." More to the point, however, the house offers an unparalleled glimpse into an architectural masterpiece before the family actually moved in.

MIDDLETON PLACE, DORCHESTER COUNTY, SOUTH CAROLINA (c. 1755)

Although the formal gardens at Drayton Hall between the house and the river have largely disappeared, the superb gardens of Middleton Place, a plantation 5 miles upriver, have survived. The Duc de la Rochefoucauld-Liancourt described them as calling "to recollection the ancient English country seats," and noted that they were extensions of the natural setting: "A peculiar feature of the situation is this, that the river, which flows in a circuitous course until it reaches this point forms here a wide, beautiful canal, pointing straight to the house."[8]

Henry Middleton acquired the plantation through marriage in 1741, and by 1755 work on the most extensive gardens in colonial America had begun. The ascent from the river to the house is a masterful combination of ponds, terraces, and plantings, juxtaposing a picturesque rice mill pond, formal butterfly lakes, and a rice field into which the water was diverted. The gardens, in short, are rooted in the topography of the rice culture. Their actual shaping was the work of slaves trained to build ditches and embankments for rice fields. The overall ambience is so English that the presence of a landscape gardener imported to supervise the work is often assumed. But that same Englishness leads to another important conclusion. Whereas the formal gardens at Middleton Place are essentially balanced and symmetrical, in England by the mid-eighteenth century landscape design of this type was being replaced by the informal garden which emphasized greater naturalness. In the New World, however, where there was all too much uncultivated wilderness already, such consciously picturesque and rustic effects were not deemed appropriate. What Middleton wanted was a garden that would express, through formal planning, his domination over nature.

Although the house at Middleton Place, an austere, three-story brick structure, possessed much less high style than Drayton Hall, the gardens gave Middleton Place a quality nearly analogous to the ancestral seats in Virginia. Henry Middleton, who owned 50,000 acres spread over twenty plantations, served as a member of the King's Council and as a delegate to the First Continental Congress. His son Arthur, who succeeded him in 1775, was a signer of the Declaration of Independence. Henry Middleton of the next generation was ambassador to Russia, and his son Williams was a signer of the Ordinance of Secession—a fact that may have prompted the Union troops to destroy the house in 1865.

ARLINGTON HOUSE, ARLINGTON, VIRGINIA (1804–1825)

The Revolutionary War and the Early Republican period were not propitious for building on the plantations. With independence, planters who had for decades lived on credit extended to them by their London agents, their staple crops serving as collateral, were thrown into the less benevolent world of international commerce. Many plantations, particularly in Virginia, were already in financial straits because tobacco cultivation was so ruinous to the soil. South Carolina fared much better by comparison: during the Early Republican period the Low Country grew the largest amount of rice and exported from Charleston the greatest tonnage in its pre–Civil War history. But the most notable architectural consequence of this wealth was the building of townhouses rather than of plantations. In both Virginia and South Carolina, by and large, plantation houses were not rebuilt or modernized except for the redecoration of interior rooms and the addition of gardens. Few new plantation houses comparable to those of the colonial period were erected until the boom first in cotton and then in sugar produced new wealth and made high-style building on a monumental scale again possible.

Historical associations and the natural setting preordained the building of Arlington House, situated on a hill across the Potomac River from the national capital. George Washington Parke Custis, the adopted

George Hadfield. Arlington House, Arlington, Virginia: 1804–1825. The monumentally overscaled portico conveys a strong visual image across the distance between the house and the National Capitol.

son of the first President of the United States, conceived the house as a monument to Washington with family heirlooms and memorabilia prominently on display.[9] The north and south wings were erected first in 1804 as living quarters in the Federal style. The central pavilion, consisting of more formal rooms, was finished in 1817, and the Greek Revival portico had been added by 1825. Notwithstanding the sequential construction and the succession of styles, a single architect, George Hadfield, was responsible for the entire design. In 1795 Hadfield had come to Washington from England to superintend the building of the Capitol, and he remained in the area until his death in 1826. The monumental portico was a brilliant way of interrelating the house with the Neoclassical architecture of Washington. Contemporary observers differed over whether the source was the Hephaisteion at Athens or a temple at Paestum; in any event, the overly massive Doric order had the effect of conveying a strong image across the space separating it from the Capitol. In this heroic setting Robert E. Lee was married to Custis's daughter in 1831, and they made Arlington House their home until the outbreak of the Civil War.

Oak Alley,
St. James Parish, Louisiana
(1837–1839)

The picturesque antebellum plantation house emerged from mid-nineteenth-century romanticism and has been sentimentally revered ever since. Its natural ambience was captured in 1856 by Frederick Law Olmsted's description of the approach to a southern plantation:

> On either side, at fifty feet distant, were rows of old live oak trees, their branches and twigs slightly hung with a delicate fringe of gray moss, and their dark, shining green foliage meeting and intermingling naturally but densely overhead. The sunlight streamed through and played aslant the lustrous leaves, and fluttering, pendulous moss; the arch was low and broad; the trunks were huge and gnarled, and there was a heavy groining of strong, rough, knotty branches. I stopped my horse and held my breath; for I have hardly in all my life seen anything so impressively grand and beautiful.[10]

Oak Alley, St. James Parish, Louisiana: 1837–1839. An alley of twenty-eight live oaks inspired the building of a plantation house with twenty-eight columns and twenty-eight slave cabins. (Sandak, Inc.)

Live oaks are indigenous to the South from South Carolina to Louisiana; one magnificent specimen at Middleton Place is estimated to be over eight hundred years old. Cultivated avenues of these trees were at Middleburg, Mulberry, and Drayton Hall. The most majestic example, however, is in Louisiana, where around the time settlement began along the Mississippi River, an unknown pioneer planted twenty-eight live oaks, running in two rows from the river to the site he had chosen for his house. More than a hundred years of growth transformed an avenue, 200 feet wide, into a vault of enormous shading branches. Between 1837 and 1839 Jacques Telesphore Roman, a sugar planter and cattle rancher, built a mansion on the site.[11] Roman was so enchanted by the setting which had already been prepared for such a monument that he designed it with twenty-eight colossal columns, corresponding to the number of trees in the avenue. (He also built twenty-eight slave cabins.) He called his plantation Beau Séjour; but it was known as Oak Alley to travelers along the river. The parasitical Spanish moss that adds to the languorous decadence of the scene was (and still is) consciously pruned to enhance the trees' architectural appearance.

The house itself represents the culmination of a type that evolved in the Mississippi River valley. The basic vernacular structure had a hipped roof extending beyond the walls and receiving support from posts on all four sides. Since the house was usually raised above the flood plain, the shaded peripheral space became in effect a gallery. It attained the status of high-style architecture in the nineteenth century when the posts were monumentalized as grandiose peripteral colonnades. At Oak Alley, whereas the house is willfully nonchalant concerning classical correctness, the live-oak avenue has the serene discipline of a veritable architectural space, combining the formal and the picturesque to create a "southern" place of sublime beauty.

Occasionally, antebellum plantation houses adhered more strictly to the Greek Revival style, and fittingly such a group exists in Athens, Georgia—although not plantation houses *per se,* many were the townhouses of planters. The John Thomas Grant House, built in 1857–1858, has a colossal two-story colonnade on three sides, but it is different from Oak Alley in that its columns, capitals, and entablature all follow the Greek Corinthian order.[12] This classicism was thoroughly imbued with a romanticism which stressed that every new planter was a southern aristocrat in the tradition of the colonial gentry in Virginia and South Carolina. Many Deep South planters were in actuality just a generation removed from frontier conditions, and in its self-conscious correctness their architecture was intended to belie that embarrassing fact. The appeal of Greek architecture was its simultaneous remoteness and familiarity, serving on the one hand to disguise humble origins and on the other to give an appearance of rootedness. Aesthetic erudition was far less important than the heroic ideals of democratic Athens and Republican Rome, whose venerable political systems had been based on

John Thomas Grant House, Athens, Georgia: 1857–1858. The colossal colonnade features the Greek Corinthian order—capitals modeled after the Choragic Monument of Lysicrates, a three-stepped architrave, a frieze, and a pediment—all having the correct classical ornamentation.

slave labor. That the South's "peculiar institution" could be exonerated through association with classical antiquity was the message of such plantation architecture.

LONGWOOD, NATCHEZ, MISSISSIPPI (1860–1861)

In the 1850s there was a shift to more picturesque architectural styles, chosen for primarily aesthetic rather than ideological reasons. In 1850, Dr. Haller Nutt, a Louisiana cotton planter, scientist, and physician, purchased the enchanting site of Longwood, just outside Natchez, that had been a favorite spot in the girlhood of his wife, where he decided to build a residence across the Mississippi from his own plantations.[13] Unlike the majority of planters who had risen up from the ranks of simple pioneers, Nutt was well educated, having studied medicine at the University of Louisville, and had traveled throughout the United States. He applied scientific methods to the farming of cotton and improved the cotton gin through the use of modern technology.

Unlike most antebellum planters, who built conventional houses and drew on the services of the available builders, or in some cases architects, Nutt went about realizing an architectural dream in a strongly individualistic way. In Samuel Sloan's *The Model Architect* (1852), he found "A Southern Mansion" described in terms he himself could appreciate:

> The southern gentleman is not circumscribed in the construction of his house, or the laying out of gardens and lawns, by the walls or fences of his neighbors, and the number of laborers at his command, the entire year, renders him less chary in the indulgence of his taste in these particulars, than he would be, if, to keep them in order, required a constant drain upon his purse. . . . Those houses are most suitable whose openings are so constructed as to permit, at pleasure, such a union of rooms and verandahs as to make them almost one and the same apartment. The laws of hospitality, observed there, require a larger number of sleeping apartments since the southern householder takes pride in converting his mansion into a sort of honorary hotel.

Nutt preferred, however, the exoticism of another design, "An Oriental Villa," in which Sloan made eclectic references to mosques at Damascus and Córdoba, to the Alhambra in Granada, and to Hagia Sophia in Istanbul. Its octagonal plan, which had a brief vogue in the 1850s, was promoted because it offered increased space, greater convenience, and better heating. In 1858 or 1859, Nutt traveled to Philadelphia, where he commissioned Sloan to design a house for Longwood based on "An Oriental Villa." Construction was begun in 1860 by a group consisting of Philadelphia workmen and local artisans; on two occasions Sloan himself inspected the work in progress. Sloan published elevations of Longwood in *Sloan's Homestead Architecture* (1861) and wrote of his clients:

> The occupants of such a residence are not only supposed to be wealthy, but fashionable people, and to possess in common with all the real aristocracy of every section, a character for hospitality, exhibited in the frequent entertainment of numerous guests, and a liberal allowance of time and money for the purpose of social and convivial enjoyment.

When the Civil War erupted in the spring of 1861, with the exterior structure virtually completed, the Philadelphia workmen returned home, and work on Longwood essentially came to an end. The basement, which had been intended for servants, was adapted for family living, and in 1864 Nutt died there, a broken man whose plantations had been destroyed. Evidence that Nutt was sympathetic to the Union makes his losses even more poignant. Above the basement, three floors with interior

Samuel Sloan. Longwood, Natchez, Mississippi: 1860–1861. The exotic mixture of Near Eastern styles, the eccentricity of the octagonal plan, and the unfinished interior give Longwood its romantic picturesqueness. (*From* Sloan's Homestead Architecture, *1861. Library of Congress.*)

surfaces of rough brick, with exposed ceiling beams, remain as they were when construction stopped.

Nutt in his dream of Longwood, notwithstanding the capriciousness of its style, was consciously trying to be modern. He not only enlisted fully professional architectural services when he commissioned Sloan to design the house, but also employed a Philadelphia landscape gardener and ordered furniture from the North. In its indulgence in northern taste, Longwood is to a considerable degree less "southern" than previous plantation houses. What makes it "southern" is mainly its unfortunate history, which in combination with nature has left behind an awe-inspiring emblem of the demise of antebellum society.

CHAPTER FOUR

SOUTHERN CHURCHES: FROM ESTABLISHED CONVENTIONS TO STYLISTIC ECLECTICISM

ST. LUKE'S CHURCH,
SMITHFIELD, VIRGINIA
(1632)

Southern churches, more than any other type of building, provide a continuous record of the evolution of architectural styles. Whereas the style of plantation houses and other dwellings ranged all the way from the grandly formal to the vernacular, the unequivocal predilection shown by churches in the South, from the earliest surviving example, is for high style. St. Luke's Church, Smithfield, was constructed in the 1630s around the same time as the Adam Thoroughgood House, about 30 miles away. The latter is solid and durable, with brickwork that displays fine craftsmanship, but its style is impossible to categorize. Any attempt to link the verticality of the end walls with the Gothic manner, or the horizontality of the façades with that of the Renaissance, would not be very meaningful. The features of St. Luke's, on the other hand, are more homogeneous stylistically, and the church can properly be described as English Gothic.

The early history of St. Luke's is obscure. A parish church had been established by 1629, and three years later it was stipulated "that in all such places where any churches are wanting or decayed, the inhabitants are tied to contribute toward the building of a church."[1] Since the work was to be completed by the end of the year, 1632 has become the generally accepted date for St. Luke's—a name it did not acquire, however, until 1828. The building, designed to accommodate the five hundred people of Newport Parish, has been preserved and restored in a quiet rural setting that retains its original ambience as the seat of the established church in a sparsely populated countryside.

The rectangular body of the church is thoroughly Gothic with exterior buttresses, traceried windows with pointed lancets, crow-stepped gables, and a steeply pitched roof. In the interior a chancel rail and rood screen characteristic of the Church of England separate the clergy from the congregation, and the trussed ceiling was typical of English churches and secular halls. The workmen did not pursue any particular style as an end in itself, but simply used the forms with which they were familiar, erecting a building that emphasized cultural dependence on the mother country. Newer motifs that were entering English architecture can be seen on the tower of St. Luke's—the curious pediment over the entrance,

St. Luke's Church, Smithfield, Virginia: 1632. Gothic features—pointed arches, buttresses, and crow-stepped gables—are combined with Renaissance details on the tower—the pediment above the entrance and corner quoins. (Sandak, Inc.)

the corner quoins added after 1657, and the third story, constructed later in the century.

ST. JAMES' CHURCH, GOOSE CREEK, SOUTH CAROLINA (1708–1719)

In Carolina, when the Church Act of 1706 mandated the establishment of the Church of England, St. James' Church, Goose Creek, was built to serve a parish of English and Barbadian planters who championed religious establishment as a means of augmenting their political ascendancy. Materials were being collected to replace an already existing wooden church with a more fashionable brick one, as early as 1707, but the building was not finished until 1719.[2] The pastel-colored stucco surfaces of St. James' are West Indian in origin, and give it a soft and delicate elegance. The style of the low, horizontal exterior has classical or Renaissance antecedents. The walls are treated as simple, smooth planes, with regularly placed windows and doors—windows with semicircular top lights, and doors framed by pilasters, entablatures, and pediments. Quoining accentuates the corners, and string courses below and above the windows integrate the adjacent sides. The rectangular floor plan is articulated by two intersecting axes—one leading from the main entrance to the pulpit, the other connecting the side doors across the nave. The large size and the frequency of the openings were both essential for ventilation, making the enclosure a skillful synthesis of function and design.

Inside, the simplicity of the exterior is transcended by four structurally unnecessary columns supporting a naïve entablature, which at once emphasizes the longitudinal axis and draws the eye to the painted plaster reredos, a masterpiece of ornamentation, that looms above the altar. In their exuberance the composite capitals, the marbleizing of the entablature, and the curved and broken pediment are decidedly Baroque, and the whole is unlike anything to be found elsewhere in America. In the center, where one might expect a cross, are the arms of George I—an explicitly political note, whose authoritarian overtones the pulpit, projecting in the center of the reredos, serves to amplify.

On the exterior, however, the imagery is entirely religious. The pediment over the main entrance features a pelican piercing her breast to feed her young, a motif often interpreted as signifying redemption in Christ. The Society for the Propagation of the Gospel in Foreign Parts, which after its founding in 1701 sent missionaries to Carolina, chose the pelican as its symbol, largely because a verse in Psalms alluding to Christ proclaims: "I am like a pelican of the wilderness." In a region where the pelican is native, no emblem could have been more appropriate. Indeed,

St. James' Church, Goose Creek, South Carolina, reredos: 1708–1719. The pulpit and its surrounding elements—the arms of George I, the Ten Commandments, the Lord's Prayer, and the Apostles' Creed—reinforced the authority of the established church.

an otherwise simple and understated building is overpowered by political and religious iconography. The overscaled enframements around both the main entrance and the reredos create a tension between function and institutional dogma.

CHRIST CHURCH, LANCASTER COUNTY, VIRGINIA
(c. 1732)

No such tension marks Christ Church, on the southeastern tip of Virginia's Northern Neck, which has been described as the most perfect building anywhere in the American colonies. It was conceived as a family chapel by Robert "King" Carter, whose mansion, Corotoman, stood nearby, and who as the owner of 300,000 acres was the wealthiest Virginian of his time.[3] He was buried outside the chancel in 1732, just after the building was finished, with this inscription in Latin on his tomb:

Here lies buried Robert Carter, Esquire, an honorable man, who by noble endowments and pure morals gave luster to his gentle birth. . . . Possessed of ample wealth, blamelessly acquired, he built and endowed, at his own expense this sacred edifice—a signal monument of his piety toward God. He furnished it richly.

Christ Church has a cruciform plan, with chancel and transepts of equal size, the nave slightly longer. The predominant feeling of the exterior is neither horizontal nor vertical, but a subtle combination of the two, with a harmoniously integrated hipped roof. A relatively small building is made to appear larger by the magnificent entrance surrounds of molded, gauged, and rubbed brick, which deemphasize the door openings themselves. The resulting monumentality expresses the meaning of the church as a family mausoleum. The Georgian style is manifest in other classical details, such as the pilasters and pediments, for which William Salmon's *Palladio Londinensis* (1734) provides the closest parallel (as it did for the doorways at Westover). That Christ Church

Christ Church, Lancaster County, Virginia: c. 1732. The cruciform plan, apparent on the exterior and in the interior, reflects the purpose of the church as the family chapel for one of Virginia's wealthiest planters. (Sandak, Inc.)

was in fact finished two years before the book was published is further testimony to the early development of high style in colonial Virginia.

In the masterfully proportioned interior, clarity of design is achieved by the vivid juxtaposition of white plaster surfaces and walnut woodwork, and above the walls a cross barrel vault logically reflects the plan and integrates the space. The altar and burial slabs for Carter's parents are located in the chancel, with the transepts and nave reserved for the congregation. The placement of the pulpit, against the wall at the intersection of the nave and transept, and diagonally opposite the Carter family pew in the chancel, signified that their rank exceeded that of the minister.

Because of its remote setting, Christ Church has survived with only minor changes and today is the most complete example of Georgian ecclesiastical architecture in existence. Like St. James', Goose Creek, Christ Church is eminently "southern" in character, embracing the ideals of the landed gentry. Their high style notwithstanding, such buildings remained primarily country chapels, whose architects were largely anonymous.

St. Michael's Church, Charleston, South Carolina (1751–1761)

The metropolitan character of Charleston, on the other hand, called for churches similar to those of Boston and Philadelphia. In 1751 the General Assembly divided Charleston into two Anglican parishes and appointed commissioners to oversee the construction of a church in the southeast corner of the square which had been platted in the original plan. Scarcely four months after the parish of St. Michael's was created, the commissioners reported that they had agreed on a design, and advertised for bricklayers, carpenters, and materials.[4] The rapidity with which the work was undertaken indicates that the local building trades were well established, and that neither the design nor the architect had to be imported from England. According to one plausible suggestion, the architect was Peter Harrison of Newport, Rhode Island, whose Redwood Library has a four-columned Tuscan portico similar to St. Michael's. He had also recently furnished the plans for King's Chapel, Boston, which was the most ambitious Anglican church before St. Michael's. Harrison was acquainted with several Charlestonians, who in turn occasionally summered at Newport. Another influence on the design of St. Michael's was the portico of St. Philip's, the church of the first Charleston parish built in the 1720s.

When the cornerstone of St. Michael's was laid early the next year, a newspaper explained that "this church will be built on the plan of one of Mr. Gibson's designs"—undoubtedly a garbled reference to James Gibbs, an English architect whose London church, St. Martin's-in-the-Fields, illustrated in his *Book of Architecture* (1728), was widely known and copied in America. The omission here of any reference to Harrison does not exclude his participation, however, as an amateur architect with commercial ties to Charleston. Similarities between St. Michael's and St. Martin's include the tripartite division into a rectangular congregation hall, a monumental entrance portico, and a tall tower with steeple. That the builder was Samuel Cardy, a native of Ireland, is known from the assertion in his obituary that he "undertook and completed the building of St. Michael's Church." The supervision of construction was a major endeavor. The brick used, including some molded with a curve for the por-

St. Michael's Church, Charleston, South Carolina: 1751–1761. While manifesting the cosmopolitan character of Charleston, the church also responded to the growing urban density by having a monumental portico projecting out to the street and a prominent tower and steeple thrust into the sky.

Joseph Hyde. St. Philip's Church, Charleston, South Carolina, interior: 1835–1838. Architectural conservatism and veneration for the previous building on the site prompted the congregation to erect a traditional eighteenth-century church at a time when the Greek and Gothic Revival styles were fashionable in the rest of America. (Carolina Art Association)

tico columns, was specially made on a Low Country plantation. The exterior was then covered in rough-cast, or stucco, providing a smooth, light surface, a hallmark of South Carolina architecture just as exposed brick was in Virginia. Native cedar was masterfully carved for the interior woodwork—the pulpit, the box pews, and the fluted columns and Ionic capitals supporting the galleries—the ornamentation in itself signifying that Charleston had many skilled artisans.

Christopher Wren had written that "handsome spires, rising in good proportion, may be of sufficient ornament to the town," and St. Michael's is to this day a dominant feature of the Charleston skyline. The 185-foot spire is a masterful series of interrelated stories which ascend through three octagonal levels before terminating in a pyramidal steeple. The portico is an impressive civic monument above and beyond its architectural function, and the interior is a solemn religious space, whose deemphasized chancel reflects the low-church liturgy of the period. The formal elegance of the rectangular, galleried nave influenced Charleston church-building for a century, and Presbyterians, Lutherans, Congregationalists, Unitarians, and Catholics, as well as Episcopalians, erected steeples whose diverse styles were all complementary to that of St. Michael's. As shown in an 1851 view, Charleston presented no less than nine church towers to ships entering its harbor.

Most specifically continuing the tradition of St. Michael's was the Episcopal parish of St. Philip's. In 1835, after their revered early-eighteenth-century church burned, its vestry had at first decided to reconstruct the destroyed building.[5] But in the following year they gave their architect, Joseph Hyde, the following instructions: "that the heavy pillars of the interior of the church be dispensed with, and that in lieu thereof Corinthian columns after the style of St. Martin's-in-the-Fields, London, be adopted." The use as a model of Gibbs's church, then over a hundred years old, was unusual in its veneration of an established architectural format. Although unprogressive stylistically, St. Philip's majestically sublime interior stands as a timeless evocation of a society whose great plantation houses were built in much the same manner.

BALTIMORE CATHEDRAL,
BALTIMORE, MARYLAND
(1804–1821)

The American Revolution separated church and state, and some of the churches of the Early Republican period reflect the ensuing religious pluralism as non-Episcopalian denominations increasingly erected churches of their own. In 1789 the Roman Catholic see of the United States was established at Baltimore, and Pope Pius VI instructed the designated bishop, John Carroll, "to erect a church in the said city of Baltimore in the form of a Cathedral, inasmuch as the times and circumstances may allow."[6] When Benjamin Latrobe offered his services to Bishop Carroll in 1804, no precedent for a cathedral of any denomination existed in the United States. Latrobe, a fully trained architect and engineer, had left England in 1795. Immediately on his arrival in the United States, he was recognized to be a professional, as distinct from the master builders and gentleman amateurs who had been designing prestigious American buildings. When Latrobe made the extraordinary gesture of presenting two proposals—one Gothic and the other Roman—to Bishop Carroll, he offered the following explanation:

> The veneration which the Gothic cathedrals generally excite by their peculiar style, by the associations belonging particularly to that style, and by the real grandeur and beauty which it possesses, has induced me to propose the Gothic style of building in the first design submitted to you. The Gothic style of the cathedrals is impracticable for the use of common life, while the Greek and Roman ar-

Benjamin Latrobe. Baltimore Cathedral, Baltimore, Maryland: 1804–1821. The Roman design Latrobe presented to the Bishop of Baltimore was a significantly new type of church having a Neoclassical portico, two towers with cupolas, and a Pantheon-like dome. (Maryland Historical Society.)

chitecture has descended from the most magnificent temples to the decoration of our meanest furniture. On this account I conceive that the former has a peculiar claim to preference, especially as the expense is not greater in proportion to the effect. The second design which is Roman, has, as far as I can judge of my own work, equal merit with the first in point of plan and structure, and I therefore submit the choice to you entirely, having myself an equal desire to see the first or the second erected, my habits inclining me to the latter, while my reasonings prefer the first.

In offering alternative designs, Latrobe not only broke with the tradition of Georgian churches, but also challenged the idea of stylistic unity within a given age. His leaving the final choice to Bishop Carroll implied that style could be freely chosen by the client. The diocese chose the Roman design because it promised a rationally articulated cathedral with a compact plan appropriate to the restricted site, and after several years of frustrating but significant revisions, construction began. Its cruciform plan made it possible for the various liturgical areas to retain their own spatial identity and yet fuse together into a larger, dynamically integrated whole, centered in a domed rotunda. In contrast to Charleston's St. Michael's—essentially a simple, rectangular enclosure with little definition between the area of the congregation and that of the clergy—the

Baltimore Cathedral is designed as a response to the nature of the liturgy. And whereas previous American churches had been spanned with wood-truss roofs—either covered by lath and plaster ceilings as at St. Michael's, or left exposed as at St. Luke's in Smithfield, Virginia—Latrobe's engineering skills led him to erect large-scale masonry vaults, the first ever attempted in a major American building. The sequence of a barrel vault and small dome in the nave, a monumental dome over the rotunda, and a half dome in the apse displays great formal virtuosity in the relating of its parts to the structural logic of the whole.

The Neoclassicism of Latrobe is stylistically distinguishable from Georgian architecture in yet another respect. Although in both styles the classical orders provided the primary source of ornamentation, the Tuscan portico of St. Michael's was simply the latest phase in a continuous evolution—from Greece to Rome, thence to the Italian Renaissance, and then to eighteenth-century England—whereas Latrobe derived his classical orders far more specifically from Greek and Roman prototypes, as in the Ionic portico of the cathedral (which when erected in 1863 followed his design). His interest in structural integrity, likewise, was inspired by antiquity, since the rotunda was in part based on the Pantheon in Rome.

Just before the cathedral was dedicated in 1821, the trustees gave to Latrobe an acknowledgment of gratitude such as clients all too frequently fail to express:

> This magnificent building, the design and plan of which are entirely yours, is fast approaching completion, and bids fair to stand for ages as a monument, not only to the piety of those who have contributed to its construction, but likewise to your genius and architectural skill and taste.

As the mother church of Roman Catholicism in the United States, the Baltimore Cathedral was national rather than regional: built for a denomination not established in the Old South, designed by an architect of international stature, and based on no indigenous traditions. Since, moreover, Baltimore was a city more like Philadelphia than Charleston, and one that would become less and less "southern" with the progress of nineteenth-century industry and urbanization, its cathedral is an example of architecture *in* the South, rather than of truly *southern architecture*.

GOVERNMENT STREET PRESBYTERIAN CHURCH, MOBILE, ALABAMA
(1835–1837)

The continued preference for high-style churches in the South in the antebellum period was determined by taste rather than tradition. Greek architecture offered Christian churches few advantages, either functionally or ideologically. Yet numerous congregations surrounded themselves with templelike enclosures because fashion advocated it. Greek temples, from whose interiors the worshiping laity were excluded, were oriented primarily to the exterior. To make the temple plan more usable for a Christian congregation, the interior space was enlarged and illuminated by replacing the side columns with walls. The columned and pedimented portico and the ornamental motifs of the interior decoration were all that remained of the ancient model.

The Greek Revival had been slow to develop in the South because of inherent conservatism and local provincialism; often the style was intro-

James Gallier and Charles Dakin. Government Street Presbyterian Church, Mobile, Alabama: 1835–1837. Exactly contemporary with the eighteenth-century-inspired St. Philip's Church of Charleston, the Government Street Presbyterian Church is an example of Greek Revival where classical correctness was particularly emphasized on the façade.

duced by architects from the North. But once it had arrived, it thrived on the very conservatism that had delayed its acceptance. Greek architecture was composed of the same basic elements as Georgian, and although a connoisseur could discriminate between the correct use of the Greek orders and the freer treatment of colonial columns and capitals, to most people the similarities were more compelling than the differences. The distinguishing quality of Greek Revival is the discreteness of elements— verticals and horizontals, smooth and articulated surfaces, and large and small motifs—integrated into a balanced, rhythmically proportioned composition.

At Mobile the advent of Greek Revival occurred in the mid-1830s with the Government Street Presbyterian Church.[7] Three New Orleans architects—James Gallier and Charles and James Dakin, all of whom had recently been associated with the New York Greek Revivalists, Ithiel Town and Alexander Jackson Davis—had a hand in the design. The chastely monumental façade is composed of distinct but interrelated Ionic columns, flanking pilasters, and a unifying entablature and pediment. The conservatism of southern architecture is apparent in the interior, whose format is essentially that of St. Michael's in Charleston—a rectangular nave with galleries on three sides. Only the ornamentation is truly in the manner of the Greek Revival: the capitals supporting the galleries were derived from the Tower of the Winds and those of the reredos from the Choragic Monument of Lysicrates—two Athenian monuments whose orders were often copied. Although the battered sides of the reredos are more Egyptian than Greek, the total effect is one of harmonious solemnity. An English visitor wrote in 1842 of the erudite taste displayed by the church:

> Its interior is unsurpassed in chasteness of style and elegance of decoration in the United States. There is a singular, but at the same time, a very happy union of the Egyptian and Greek in the elevated platform, answering the purposes of the pulpit, and the semi-Theban and semi-Corinthian [reredos], which seems to rise behind the platform, with the rich diagonally-indented ceiling, and luxurious sofa-like pews, make this interior altogether the most strikingly beautiful I ever remember to have seen.[8]

First Presbyterian Church, Nashville, Tennessee (1848–1851)

Egyptian Revival, of which the Government Street Presbyterian Church reredos was a forerunner, like Greek Revival, was employed for aesthetic rather than ideological reasons. Egyptian architecture implied solidity and permanence; hence the Revival style was used for churches, cemeteries, and even prisons. One of the finest surviving examples is the First Presbyterian Church in Nashville, designed by William Strickland and built in the late 1840s.[9] Strickland had gained a national reputation as a Greek Revivalist and had come to Nashville to supervise the construction of the Tennessee State Capitol. A Nashville newspaper reporter admitted to bewilderment over a church "constructed (it is said) chiefly according to the Egyptian style of architecture. Not being a student or learned in that style, we would not venture an opinion as to its appropriateness for a modern Christian church."[10]

The basic plan was conventional—a rectangular auditorium and a colonnaded entrance between two towers. The portico columns are com-

William Strickland. First Presbyterian Church, Nashville, Tennessee, interior: 1848–1851. The interior ornamentation was heightened in the 1880s by the vivid painting of the columns and the illusionistic fresco, giving the effect of an Egyptian hypostyle hall. (Historic American Buildings Survey, photo: Jack Boucher.)

posed of bundled stalks which burst free at the top to form capitals, and the entablature has the typical moldings of an Egyptian pylon. Similar moldings characterize the window surrounds, which together with the battered sides reveal that the ornament was primarily superficial. The same motifs are used in the interior (redecorated in the 1880s in an even more intensely Egyptian manner). The lotus capitals on both sides of the chancel and the illusionistic painting of columns on the walls offered a fitting, if theatrical, background for Old Testament readings concerning the Israelites in Egypt—but were less relevant to the New Testament Gospels, or to the life of nineteenth-century Nashville. The overwhelmingly heavy architectural features emblazoned with rich polychromy are explicitly Victorian—vivid testimony to the capriciousness of taste when ecclesiastical architecture was a matter of style rather than tradition.

Church of the Nativity, Union, South Carolina (1855–1859)

Mid-nineteenth-century eclecticism also included a revival of Gothic—a style that had influenced St. Luke's, Smithfield, the earliest surviving southern church. But with the advent of ecclesiology, a movement within Catholic and Episcopal circles toward liturgical reform, Gothic was promoted as truly Christian architecture capable of inspiring religious devotion. The Episcopal Church of the Nativity in Union, South Carolina, is a southern example of ecclesiological Gothic Revival.[11] The parish was a missionary venture in the Piedmont area, where liberal Protestants far outnumbered Episcopalians. Services were held sporadically in the 1840s and early 1850s, but the congregation was kept alive largely by the efforts of three sisters—Mary Poulton Dawkins, Charlotte Poulton, and Jane Poulton McLure. Mary Poulton, after beginning "life in England, a child of the Church," had come to the United States with her family in 1833. She had been educated at the Emma Willard Seminary in Troy, New York, and became a teacher at a school near Union, where she soon married a prominent South Carolina lawyer and judge, Thomas N. Dawkins. She remained proudly English, however, asserting on one occasion that nothing "would induce me to forfeit the privilege of being an English woman." When she and her husband visited England in 1852, they found in the village of Isleworth, near the family estate 10 miles outside London, a small Gothic nineteenth-century church (now destroyed), which Mary Dawkins decided to replicate in Union. She obtained plans of it from London, and the cornerstone was laid in 1855. Construction was slow because members of the parish did most of the labor themselves. Granite was quarried nearby and hauled to the site by Judge Dawkins's

Church of the Nativity, Union, South Carolina: 1855–1859. Ecclesiological Gothic Revival stressed the purity of worship through a return to the historically Christian architecture of the Middle Ages.

teams of horses. Contemporary references chart the progress of the work up until the church was consecrated in 1859:

> There is in the process of erection, a very handsome stone church, built entirely by the citizens of the place, and chiefly by the liberality of two gentlemen. . . . A beautiful sanctuary is progressing toward completion, by means of the zealous efforts of the churchmen of that vicinity. . . . The church edifice is said to be one of the handsomest in the state. It is of stone and of Gothic architecture.[12]

The plan of the Church of the Nativity—typical of English parish churches promoted by the great leader of ecclesiology, Augustus Welby Pugin, and also manifest in two North American churches begun in 1846, St. James the Less, Philadelphia, and St. Anne's, Fredericton, New Brunswick—is composed of two rectangular parts, nave and chancel, separated by the break in the roof surface. Gabled porches provide entrances on both sides of the nave, and the five lancet windows on the wall opposite the altar lead upward to the bell cote. The Gothic verticality of pointed arches and steeply pitched roofs is balanced by the human scale of the doorways and the ecclesiastical furnishings inside. The overall effect, therefore, is an uplifting but intimate experience for a small parish of zealous communicants. The nave space is unbroken by columns, and the wall surfaces of stucco over granite give a feeling of secure enclosure, whose austerity is softened by the oak pews and reredos—the latter carved by the rector—and by the stained glass that was added later in memorial to the Poulton sisters and others.

The missionary purpose and the conception of a hallowed space are reminiscent of colonial parish churches. The Church of the Nativity, however, is distinguished by the strength and ruggedness of its granite masonry from such Georgian churches as St. James', Goose Creek, with its soft-colored stucco surfaces, and Christ Church, Lancaster County, with its formal brickwork. Whereas the Gothic elements of St. Luke's, Smithfield, amount to an unconscious survival, the Church of the Nativity is a late, purposeful attempt to erect an English building in the South—one of the last before the Civil War brought traditional southern architecture to a halt.

CHAPTER FIVE

PATRONS AND ARCHITECTS: THE SHAPING OF SOUTHERN LIFE

The country house, England's greatest contribution to the history of architecture, developed during the seventeenth and eighteenth centuries into a consummate work of art, designed to meet the formal and functional requirements of a more fluid society, based on an increasingly mercantile economy and a changing political structure that gave new power to Parliament. The southern plantation house was a variation on the theme of the English country house; its architecture was influenced by English taste, its manner of living defined by English fashion. Yet it was also shaped by indigenous factors such as climate and topography, which differed significantly from the English landscape. High-style living in the South was an achievement in itself; but even more remarkable was its enduring relation to the mother country.

Both English and southern houses emanated more often from the patron's aspirations than from an architect's design. The English amateur architect Roger Pratt summarized, about 1660, the way in which a country house was conceived and erected:

> First resolve with yourself what house will be answerable to your purse and estate, and after you have pitched upon the number of rooms and the dimensions of each, and ... if you be not able to handsomely contrive it yourself, get some ingenious gentleman who has seen much of that kind abroad and been somewhat versed in the best authors of architecture: viz. Palladio, Scamozzi, Serlio, etc., to do it for you, and to give you a design of it in paper.... Show this afterwards to men of ingenuity, ... and after you have had the advice and heard the discourses of many such, ... get a model to be most exactly framed accordingly, and ... so go on with your building, or change it till it pleases you.[1]

65

Pratt had collaborated with his cousin George Pratt in the building of Coleshill, the most important English country house of the mid-seventeenth century; its formal planning centered around a two-story stairway hall, a great parlor on the main floor, and directly above it a state dining chamber—an arrangement Pratt specifically recommended:

> Let the fairest rooms . . . be placed in the very midst of the house, . . . for so the grace of them will appear the greater, and as for the other rooms which shall be thought necessary to be added, let them be equally placed both as to dimension and number, on one side and the other.

The secondary rooms were flexible in function, serving as parlors, withdrawing rooms, or bedrooms for the host and his guests. Such a house was a hierarchical sequence of spaces, reflecting the social etiquette of the period.

In the colonial South, Stratford Hall and Drayton Hall followed the same basic organization. Any given room could be used for more than one different purpose; dining, for example, instead of being localized in one place, might occur in any of several separate rooms, depending on the formality of the occasion and the status of the guests. The great hall at Stratford Hall was without heating, and it interrupted normal circulation through the house. But it provided a center to which the host and his guest of honor could come from the apartments assigned to them in the wings of the house and meet as social equals. When no visitor of distinction was present, the family could live comfortably in its own wing. In its Palladian symmetry, Drayton Hall is an even more specific re-creation of the English formal house, with pretensions that lift it beyond the mundane realities of a Low Country rice plantation.

MILES BREWTON HOUSE, CHARLESTON, SOUTH CAROLINA (1765–1769)

The emulation of English social customs also occurred in the townhouses of southern cities. The initial plans of the Miles Brewton House in Charleston presumably had been formed in typical eighteenth-century fashion, out of the ideas of an informed and sensitive client, the use of architectural handbooks, and the influence of nearby Drayton Hall. The architect directly responsible was Ezra Waite, who in a professional résumé described himself as "civil architect, house-builder in general, and carver, from London."[2] He had, the résumé continues, "finished the architecture, conducted the execution thereof, . . . and carved all the said work in the four principal rooms; and also calculated, adjusted, and drew at large for to work by, the Ionic entablature, and carved the same in the front and round the eaves."

That Brewton aspired to the style of the English gentry is evident from the countrified appearance of his house, a freestanding structure on a large lot which had not been subdivided as Charleston's urban density increased. Its plan, with four rooms on each floor divided by an entrance hall and stairway, was common in pre-Revolutionary Charleston. Somewhat less formal than Drayton Hall, it offered an urbane setting more appropriate for a prominent merchant. Four entertaining rooms are located on the front of the house: on the first floor a reception room and dining room, on the second a drawing room and a withdrawing room, which provided for the separation of the sexes after dinner according to the English custom, allowing the men to drink, smoke, and converse by themselves. As with the English formal house, admission to the various rooms indicated the status of the guest. A business acquaintance or a daytime caller would be entertained in the reception room; the dining room was used primarily by members of the family; only a specially invited guest

Ezra Waite. Miles Brewton House, Charleston, South Carolina: 1765–1769. High style, rather than vernacular adaptations to the subtropical climate, characterizes one of the earliest Charleston houses for which a specific architect has been identified.

ascended to the drawing room where lavish formal dining, dancing, and musical events took place.

What distinguishes the Brewton House from numerous other Charleston houses of similar plan is sumptuous ornament, including imported marble fireplaces, columns of Portland stone, and the carved work for which it is likely that Waite was specifically brought from London. By claiming in his résumé "twenty-seven years experience, both in theory and practice, in noblemen and gentlemen's seats," Waite reveals not only his credentials but also the high-style aspirations of his client. Waite advertised for further commissions when the house was finished in 1769; however, he died in Charleston within three months. Brewton himself was to enjoy the architectural masterpiece only briefly: he and his family were lost at sea in 1775.

GUNSTON HALL, FAIRFAX COUNTY, VIRGINIA (1755–1759)

Unlike Waite, whose career was entirely established in England, William Buckland became an architect after arriving in America. Born at Oxford in 1734, he was apprenticed at thirteen to his uncle, a member of the London Joiners' Company and a publisher and seller of architectural books. During his seven-year apprenticeship Buckland learned to make wood paneling and the surrounds for chimneypieces, doors, and windows—the same skills Ezra Waite had mastered. In 1755 Buckland signed an indenture to Thomson Mason, who after finishing his law studies in London was about to return to Virginia, where his older brother, George Mason, had already begun building a plantation house on the Potomac River.[3] The terms of the contract were a legacy of the medieval craft system:

> That he the said William Buckland shall and will, as a faithful covenant servant, well and truly serve the said Thomson Mason, his executors and assigns in the plantation of Virginia beyond the seas, for the space of four years, next ensuing his arrival in the said plantation, in the employment of a carpenter and joiner.

Buckland probably crossed the Atlantic with Mason, bringing along the architectural handbooks that were his most important possession (Buckland's estate in 1774 included fourteen such volumes, half of which were published before 1755).

Gunston Hall, for whose interior woodwork the twenty-year-old carpenter and joiner had been indentured, is a restrained, one-and-a-half-

William Buckland. Gunston Hall, Fairfax County, Virginia: 1755–1759. The simple story-and-a-half house was already under construction when Buckland arrived in Virginia. He added the semioctagonal porch, modeled after plate XXXI in Batty Langley, Gothic Architecture Improved by Rules and Proportions in Many Grand Designs (*1742*).

story house placed comfortably on the land, its simple brick walls and restful horizontal profile, under a sheltering roof, expressing domestic tranquillity. Exterior ornament is limited to the stone quoins at the corners and the modillioned cornice of the eaves. Mason apparently wanted a house in which he could enjoy a private life with his immediate family, and this he accomplished in the half of the house where the office-library and his bedchamber were located; the second story was a series of bedrooms for his nine children. But his public career as an eminent constitutional lawyer increasingly associated him with Virginia political leaders, and the house had to be sufficiently elegant for the visits of men such as George Washington and Thomas Jefferson. Accordingly, the other side consisted of a spacious hall, a dining room, and a drawing room for formal entertaining.

With youthful boldness, Buckland proceeded to apply his newly acquired skills in joinery to ornamenting these formal rooms. The Palladian drawing room was modeled after details in Batty Langley, *The City and Country Builder's and Workman's Treasury of Designs* (1740), and Abraham Swan, *The British Architect* (1745). The Chinese Chippendale dining room was more precocious in its derivation from Thomas Chippendale, *The Gentleman and Cabinetmaker's Director* (1754). These innovations introduced Palladianism and Chinese Chippendale, two artistic movements which previously had not influenced Virginia interiors. A third style, Gothic, characterized the semioctagonal porch which Buckland added on the south front, combining ogee arches adapted from Batty Langley, *Gothic Architecture Improved by Rules and Proportions in Many Grand Designs* (1742), with classical pilasters and triglyphs. In approving the eclectic designs of a craftsman trying to prove himself several thousand miles from his roots, Mason was doing very much the same thing. The house as a whole reveals the tension between simple family living, on the one hand, and sumptuous entertainment on the other.

When Buckland's indenture came to an end in 1759, Mason wrote the following recommendation:

> During the time [Buckland] lived with me he had the entire direction of the carpenters and joiners work of a large house; and having behaved very faithfully in my service, I can with great justice recommend him to any gentleman that may have occasion to employ him, as an honest sober diligent man, and I think a complete master of the carpenter's and joiner's business both in theory and practice.

Gunston Hall, drawing room. The overscaled ornament, modeled after English architectural handbooks, exudes Buckland's youthful enthusiasm for his first commission in the New World, as well as George Mason's desire to decorate his house in the latest Palladian fashion. (Sandak, Inc.)

Having established his credentials, Buckland remained in Virginia, where he received subsequent commissions for the interior decoration of country houses, most notably Colonel John Tayloe's Mt. Airy (1758–1762) in Richmond County. In 1771, after one of Tayloe's daughters married a Maryland planter, Edward Lloyd, Buckland was summoned to Annapolis to complete the Chase-Lloyd House (1769–1774). By then his own fortunes had risen: his household in 1772 included, besides his wife and three children, a former apprentice, five indentured servants, and five slaves. A portrait by Charles Willson Peale in 1774 shows him dressed as a gentleman with draftsman's instruments and a plan and elevation of another house he had just built.

Matthias Hammond House, Annapolis, Maryland (1773–1774)

Buckland not only supervised the construction and designed the ornament but was also the architect of the Matthias Hammond House (the one shown in his portrait).[4] Handbooks still inspired such details as the entrance doorway and the dining-room chimneypiece, which were derived from Swan, *The British Architect*. But unlike Gunston Hall, where the ornament is overscaled to the modest-sized rooms, the Hammond House is skillfully integrated in every respect—a development from the natural maturing of the craftsman-architect, given scope by a commission which allowed him to design as well as decorate.

Built on the eve of the American Revolution, the Hammond House shows many characteristics of domestic architecture in the Federal period. The overall plan, consisting of five discrete but connected volumes, allowed for functional use of the flankers as a law office and kitchen respectively, while the dominant central block contained the living areas. Exterior ornament is restricted to the axial bay on both front and back, and to the stairway window on the south side. Because the stairway is not part of the central hall, the plan permits the rooms to vary in size, use, and embellishment, from a small library and bedroom to the spacious dining room and ballroom. This diversity reflected a desire to locate domestic functions in specific areas—an innovative feature of the Federal house. Even the ornament of the main rooms is progressive, in that plaster surfaces replaced the wood paneling characteristic of Georgian walls. Buckland had become an architect capable of designing a house to meet the future needs of independent Americans.

Would Buckland have developed in the same way if he had stayed in England? A comparison with a contemporary architect may suggest an answer to this intriguing question. Robert Adam, five years older than Buckland, was the son of a prominent Scottish architect and was edu-

William Buckland. Matthias Hammond House, Annapolis, Maryland, dining room: 1773-1774. Buckland's talents as an architect as well as a craftsman are apparent in the masterful design of the dining room, with no element out of place or overscaled. (Sandak, Inc.)

cated at the University of Edinburgh. Adam left England, just one year before Buckland's departure for Virginia, on a trip which would irrevocably set the course of his career. But instead of going to the New World, Adam traveled to Italy and Dalmatia to study Roman domestic architecture. Upon his return he proceeded to revolutionize English interior house planning and ornamentation. Buckland, had he remained in England, might have become a mere follower of Adam. Instead, his journey to America provided the means by which he became an architect, since his talents in carpentry and joinery were precisely those which colonists used to emulate English high style.

Buckland's own synthesis of formality and functionalism in the Hammond House could hardly have been derived from Adam, since the *Works in Architecture of Robert and James Adam,* first published in 1773, was not listed in Buckland's inventory of 1774. Rather, it was a direct response to his client's requirements—a townhouse in which he could practice law and also entertain as a member of Annapolis society. The Hammond House and Adam's virtually contemporary work emerge from two very different worlds, whose divergence the coming American Revolution confirmed.

JOSEPH MANIGAULT HOUSE, CHARLESTON, SOUTH CAROLINA
(1802–1803)

While the Adam brothers' *Works in Architecture* was being published in installments, during the 1770s, the Revolutionary War slowed down American building and eventually brought it to a halt. When recovery finally came in the 1790s, however, the influence of Adam was overwhelming. Adamesque style tended to be acceptable in America because it differed significantly from Georgian, the style associated with the colonial phase of American history, although another reason may have been the nature of Adamesque style itself. By combining Neoclassical motifs and functional planning, Adam invented an ornamental vocabulary consisting of, in his own words, "a beautiful variety of light mouldings, gracefully formed, delicately enriched, and . . . a great diversity of ceilings, friezes, and decorated pilasters," to which he had "added grace and beauty . . . by a mixture of stucco and painted ornaments, together with the flowing rainceau, with its fanciful and winding foliage."[5]

Notwithstanding the acceptance of the new style in decoration, the practice of architecture in America was slow to change. In the North, Samuel McIntire was influenced by the Adamesque style, but remained a craftsman-architect in the tradition of Buckland. Asher Benjamin compiled in 1797 the first American handbook popularizing Adam's work, even though during this phase of his career he was more a builder than a professional architect. In the South the Adamesque style was introduced with the banquet hall which George Washington added at Mount Vernon in 1784–1787. A decade later, a gentleman–amateur architect, Gabriel Manigault, used it in several of his buildings in Charleston. Born in 1758, Manigault was descended from well-established Low Country families. His maternal grandfather, a member of the Royal Council of South Carolina, possessed a small collection of architectural handbooks (a fact perhaps no more than coincidental, since he died before Manigault was born), and his paternal grandfather was one of the commissioners responsible for the building of St. Michael's Church. After studying law in London during the late 1770s, Manigault returned to South Carolina in 1780, bringing with him his own small architectural library. In the 1790s he began to design buildings in a style largely derived from Adam, whose London work of the 1770s dates from just before Manigault's stay and whose *Works in Architecture* could have been among the volumes Manigault brought back with him.

By the end of the century, several popular handbooks espousing Adamesque ideas had appeared, including William Pain's *British Palladio* (1798) and Asher Benjamin's *The Country Builder's Assistant* (1797). Whether or not Manigault had access to these volumes, his work parallels them in tending to reduce the scale of Adam's ornamentation to

Gabriel Manigault. Joseph Manigault House, Charleston, South Carolina: 1802–1803. After the Revolutionary War, Georgian ornamentation was considered inappropriate; hence, the Federal style featured simpler wall surfaces and, frequently, curving elements.

one more appropriate to the early republic. As a gentleman-amateur who was primarily a rice planter (he owned five Low Country plantations), Manigault designed no fewer than five buildings in Charleston—the Bank of the United States (now the City Hall), South Carolina Society Hall, the Orphan House Chapel, his own townhouse, and his masterpiece, a house for his brother Joseph.[6] Virtually no contemporary documentation associates Manigault with any of these buildings (the attributions come almost entirely from a family history of 1897), and there is no record that he was ever paid for his services. But in these commissions, he acted as a professional in the sense that, unlike the craftsman or builder architects of his time, he furnished plans to a client who then turned them over to a contractor for construction.

During the first two decades of the nineteenth century, the great southern residences were townhouses in Richmond, Charleston, and Savannah; they were without the aristocratic pretensions of the houses that had been built before the Revolutionary War or of those that characterized the antebellum period. The Manigault House is a gauntly vertical, freestanding structure of brick with austere wall surfaces, whose uneasy relation to a fairly ample lot is very different from the way a Georgian plantation house takes possession of its site. The only variations in its rectangular volume are three semicircular projections and a two-story porch. These features are the result of the interior plan, rather than any effort to integrate the house with its surroundings. The entrance on the north leads under a gracefully cantilevered stairway to the hall, which divides the first floor between, on one side, the library and music room, and the dining room on the other. The ornamentation is scaled to the size and function of each room, varying from simple details in the library to elaborate moldings in the dining room. On the second floor a similar contrast exists between the master bedroom and the drawing room, the most elegantly decorated in the house.

The ornament, derived from Adam, consists of attenuated columns and pilasters framing doors, windows, and chimneypieces; lyrical swags, foliate chains, and spiraling rainceaux extending across mantels and cornices; and a ceiling medallion above the stairway. Whereas Adam had adapted classical motifs in marble by reducing the sense of weight and three-dimensionality of the various elements, the materials used in the Manigault House are wood and plaster. The overall effect is a light, airy net of details stretched two-dimensionally across surfaces, rhythmically

Joseph Manigault House, drawing room. In typical Charleston fashion the main entertaining room is on the second floor, where it could receive the maximum amount of the available breezes. (Charleston Museum.)

William Jay. Richard Richardson House, Savannah, Georgia: 1817–1819. In design the house is thoroughly English, but local materials were used, particularly the "tabby" of which many of the walls were made. "Tabby," a mixture of burnt oyster shells, sand, and water, approximates concrete. (The Owens-Thomas House of the Telfair Museum of Art.)

unifying the design of the whole, which can be described as proceeding outward from within. In this sense, it anticipates the functional architecture of Louis Sullivan and Frank Lloyd Wright. Even circulation appears to have been carefully considered: the house has a service corridor and stairway, such as were not usual in contemporary Charleston "single houses." The masterful handling of inherently architectural aspects indicates that Manigault, although a gentleman-amateur, was a true architect in spirit.

RICHARD RICHARDSON HOUSE, SAVANNAH, GEORGIA (1817–1819)

During the first two decades of the nineteenth century, Savannah enjoyed exceptional prosperity. Until then the humble origins of the colony, its hesitant growth in the eighteenth century, and a disastrous fire in 1796 precluded progress comparable to that of Charleston, Savannah's more cultivated neighbor to the north. A traveler in 1804 unflatteringly described Savannah as "a wooden town built on a sand heap."[7] The squares were still open, unlandscaped spaces in 1810 when—following a boom in the cotton industry, made possible by Eli Whitney's invention of the cotton gin on a plantation near Savannah—the urban improvement finally began.

Savannah's sudden emergence as a cultural center paralleled the rise of Bath, a sleepy English village until the rediscovery of Roman baths made it a fashionable spa and a major center of Georgian architecture. William Jay, who had been born there in the early 1790s, attempted a similar transformation at Savannah. After developing a personal style under the influence of the Neoclassical architect John Soane, Jay moved to Savannah in 1817, following the marriage of his older sister into one of the city's prominent families. For another relative by marriage—the prosperous banker and cotton merchant Richard Richardson—Jay designed a house, probably before he left England.[8] The circumstances appear to have been similar to Gabriel Manigault's designing of a house for his brother Joseph. Unlike Manigault, however, Jay was by training and aspiration a professional architect eager to establish a career for himself in America.

Based on the work of Soane, the Richardson House introduced the Regency style to Savannah. In its freedom of plan, and the varied room sizes and shapes, it continued the Adamesque, or Federal, style, but with

Richard Richardson House, dining room. The Regency style is apparent in the exuberantly dramatic space generated by the curving walls and defined by bold Greek-inspired ornamental motifs. (The Owens-Thomas House of the Telfair Museum of Art.)

a more precise use of the classical orders. In its attenuation the Adamesque column had lost most of its supportive character, functioning primarily as a two-dimensional element. Soane had returned the column to
its original purpose, as a robust support with a capital and entablature
derived from Greek sources. He had also emphasized architectural volumes rather than surfaces. Whereas Adamesque interiors had been articulated by a decorative net stretched lightly across surfaces, Soane
molded space three-dimensionally, using ornament to define rather than
embellish it.

Jay's understanding of Soane is illustrated by the entry portico of
the Richardson House, which boldly projects with a curving base and
entablature. The circular stairs and the door recessed in a semicircular
niche turn the experience of entering into a spatial event. Inside the door,
and screening the vestibule from the stairway, are two Corinthian columns with capitals derived from the Choragic Monument of Lysicrates,
the Greek archetype for that order illustrated in Stuart and Revett's *Antiquities of Athens* (1762). By means of subtle contrast, the dining room
sets up a spatial dialogue among the oblong plan, the semicircular end
wall, and the rectangular chimneypiece. On the north wall the concavity
and convexity of a skylight interrupt the planar surface. The Greek fret
and cornice antefixes complete an architectural *tour de force* which only
a professional could have managed.

WILLIAM SCARBROUGH HOUSE, SAVANNAH, GEORGIA (1818–1819)

In embracing London fashion, the normal responses to building in a subtropical climate (sheltering piazzas, vertical orientation, and internal circulation) were almost entirely overlooked in the Richardson House. The
same is true of William Jay's next commission, a house for William Scarbrough, another prominent Savannah merchant. Here Jay used a simplified Doric portico on otherwise unornamented surfaces, so as to convey
heroic monumentality. Inside, a two-story skylighted atrium, one of the
most impressive interiors in American architecture, featured the most ar-
chaeologically correct Greek Doric to be found in the South at that date.
In 1819, shortly after it was built, the house was chosen as the place to
entertain President James Monroe. In prospect of the event, Scarbrough
wrote to his wife:

> Our house is quite in readiness for him. It is most tastefully and ele-
> gantly decorated and furnished—and seems to bring to the recollec-
> tion of all who have lately visited it—the house of the Lord Gover-

nor in the neighborhood of Chester and Liverpool. . . . The President must be pleased with Savannah; as in the whole course of his extended tour, he may be received at costly and splendid rate; but no where with such pure and genuine taste—Jay will begin to attain the prominence, which low jealousy and perverted judgment would not before award him.[9]

Jay's architecture was apparently considered fit for a President even though it was more English than American.

Jay established an office in Charleston and was appointed architect of the South Carolina Board of Public Works when it was organized in 1820. The year of what looked like the beginning of an impressive career brought with it not only a disastrous fire and an epidemic of yellow fever in Savannah, but also new tariff laws and an economic depression, such that the promise of work in Georgia and South Carolina failed to materialize. Jay's plans for a series of Charleston civic buildings were not implemented, and late in 1820 his place on the Board of Public Works was taken by Robert Mills. By 1824 he had returned to England. But as the architect responsible for giving Savannah the dignity implicit in the city's original plan, Jay had imparted a distinctive character that had no counterpart anywhere in America. Regency Savannah was described as early as 1836 as having "several very ambitious-looking dwellings, built by a European architect for wealthy merchants during the palmy days of trade; these are of stone or some composition, showily designed, and very large, but ill-adapted . . . for summer residences in this climate."[10]

CHAPTER SIX

WASHINGTON AND JEFFERSON: ARCHITECTS OF THE AMERICAN REPUBLIC

Conceived in emulation of the English landed gentry, plantations became the dynastic seats from which political leaders could be expected to emerge. The ascendancy of Virginia during the early years of the American republic gave two eminently southern plantations—George Washington's Mount Vernon and Thomas Jefferson's Monticello—a national character. And together the two men charted the initial course for the architecture of the United States.

MOUNT VERNON, FAIRFAX COUNTY, VIRGINIA (1759–1787)

A patent on Mount Vernon's spectacular site, overlooking the Potomac River, had been obtained by a great-grandfather of George Washington in 1674, and the property had been continuously in the family when Washington purchased it in 1754 after the death of his half-brother. When Washington's military assignment with General Edward Braddock in the French and Indian War ended, he brought his new bride, Martha Dandridge Custis, to Mount Vernon with every expectation of retiring from public life: "I am now, I believe, fixed at this spot with an agreeable consort for life and hope to find more happiness in retirement than I ever experienced amidst a wide and bustling world."[1]

The house on the property, a simple story-and-a-half building, was similar in plan to George Mason's Gunston Hall, just a few miles downriver, with four rooms and a central hall on the main floor. Washington stripped the house to its wooden frame and then added one story to its height, redecorating the interior with chimneypieces, door and window surrounds, and cornices in the finest Georgian style. He covered the exterior with "rusticated boards" which simulated masonry in the beveling of their edges and the mixing of sand with the paint that covered them. Out of these origins emerged an asymmetry that would not have been present had the design been laid down all at one time—as the extent of the changes suggests that Washington might as easily have done. Thus, the renovations indicate respect for the existing structure, small and unpretentious though it was. In comparison with the brick plantation houses at Stratford Hall and Westover, and with the virtually contemporary Gunston Hall, the wood construction of Mount Vernon was architecturally far less sophisticated. By retaining the core of the house, Washington rooted his destiny in that of his ancestors.

Washington's country retirement was interrupted in 1775, when he assumed command of the Continental Army. Even though he was almost continually away from Mount Vernon during the Revolutionary War, however (he stopped there briefly on his way to and from Yorktown), work on the enlargement of the house continued. As early as 1773, he had begun additions at both ends of the house—a library on the south and a banquet hall on the north. Since these were not family rooms, they appear to contradict Washington's earlier statement that simple country living was his most cherished dream. In the 1780s the library became the

Mount Vernon, Fairfax County, Virginia: 1759–1787. The monumental portico, added to the river front, was George Washington's way of integrating the successive building campaigns into a formal design that belied the humble origins of the house. (Gerald Allen.)

place where he did most of his thinking and writing about constitutional government, and the banquet hall was sufficiently elegant for his use as the first President of the United States (1789–1797). If Washington had planned the rooms in the 1790s rather than before the Declaration of Independence, all this would have been less surprisingly prophetic. In any event, Washington did not actively seek public life; persistently stalked by it, he reluctantly acquiesced. The development of Mount Vernon is made still more remarkable by the fact that Washington was childless. Although he raised his wife's children by her first marriage and in 1781 adopted two grandchildren, the Custis heirs did not figure prominently in his will. After his wife's death the mansion went to his nephew, Bushrod Washington, who from 1799 to 1829 was an associate justice of the Supreme Court. Transcending the usual functions of a southern plantation, Mount Vernon became a symbol of the transformation of colonial America into an independent republic.

The piazza erected in 1777 on the east front exemplifies this transformation. Its square columns are not high style, nor were they patterned after English sources. From every point of view the piazza is additive, yet it integrates, more fully than any other single element, the house with its site on a promontory above the river, providing a shaded breezeway so necessary for the humid climate of Virginia. The colossal portico rising two full stories, the first of its kind in American domestic architecture, became a prototype, the distinguishing feature of the antebellum plantation house.

Such an accomplishment would suggest the hand of a trained architect; but none has ever been definitively associated with Mount Vernon, during either the renovation of 1757–1759 or the enlargement of 1773–1787. Washington proceeded as a gentleman-amateur; his training as a surveyor enabled him to make measured drawings. Even during his absence he supervised the work through letters to his plantation manager, giving such instructions as these, in 1776: "The chimney of the [banquet] room should be exactly in the middle of it—the doors and every thing else to be exactly answerable and uniform—in short I would have the whole executed in a masterly manner." In the banquet hall, upon which Washington lavished his greatest attention, the chimney-piece was balanced on the opposite wall by a Palladian window specifically derived from Batty Langley's *Treasury of Designs* (1745). To an English friend whom he had met in Philadelphia, and who provided the marble mantel, Washington wrote in 1785: "I have the honor to inform you that the chimney piece is arrived, and, by the number of cases (ten) too elegant and costly by far, I fear for my own room and the republican style of living." What Washington meant by a "republican style of living" is not altogether clear, but his taste obviously was moving away from the ebullient Georgian of the earlier rooms. "I want," he asserted, "to finish [the banquet hall] in stucco. It is my intention to do it in a plain neat style; which, independently of its being the present taste (as I am informed) is my choice."[2] To the combination of reliance on architectural handbooks with a patron's connoisseurship which was generally characteristic of the eighteenth century, a progressive idea had been added: that a style could express an individual and even a nation.

Among the details of the banquet-hall ceiling, in addition to its Adamesque foliate chains and flowing rainceaux, were the shapes of agricultural implements—spades, pickaxes, and sickles—conveying Washington's delight in being a farmer. Under his direction Mount Vernon grew from 2,000 to more than 8,000 acres, divided into five separate farms. Among Virginia plantations it was neither the largest nor the most profitable. But Washington brought to it an unmistakable pride as well as affection:

> I think that the life of a husbandman of all others is the most delectable. It is honorable. It is amusing, and, with judicious management, it is profitable. . . . I do not hesitate to confess, that reclaiming, and laying the grounds down handsomely to grass, and in woods thinned, or in clumps, about the mansion house is among my first objects and wishes.

Toward the end of Washington's life, Mount Vernon was described by a Polish visitor:

> The whole plantation, the garden, and the rest prove well that a man born with natural taste may guess a beauty without having seen its model. The General has never left America; but when one sees his house and his home and his garden it seems as if he had copied the best samples of the grand old homesteads of England.

Mount Vernon was, however, anything but a copy of an English country house. It was rather, in its final form, one of the first consciously "republican" houses in America. When he died in 1799, Washington was eulogized as "first in war, first in peace, and first in the hearts of his countrymen." But equally important to the meaning of Mount Vernon is the concluding statement: "He was second to none in the humble and endearing scenes of private life."

MONTICELLO,
CHARLOTTESVILLE, VIRGINIA
(1769–1782)

George Washington, whose interests included architecture, landscape gardening, interior decoration, painting, and music—avocations typical of an eighteenth-century Virginia gentleman—was in vivid contrast to the second President of the United States. John Adams of Massachusetts, in a plaintive letter to his wife, expressed his vow that statecraft must take precedence over the arts:

> I must study politics and war, that my sons may have liberty to study mathematics and philosophy. My sons ought to study mathematics and philosophy, geography, natural history and naval architecture, navigation, commerce, and agriculture, in order to give their children a right to study painting, poetry, music, architecture, statuary, tapestry, and porcelain.[3]

Thomas Jefferson, the third President, not only acknowledged himself to be "an enthusiast on the subject of the arts," but as a matter of public policy set out "to improve the taste of my countrymen, to increase their reputation, to reconcile to them the respect of the world and procure them its praise."[4] Thus, architecture was aggressively linked with the development of the republic.

Jefferson's architectural theory is inseparable from his political philosophy, whose underlying concept of the necessity for rational change is also central to his phrasing of the Declaration of Independence: "That whenever any form of government becomes destructive of these ends, it is the right of the people to alter or to abolish it, and to institute new government." In 1787, the year after Shays's Rebellion threatened the peace of the Confederation, Jefferson declared his belief "that a little rebellion now and then is a good thing, and as necessary in the political world as storms in the physical. . . . It is a medicine necessary for the sound health of government. . . . God forbid we should ever be twenty years without such a rebellion."[5] Similarly, he thought of architecture not as fixed for eternity, but as constantly in evolution.

As a student at the College of William and Mary, Jefferson acquired an extracurricular knowledge of architecture, as well as an adverse opinion of the Wren-inspired Georgian style. He wrote of Williamsburg twenty years later:

> The college and hospital are rude, misshapen piles, which, but that they have roofs, would be taken for brick-kilns. . . . The genius of architecture seems to have shed its malediction over this land. Buildings are often erected, by individuals, of considerable expense. To give these symmetry and taste, would not increase their cost. It would only change the arrangement of the materials, the form and combination of the members. This would often cost less than the burthen of barbarous ornaments with which these buildings are sometimes charged. But the first principles of the art are unknown, and there exists scarcely a model among us sufficiently chaste to give an idea of them. Architecture being one of the fine arts, and as such within the department of a professor of the college, according to the new arrangement, perhaps a spark may fall on some young subjects

of natural taste, kindle up their genius, and produce a reformation in this elegant and useful art.[6]

This statement contains the dominant themes of a lifelong architectural avocation, which Jefferson first expressed in the building of Monticello. The most distinctively personal plantation house of the colonial period, it was placed triumphantly at the top of an 857-foot elevation near Charlottesville, on land he inherited from his father. Its topography differed significantly from the James River plantations Jefferson had known during his college years. Romantic in its rapport with nature and classical in its architectural style, Monticello resulted from "a spark [falling] on some young subject of natural taste." A site plan of 1771–1772 and contemporary diary entries describe the clearing and leveling of a plateau and the domestication of it through gardens and paths. With time and labor the house and the site became integrated. Monticello was to the Piedmont what a cultivated plantation was to the wilderness—a willful testament of man's presence amid primeval nature.

The history of Monticello is exceedingly complicated. Begun in the late 1760s, the house evolved over a period of forty years. Jefferson had acquired drafting skills from his father, a surveyor, and the precise and technically competent drawings that have survived reveal how thoroughly he controlled the design and construction. The initial concept grew from Jefferson's acquaintance with the Palladian-inspired architectural volumes at the College of William and Mary and in William Byrd's library at Westover. These influences are evident in the crisp geometry of the plan and the two-story portico of the façade. But instead of a cubical block like Drayton Hall or the Miles Brewton House in South Carolina—either of which would have appeared awkwardly heavy on the elevated site—Jefferson gave Monticello a cruciform plan, horizontal roof lines, and polygonal terminal bays. Villas in the *Select Architecture* (1755) of Robert Morris have similar features, and for one of them the author suggests a site much like Monticello's: "The situation for this structure should be on an eminence whose summit should overlook a long extended vale, and, if attainable, quite round the horizon."

Jefferson was innovative in dealing with the dependency structures essential to a plantation. Palladian precedent called for flanking wings either nearby or actually connected to the main house. Since at Monticello these would have limited the view and have detracted from the consummate idea of a structure to crown the site, Jefferson skillfully located below grade, in a U-shaped configuration extending from the house, not only the brewing and smoke rooms, the laundry, the kitchen and pantry, the wine, rum, and beer cellars, and the storeroom, but also the servants' quarters, stables, and carriage house. Since the terrain sloped on either side of the hilltop, colonnaded walkways allowed light and breeze to enter the various areas. Wholesome amenities were thus provided for the slaves without compromising the siting advantages of the main house. This arrangement gave Monticello a quality of life quite different from that of the typical Virginia plantation. At Westover and Mount Vernon one imagines bustling movements of slaves, overseers, and the family among the various buildings. At Monticello the mood must have been more serene, with all such activities largely invisible from the house and garden. In this way, Monticello ennobled the dignity of man and his bond with awe-inspiring nature.

A French traveler, the Marquis de Chastellux, described the interior of Monticello in 1782:

> This house, of which Mr. Jefferson was the architect, and often the builder, is constructed in an Italian style, and is quite tasteful, although not however without some faults; it consists of a large square pavilion, into which one enters through two porticos ornamented with columns. The grand floor consists chiefly of a large and lofty salon, or drawing room, which is to be decorated entirely in the antique style; above the salon is a library of the same form; two small wings, with only a ground floor and attic, are joined to this pavilion, and are intended to communicate with the kitchen, offices, etc. which will form on either side a kind of basement topped by a terrace.... It resembles none of the others seen in this country; so that it may be said that Mr. Jefferson is the first American who has consulted the fine arts to know how he should shelter himself from the weather.[7]

STATE CAPITOL, RICHMOND, VIRGINIA (1785–1789)

With the Revolutionary War over, Jefferson, like Washington before him, desired only retirement to the life of gentleman-planter. But after this ideal was destroyed by the death of his wife in 1782, partly to ease his own gloom he returned to government service. Work on Monticello stopped; it would not be resumed until eleven years later. In 1784 Jefferson sailed for France to negotiate commercial treaties between that country and the new American republic, and from 1785 to 1789 he served as minister to France. There, on a trip to Nîmes, the glories of classical antiquity, as revealed in one particular building, evoked his astonished adulation. "Here I am," he wrote, "... gazing whole hours at the Maison Carrée, like a lover at his mistress.... From Lyons to Nîmes I have been nourished with the remains of Roman grandeur."[8]

The Roman architecture of the Maison Carrée had excited Jefferson before he actually saw it. In 1780, when the Virginia state capital was moved from Williamsburg to Richmond, he had offered suggestions for a

Virginia State Capitol, plaster model: 1786. Thomas Jefferson and Charles-Louis Clérisseau adapted the design of the Maison Carrée at Nîmes for the Virginia State Capitol, and a plaster model made by Bloquet was then sent from France to Richmond. (Virginia State Library.)

governor's house and the capitol. His plans for the latter drew its temple format with an eight-columned portico from a volume by a French Neo-classicist, the *Monuments de Nîmes* (1778) of Charles-Louis Clérisseau, which contained views of the Maison Carrée. In 1785, Jefferson worked with Clérisseau on drawings for the capitol, which were sent to Rich-mond the following year with a plaster model. As Jefferson explained in a letter to James Madison:

> We took for our model what is called the Maison Carrée of Nîmes, one of the most beautiful, if not the most beautiful and precious morsel of architecture left us by antiquity. . . . It is very simple, but it is noble beyond expression, and would have done honor to our country as presenting much for our maturer age. . . . How is a taste in this beautiful art to be formed in our countrymen, unless we avail ourselves of every occasion when public buildings are to be erected, of presenting to them models for their study and imitation.[9]

Constructed between 1786 and 1789, the Virginia State Capitol marked a conscious break with the English architectural tradition, which until then had influenced virtually every colonial building. Neither inde-pendence nor Jefferson's preference for French culture alone fully ex-plains the importance of the shift. Ideologically appropriate architecture for the new American republic was difficult to find in 1785. Continued use of English style would imply cultural dependence rather than political independence. French architecture, as the product of a monarchy, was abhorrent to a country that had just overcome the "tyranny" of George III. Germany and Italy both consisted merely of disparate principalities offering little sense of national consciousness. Classical Rome, on the other hand, conjured up associations of heroic virtue, patriotic duty, and antique grandeur. For Jefferson the imagery of the Roman temple was so apt that in his mind it overrode the functional deficiencies of such a style as a setting for state government.

The ultimate meaning of the Virginia State Capitol lies in its overall purpose. Colonial buildings had often been expressions of the institutions which had erected them. But no American building had ever been quite so consciously exemplary. Jefferson truly believed that a properly designed building could influence the public as beneficially as a well-drafted piece of legislation. Buildings were more than utilitarian structures, status symbols, or objects of private delectation; they measured the cultural achievement of a nation.

That the Virginia State Capitol derived its classical form more directly from a specific antique source marks it as Neoclassical. Earlier American buildings such as St. Michael's Church in Charleston and Mount Vernon on the Potomac River, both featuring monumental porticos, had evolved from a continuum of Greek, Roman, Renaissance, Baroque, and English Palladian architecture. Implicit in the sequence of styles was the idea that each age assumed the architecture of its predecessor but altered it freely. Although before Jefferson English and French architects worked in a Neoclassical style, the Virginia State Capitol— with its strict archaeological approach to the classical orders—was its first American exemplar, the achievement of an amateur architect whose duties as a statesman actually prevented him from traveling to Rome.

MONTICELLO, CHARLOTTESVILLE, VIRGINIA (1796–1809)

Before leaving Paris, Jefferson was, in his own words, "violently smitten with the Hôtel de Salm, and used to go to the Tuileries almost daily to look at it."[10] The innovative plan of this house, which was under construction from 1782 to 1787, emphasized comfort and privacy rather than formality. What Jefferson admired most, however, was the Neoclassical façade, whose low horizontality gave the house the appearance of being one story high. When Jefferson traveled to England in 1786, he visited several country houses, including Chiswick House, the most influential of English Palladian villas. On his return to the United States, a second phase of construction of Monticello began, reshaping it in the combined images of Chiswick and the Hôtel de Salm. The alterations were substantial. Jefferson wrote in 1796: "I have begun the demolition of my house, and hope to get through its re-edification in the course of the summer."[11]

The Monticello that was built between 1796 and 1809, and which largely exists today, is proof of Jefferson's assimilative genius. The two-story portico was replaced by a one-story exterior, with second-floor rooms concealed behind the entablature and balustrade. To create a sense of center and to integrate the garden portico with the wings, he added an octagonal dome over the parlor—a significant change in which Jefferson sacrificed his second-story library, with its magnificent view, for a domed room that never had a specific purpose.

For all its evident debt to its models abroad, Monticello in its totality stands independent of both Chiswick, whose cool gray planar surfaces owe their beauty to geometrical precision, and the Hôtel de Salm, an urban villa oriented to the street with an ornamental sophistication that is entirely European. In adapting his sources, Jefferson drew on the earthy

Thomas Jefferson. Monticello, Charlottesville, Virginia: 1769–1782 and 1796–1809. Monticello is a series of studied contrasts: undoubtedly the most personal American house of its time, yet meant to be exemplary of how Americans should live; formal in its Old World sources, yet romantic in its relation to nature; and high style in its cultivation of the arts, yet scientific in its technological gadgetry. (Sandak, Inc.)

Monticello, parlor. Jefferson conceived the parlor as an art gallery where he could display his collection of Neoclassical paintings and sculpture, largely acquired during his years in France. (Thomas Jefferson Memorial Foundation, photo: Ed Roseberry)

colors and textures of brick. The polygonal and rectangular projections of the exterior softened its outlines, allowing the masonry forms to blend into the landscape. Classical ornament highlighted the surfaces without overwhelming the warmth of the brick. Combining English Palladianism and French Neoclassicism, Jefferson had nevertheless produced an American building.

In 1782 Monticello had consisted of a central parlor with a drawing room and dining room on either side, and bedrooms in the polygonal projections—a plan whose symmetry was typically Georgian, and also deficient in circulation. In the reconstruction Jefferson preserved the first-floor rooms and added a tier of rooms to the east, providing greater variety and internal corridors—both features of the Federal period. The new rooms were skillfully connected, and their sizes and shapes were in harmony with those of the old rooms. Functional zoning had made the house more comfortable. A large entrance hall was added to the east of the original Georgian parlor; these rooms designed for entertaining formed a major axis between the two porticos. On the south were Jefferson's private quarters, consisting of his bedroom, study, and library. On the other side were family rooms for more general use, including the dining room, the tea room, and two bedrooms. Where functions interrelated (as in Jefferson's own quarters), the spaces flowed freely; where different uses were juxtaposed (as in the north set of rooms), the spaces were clearly separated.

Jefferson positioned his bed in an alcove between the bedroom and study, allowing for a cool breeze in summer. In winter the location of the bed kept it away from drafty exterior walls, and curtains enclosed it for even greater warmth. Gadgets abounded in the house—a weathervane, a hallway clock, double opening doors, and a dumbwaiter—showing Jefferson to be a technical innovator as well as a theorist. And he developed every opportunity for symbolic meaning. In the parlor, the most formal room, the friezes of the mantelpiece and cornice depict agricultural implements similar to those of the banquet-hall ceiling at Mount Vernon, celebrating the fact that, like Washington, he was above all else a farmer.

The parlor was at the same time designed to serve as a gallery where Jefferson's collection of more than sixty paintings and many sculptures (one of the first American art collections) could be displayed. The entrance hall eventually became a veritable museum of natural history, housing specimens brought back by Lewis and Clark from their expedition through the Pacific Northwest. Jefferson's library contained more than sixty books on architecture, representing virtually all the authors and periods he had admired and assimilated to his own use. As a reflection of Jefferson's encyclopedic humanism, Monticello is a fascinating combination of contrasts: Old World and New World, formality and functionalism, and even art and science.

A site plan of 1771–1772 shows Monticello situated in a cultivated garden, whose straight or semicircular walkways and regular plantings were appropriate to the Palladian character of the early house. During his trip to England in 1786, Jefferson had discovered, in the beauty of the informal garden, one aspect of English art he could truly admire. He wrote near the end of his presidency:

> The grounds which I destine to improve in the style of the English gardens are in a form very difficult to be managed. They compose the northern quadrant of a mountain for about two-thirds of its height and then spread for the upper third over its whole crown. . . . [To England] without doubt we are to go for models in this art. Their sunless climate has permitted them to adopt what is certainly a beauty of the very first order in landscape. Their canvas is of open ground, variegated with clumps of trees distributed with taste.
>
> Of prospect I have a rich profusion and offering itself at every point of the compass. Mountains distant and near, smooth and shaggy, single and in ridges, a little river hiding itself among the hills so as to show in lagoons only, cultivated grounds under the eye, and two small villages. To prevent a satiety of this is the principal difficulty. It may be successively offered, and in different portions through vistas, or which will be better, between thickets so disposed as to serve as vistas, with the advantage of shifting the scenes as you can advance on your way.[12]

THE PLANNING OF
WASHINGTON, D.C.

During the Revolutionary War, the seat of American government was not in a fixed location; Philadelphia, Baltimore, Lancaster, and York served at various times as the place where the Continental Congress met. Weak federal authority prolonged into the period of the Confederation this wandering of the capital, from Philadelphia, successively, to Princeton, Annapolis, Trenton, and New York. The Constitutional Convention of 1787 proposed a permanent national capital, and after much controversy Congress approved in 1790 a site near Georgetown on the Maryland side of the Potomac River. Washington was authorized to choose the actual boundaries, and late in the year he and Jefferson formulated plans for the new capital.

Jefferson wrote: "I should propose [the streets] to be at right angles as in Philadelphia."[13] He listed among the requisite buildings: a capitol, federal offices, the president's house and gardens, a city hall, a market, public walks, and a hospital. No detail was neglected: the specific widths of streets, the appropriate size of public gardens, and the logical relation of houses to the whole:

> I doubt much whether the obligation to build the houses at a given distance from the street, contributes to its beauty, it produces a disgusting monotony, all persons make this complaint against Philadelphia, the contrary practice varies the appearance, and is much more convenient to the inhabitants.

> In Paris it is forbidden to build a house beyond a given height, and it is admitted to be a good restriction, it keeps the houses low and convenient, and the streets light and airy, fires are much more manageable where houses are low.

In early 1791 two surveyors were appointed: Andrew Ellicott, who was to fix the boundary of the federal district, and Pierre Charles L'Enfant, who was to ascertain the appropriate sites for government buildings. Around this time Jefferson sent Washington a sketch showing a gridiron plan, three blocks wide and eleven blocks long, beside the Potomac River immediately north of Tyber Creek. Where earlier he had suggested public gardens, he now proposed a mall that would link the President's house with the Capitol. Forwarding Jefferson's sketch to L'Enfant, Washington wrote: "Although I do not conceive that you will derive any material advantage from an examination of the enclosed papers, yet . . . they may be compared with your own ideas of a proper plan for the Federal City." L'Enfant responded that a gridiron plan was applicable only on level ground: "It would never answer for any of the spots proposed for the Federal City, and on that held here as the most eligible it would absolutely annihilate every of the advantages enumerated and . . . alone injure the success of the undertaking." Realizing that he had been advocating a significantly different conception, Jefferson wrote L'Enfant to offer his cooperation:

> I have examined my papers, and found the plans of Frankfurt-on-the-Main, Karlsruhe, Amsterdam, Strasbourg, Paris, Orléans, Bordeaux, Lyons, Montpellier, Marseilles, Turin, and Milan, which I send in a roll by the post. . . . I am happy that the President has left the planning of the town in such good hands, and have no doubt it will be done to general satisfaction. . . . Having communicated to the President, before he went away, such general ideas on the subject of the town as occurred to me, I make no doubt that, in explaining himself to you on the subject, he has interwoven with his own ideas, such of mine as he approved. . . . Whenever it is proposed to prepare plans for the Capitol, I should prefer the adoption of some one of the models of antiquity, which have had the approbation of thousands of years; and for the President's house, I should prefer the celebrated fronts of modern buildings, which have already received the approbation of all good judges.

This remarkable letter captures the essence of Jefferson's open and inquiring mind. He now understood that his earlier gridiron plan was inferior to L'Enfant's Baroque design of radiating avenues imposed on a grid of streets, although the two men had both envisioned the same location for the Capitol; L'Enfant, writing of Jenkin's Hill, described it as "a pedestal waiting for a superstructure." Jefferson, having built Monticello to crown a hilltop, would naturally have perceived in it the opportunity for another monument of romantic classicism. When L'Enfant publicly revealed his plan, two of Jefferson's ideas were embodied in it: the placing of the President's house in relation to the Capitol and the mall between the two.

Jefferson's proposal for a Capitol in the classical style and a modern residence for the President recalls the respective styles of the Virginia State Capitol and his own house, Monticello: a government building expressing the republican virtues of antiquity, with a President's house avoiding the appearance of a royal palace. When L'Enfant's appointment came to an end in 1792, through his arrogance toward the commissioners charged with overseeing the work, Jefferson recommended a competition to select architects for the two buildings. Under circumstances that are not altogether clear, he anonymously submitted plans for a President's house based on Palladio's most influential building, the Villa Rotonda at Vicenza. He may have entered the competition after realizing that the other submissions were mediocre architecturally, and that here was another occasion to "improve the taste of [his] countrymen." Although the design of James Hoban was chosen over his own, Jefferson had an opportunity to perfect the White House when he became President in 1801.

James Hoban. Competition drawing for the President's House, Washington, D.C.: 1792. The winning entry was based on plate LIII in James Gibbs, Book of Architecture (1728), and it has been suggested that Leinster House in Dublin also influenced the Irish-born and -trained Hoban. (Maryland Historical Society.)

William Thornton. Design for the National Capitol, Washington, D.C.: 1794. The dome of the Capitol began with Jefferson's recommendation that one based on the Pantheon be added. (Library of Congress.)

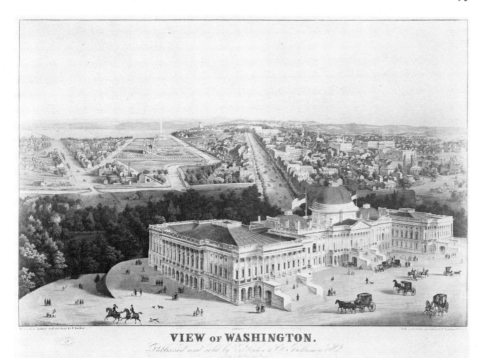

VIEW OF WASHINGTON.

View of Washington, D.C.: 1852. The monumental scale of the L'Enfant plan is apparent from the vast open spaces between the Capitol, the White House, and the Washington Monument (designed in 1836 but not finished until after the Civil War). (Drawn by E. Sachse: 1852. Library of Congress.)

Under Benjamin Latrobe's supervision, the interior was finished, low pavilions were added on the east and west sides, and the gardens were landscaped. Porticos were also planned for the north and south fronts, but these were not erected until the 1820s.

Although Jefferson made no formal submission of plans to the competition for the Capitol, in which the winning design was by William Thornton, he nonetheless participated in its formulation. A surviving sketch shows his concept of a rotunda divided into four elliptical spaces—an entrance hall and chambers for the Senate, House of Representatives, and Supreme Court—with the Roman Pantheon as its ultimate source. He persuaded the architects involved in the early stages of construction to add a domed rotunda, which with each successive architect grew in magnitude until Thomas Ustick Walter's colossal dome of 1855–1864—one so large that it required a cast-iron structure. Another of the distinctive features of the national capital was thus initiated by Jefferson.

As the competitions for the White House and Capitol suggested, America had no architects capable of accommodating the republican ideals of Washington and Jefferson to the grandiose design of L'Enfant. As a result, the intended dignity of the federal capital was slow in being achieved. In the 1840s Charles Dickens could still refer to the capital as the City of Magnificent Distances and of Magnificent Intentions. The initial vision simply awaited an architect who could revive and further its aspirations. Robert Mills was responsible, in 1836, for proposing what became the Washington Monument, at the intersection of the axes of the Capitol and White House. Having stayed at Monticello during 1802 and 1803 (while he used the library for architectural study), Mills was undoubtedly acquainted with Jefferson's objectives, and through him with those of L'Enfant. In a European city a monument over 600 feet high would have been ludicrous, but the spaciousness of the mall required a structure of that size. By creating a sense of center, Mills anticipated several developments of the twentieth century—the reclaiming of land along the Potomac River and the extension of the axes westward and southward to the present locations of the Lincoln and Jefferson memorials, erected respectively in 1914–1922 and 1937–1943.

The location of the city of Washington, along with the prominent role played by the two Virginians in its planning, made the federal capital a southern city. But in addition to the accidents of geography and of political leadership, Washington displays a kinship to the idea of the plantation house—an expansive classical design in a natural setting. Louis XIV's château and gardens at Versailles have often been cited as possible sources for L'Enfant's concept, and he must certainly have been influenced by this aspect in his background. But whereas Versailles is absolutist—the unitary plan of a king asserting the divine right in domination over nature—Washington sets forth the balance between the legislative and executive functions, with the Capitol and White House subtly connected by the hypotenuse of a triangle, whose effect is to preclude a physical confrontation between the two. The legs of the triangle were designed as public and private gardens in a manner analogous to those of a plantation. Washington and Jefferson had conceived an urban plan with undeniable similarities to Mount Vernon and Monticello—one that drew, moreover, on the plan of eighteenth-century Williamsburg, where the Virginia Capitol and Governor's Palace were related in precisely the same way as their federal counterparts in Washington.

CHAPTER SEVEN

SOUTHERN COLLEGES: PLANTED CAMPUSES

THE COLLEGE OF WILLIAM AND MARY, WILLIAMSBURG, VIRGINIA

Southern colleges during the early stages of settlement were, like southern churches, idealistic creations amid a world of frontier rusticity, and even later required constant nurturing. Education was promoted primarily by the clergy, whose missionary zeal had been a motivation for going to the New World. The concept of civilized society based on communal institutions gave rise to the unrealistically ambitious program of the College of William and Mary—a common school for Indians, a grammar school for the teaching of Latin and Greek, a college of liberal arts, and a graduate college of theology. In 1724, Hugh Jones praised the architecture of the college building, but remarked that the program had not attained its intended objectives.[1] Although its charter called for professorships in Divinity, Mathematics, Philosophy, Languages, History, and Humanity, the entire faculty comprised two professors of philosophy, two of divinity, one master for the grammar school, and another for the Indian school. It was not until the time of the American Revolution, while Jefferson was governor of Virginia, that the curriculum was broadened to include professorships in Law and Police; Anatomy and Medicine; Natural Philosophy and Mathematics; Moral Philosophy, the Law of Nature and Nations, and the Fine Arts; Modern Languages; and the Indian school.[2]

Jefferson's attitudes toward William and Mary are ambiguous. Even though he thrived on his education there, from an early date he conceived of a university based on his own very different principles. Harshly critical though he was of Williamsburg architecture, his designs in 1771–1772 for completing the college quadrangle were in the spirit of the original plans (its construction came to an end with the outbreak of the Revolutionary War). In 1779 Jefferson also oversaw the curricular revisions which redirected it toward more worldly studies—a change that students at William and Mary had championed eighty years earlier in their support of Williamsburg as the capital. But at the same time he urged the shift of the capital to Richmond, which deprived the college of its favored position.

The fortunes of William and Mary declined along with the town. A proposal for moving it to Richmond in the 1820s was barely averted. After a fire in 1859 the college building was reconstructed in the then popular Italianate fashion, only to be destroyed by Union troops three years later. Owing to the hardships of Reconstruction, the rebuilding of 1867–1869 was far from stylish, but its results survived up until 1928, when the college was chosen as the initial venture of Colonial Williamsburg. Today, the proud dignity of the College of William and Mary as the oldest and also one of the most distinguished universities in the South has been reestablished, and after only fifty years the restored college building has assumed the aura of a historic structure.

South Carolina College, Columbia, South Carolina

The founding of state universities, which began in the South after the long-standing practice of sending young men to England to be educated was curtailed by the Revolutionary War, brought with it a shift in emphasis from theology to a more diversified and secular curriculum. To some degree this change had been anticipated at William and Mary. The charter of the University of Georgia (initially named Franklin College), approved by the state legislature in 1785, expressed even more fully the new educational philosophy:

> It should therefore be among the first objects of those who wish well to the national prosperity, to encourage and support the principles of religion and morality, and early to place the youth under the forming hand of society, that by instruction they may be moulded to the love of virtue and good order. Sending them abroad to other countries for their education will not answer these purposes, is too humiliating an acknowledgment of the ignorance or inferiority of our own, and will always be the cause of so great foreign attachments, that upon principles of policy it is not admissible.[3]

The actual development of the campus at Athens and of the one at Chapel Hill, designated four years later in the charter of the University of North Carolina, was slow and haphazard. South Carolina College, the third southern state university, was more ambitious. Its beginnings in 1801 were analogous to those of William and Mary, though without the religious establishment. A new state capital at Columbia had been surveyed in 1786, and as conceived and promoted by Governor John Drayton the college was needed to justify moving the capital from Charleston, the most urbane city in the South. As Drayton described Columbia in 1802, the capitol and the college were the only institutions meriting specific mention:

> Here the statehouse situated on a beautiful eminence, is to be seen, at the distance of many miles, from various parts of the country. And soon, we hope, the South Carolina College will rise an ornament to the town; respectable from its establishment; but still more from the learning and friendship, which a national institution, like this, cannot fail to promote among the young from all parts of the state.[4]

At about the same time, the trustees decided to hold a competition to secure "original plans for the erection of a college capable of accommodating the greatest possible number of students; besides having a sufficient number of public rooms adapted to the exercises of the institution, and, for the accommodation of the professors." The building was to cost no more than $50,000, and a prize of $300 was offered for the best plan. The trustees also requested from "the presidents of colleges in the United States, a description or plan, of the college over which they preside." In proposing a competition (not the usual way of choosing an architect), the trustees were probably influenced by the recent competitions for the Capitol and White House in Washington; the chosen architect of the latter, James Hoban, had designed the South Carolina statehouse of 1790. Among the major entrants in the South Carolina competition, Peter Banner was a builder who had supervised the construction of dormitories at Yale; Benjamin Latrobe was a thoroughly professional architect, his office in Philadelphia; and Robert Mills was Charleston-born and just beginning his career in Washington. The trustees, "inasmuch as the plan adopted is founded upon some principles taken from [their] plans," divided the prize between Mills and another architect, who may have become the builder. In overall format the proposed structure was similar to Nassau Hall at Princeton and University Hall at Brown, both of whose presidents had contributed information, as requested by the trustees.

The plan of the college building was conventional, if not old-fashioned. Included in the three-story rectangular building were a chapel, a library, two lecture rooms, dormitory space for one hundred students, and living quarters for three professors. The one innovative aspect was the clustering of student rooms around entry stairwells, which eliminated long, monotonous corridors. Before construction began, however, the trustees suddenly decided to erect not one but two buildings, "fronting each other, at such a distance apart, as will be suitable to the land," and a committee was appointed to "decide upon the style in which the college shall be finished." By 1805 the beginning of a mall plan with a horseshoe configuration, in which Rutledge and DeSaussure colleges faced each other across the lawn, was under construction (the University of South Carolina campus to this day is known as the Horseshoe). Three other buildings were planned and eventually built: the president's house, closing the short end of the mall; a dining hall; and a professor's house continuing the long axes of the main buildings at the open end. This plan continued to govern the expansion of the college throughout the antebellum period.

The importance of cross-influences between Robert Mills and Thomas Jefferson that made South Carolina College a major contribution to American college planning has only recently been recognized.[5] There is evidence that Mills continued to advise the trustees, and in that capacity he could have been responsible for suggesting the mall plan. Since he was using Jefferson's architectural library at Monticello at the time he prepared his competition entry, it is not surprising to discover that it drew on Jefferson's plan to complete the quadrangle at William and Mary. Indeed, since Jefferson was already formulating his plans for a university, he may have been responsible for the idea of a mall. In any event, the South Carolina College horseshoe was an innovation that led directly to the plan at Jefferson's own University of Virginia.

UNIVERSITY OF VIRGINIA, CHARLOTTESVILLE, VIRGINIA

Long before the University of Virginia was formally established in 1817, the idea had been in Jefferson's mind. As early as the Revolutionary War he advocated comprehensive education ranging from primary instruction, which would impart "to every citizen the information he needs for the transaction of daily business," to higher education for those "whom nature hath endowed with genius and virtue." He envisioned a program based not on the privileges of birth or wealth but rather on an aristocracy of the mind. He wrote to his former teacher George Wythe in 1786:

> I think by far the most important bill in our whole code is that for the diffusion of knowledge among the people. No other sure foundation can be devised for the preservation of freedom and happiness.... Preach, my dear sir, a crusade against ignorance; establish and improve the law for educating the common people. Let our countrymen know that the people alone can protect us against these

evils, and that the tax which will be paid for this purpose is not more than the thousandth part of what will be paid to kings, priests, and nobles who will rise up among us if we leave the people in ignorance.[6]

The philosophy, curriculum, and plan of Jefferson's ideal university, based on the principles of the Enlightenment and the needs of the new American republic, had been formulated by 1805:

Convinced that the people are the only safe depositories of their own liberty, and that they are not safe unless enlightened to a certain degree, I have looked on our present state of liberty as a short-lived possession unless the mass of the people could be informed to a certain degree. . . .

[The university] should be defined only generally for the teaching of the useful branches of science, leaving the particulars to the direction of the day. Science is progressive. What was useful two centuries ago is now become useless, e.g., one-half the professorships at William and Mary. . . .

The greatest danger will be their overbuilding themselves by attempting a large house in the beginning, sufficient to contain the whole institution. Large houses are always ugly, inconvenient, exposed to the accident of fire, and bad in cases of infection. A plain, small house for the school and lodging of each professor is best. These connected by covered ways out of which the rooms of the students should open would be best. These may be built only as they shall be wanted: in fact, a university should not be a house but a village.[7]

Although in 1816 the Virginia legislature passed "An Act to Establish a System of Education," as envisioned by Jefferson, out of his comprehensive program, only the university actually came into being. The Charlottesville site, which Jefferson favored, was chosen because (with West Virginia still part of Virginia) it was in the center of the state. A curriculum was proposed consisting of ten professorships: in both ancient and modern languages, pure mathematics, physico-mathematics, physics or natural philosophy, botany and zoology, anatomy and medicine, government, political economy, and history, law, and ideology (this latter covering grammar, ethics, rhetoric, belles-lettres, and fine arts).

Work began, Jefferson furnishing the drawings and supervising the construction of an "academical village": ten pavilions, five on each side of a rectangular lawn, providing classrooms and residential quarters for the faculty; student rooms opening onto a colonnaded walkway connecting the pavilions; and running parallel to these, separated from them by gardens, two ranges of refectories and additional rooms for students.

Among the architectural sources for the complex was the Château de

View of the University of Virginia, Charlottesville, Virginia: 1845. The
variety among the ten pavilions was Jefferson's way of adding an
architectural curriculum to the university. (Thomas Jefferson. "University of
Virginia at Charlottesville," from Henry Howe, Historical Collections of
Virginia, *1845. Library of Congress.)*

Marly, which Jefferson had visited in 1786.[8] Built for Louis XIV in 1679,
it had a strictly regular plan like that of Versailles; Jefferson's adaptation
for the University of Virginia was looser and more varied in concept.
The orders of the pavilions were derived mainly from either Palladio or
Chambray, with one exception, based on the Hôtel Guimard, a contemporary Neoclassical building designed by Claude-Nicolas Ledoux. According to a remarkable system devised by Jefferson, the Doric, Ionic,
and Corinthian orders are clearly distinguished, with no order repeated
from one pavilion to the next or in its counterpart across the lawn.[9] The
corresponding orders are placed diagonally: Pavilions I and X are Doric,
II and IX are Ionic, III and VIII Corinthian; and IV and VII, once again,
are Doric. Pavilions V and VI, which face each other, are technically
both Ionic; however, Jefferson specified that Pavilion VI "is to have no
columns," with the effect that it is Ionic only in its entablature—a subtle
means of completing the series by relating to Pavilion V while retaining
its distinct identity.

    In a letter to William Thornton, one of the two architects whose ad-
vice he solicited, Jefferson wrote: "Now what we wish, is that these pavilions, as they will show themselves above the dormitories, shall be models
of taste and good architecture, and of a variety of appearance, no two
alike, so as to serve as specimens for the architectural lecturer."[10] He
wrote similarly to Benjamin Latrobe, who responded with a sketch of a
domed rotunda to give the campus a central focus: "I have found so much
pleasure in studying the plan of your college. . . . [The] center building

. . . ought to exhibit in mass and details as perfect a specimen of good architectural taste as can be devised."

The Rotunda, which Jefferson added to the plan at Latrobe's suggestion, was based on the Roman Pantheon, and constructed half-scale, it presented "one of the models of antiquity, which have had the approbation of thousands of years." Jefferson transformed his source from a temple dedicated to "all the gods" (the meaning of Pantheon) to a functional building for his ideal university. Whereas the dominating building in an English university or a colonial college had generally been a chapel, Jefferson designated the Rotunda as primarily a library—a treasury of wisdom and virtue rather than of theological doctrine. The oval rooms on the first floor were used for instruction in drawing and music, and for examinations, as well as for religious worship. The circular room above had book stacks around its circumference, a reading room in the center, and a dome on which the celestial constellations could be charted. The oculus of the Pantheon, which allows a shaft of light to illuminate the interior, may have suggested an astronomical function for the Rotunda: Etienne-Louis Boullée, in 1784, had designed a cenotaph for Isaac Newton whose form and intent were similar. In the university's central building Jefferson had combined a Roman source with references to French Neoclassicism, to science, and to his vision of America's future.

Each of the ten pavilions was a separate building within a comprehensive whole. Freely adjusting the various elements, an effort to reconcile individuality and unity, Jefferson produced a number of anomalies. The juncture of the continuous, human-scaled colonnades and the monumental columnar porticos is occasionally forced and awkward. The increased spacing between the pavilions at the south end of the quadrangle, away from the Rotunda, is either a conscious device, intended to give an illusion of distance, or an accommodation made after the Rotunda had been added to the plan. Because of sloping terrain, the east range is farther away from the pavilions than the west range. Instead of receiving uniform emphasis, the pavilions ascend in what appears to be a hierarchical sequence from the open end of the lawn to the Rotunda, as a result of two rises of the ground level—at Pavilions IX and X, and again at V and VI. The temple fronts of the pavilions near the Rotunda tend, moreover, to be more monumental than those near the open end, which suggest a more domestic scale and a more contemporary style. The careful individualizing of the pavilions manifests Jefferson's faith in democracy, and as exemplary buildings they differ from their sources (both Roman and Neoclassical) in the way they have been liberated from rigid absolutism.

When the university opened in 1825, Jefferson once again proclaimed his optimistic idealism: "Withdrawn by age from all other public services and attentions to public things, I am closing the last scenes of life fashioning and fostering an establishment for the instruction of those who are to come after us. I hope its influence on their virtue, freedom, fame, and happiness, will be salutary and permanent."[11] He chose to be remembered in his epitaph as "Father of the University of Virginia," as well as "Author of the Declaration of American Independence" and of the "Statute of Virginia for Religious Freedom." More than any other of his architectural projects, the University of Virginia embraced his life-long belief in the perfectibility of man.

WASHINGTON AND LEE UNIVERSITY, LEXINGTON, VIRGINIA

Jefferson's influence extended to a small college, 65 miles to the south-west of Charlottesville, which grew into Washington and Lee University.[12] Under the name of Augusta Academy, it began in 1749 as a Presbyterian school near Staunton, Virginia, supported by the Scots-Irish who were settling the Appalachian frontier. Renamed Liberty Hall during the Revolutionary War, it was moved in 1782 to Rockbridge County, where it continued a tenuous existence. In 1796 George Washington gave it one hundred shares of James River Company stock, a benefaction that led immediately to a proposal for a college with four professorships covering Languages; Mathematics; Natural Philosophy and Astronomy; and Logic, Moral Philosophy, and Belles-Lettres. The name was changed two years later to Washington Academy, and in 1803 it was moved to a com-

View of Washington College, Lexington, Virginia: 1845. From the central building of the early 1820s, the campus developed into an integrated complex resembling one range of the University of Virginia. (Woodcut by Henry Howe: 1845. Washington and Lee University.)

*Washington College: 1870. The campus at the time of Robert E. Lee's
funeral (October 15, 1870) shows the dramatic juxtaposition of styles
between the classical Washington Hall and the Victorian chapel, which Lee
had built. (Michael Miley Collection, Washington and Lee University.)*

manding hilltop overlooking the town of Lexington. Its transformation
into a college did not occur, however, until 1813.

The first buildings on the new site were simple ones of brick, distinguished only by their honest, utilitarian character. In 1822 a more ambitious classroom building, Washington Hall, was authorized by the trustees; it was completed in 1824 from a design attributed to James
McDowell and Andrew Alexander, with the construction supervised by
John Jordan, a local builder-architect who had been a bricklayer at Monticello and a contractor at the University of Virginia. Described as "a
Maison Carrée, like the State Capitol," the building is thus unique in
bearing an intimate association with all three of Jefferson's major structures. Flanking buildings connected to Washington Hall were constructed in the 1830s and 1840s, along with four faculty houses placed
two on either side but in front of the college buildings. The same Jeffersonian red brick as at the University of Virginia, with its dramatically
contrasting white columns, piers, and pilasters, was used from the start,
and the plan based on one range at Charlottesville permitted the campus
to evolve as an integrated whole over the years.

With a proud but unsophisticated directness, the humble origins of
Washington College as a frontier academy were retained even after the
donation of Washington and despite the architectural influence of Jefferson. Washington Hall and its later wings stand upright, simple and well-
proportioned, their volumes pleasingly related to the site. The variation
in the mass between the porticoed pavilions and the smaller connecting
units creates a rhythmical sequence scaled to human usage. The orna-

mentation, limited mainly to columns and pilasters, is not of the high style derived from ancient prototypes, but expresses the character of the nineteenth-century Appalachian setting, geographically and culturally removed from the long-established and more fashionable regions of the state. This stylistic naïveté is best shown in the cupola of Washington Hall (added in 1841–1842). Its purpose was fundamentally utilitarian, an enclosure for the college bells, yet architecturally it forms the visual center of the campus—an upcountry attempt to re-create the Tower of the Winds, an Athenian structure frequently copied during the Greek Revival period. At the top of the cupola, a statue of Washington, carved in oak by a local cabinetmaker, expressed esteem for a benefactor with the eclectic symbolism of a Roman toga over a Continental Army uniform, together with the attributes of sword and scroll.

After the Civil War, when Robert E. Lee accepted the presidency of the college, he added a chapel and a president's house, whose Victorian style made them discrete from the earlier Neoclassical buildings. The chapel, in which Lee himself was buried in 1870, is on an axis with Washington Hall, but at a considerable distance down the sloping lawn—thus providing a historic dialogue between Virginia's two greatest military leaders, who in 1871 were united with the renaming of the institution, Washington and Lee University.

The College of Charleston, Charleston, South Carolina

The architectural development of the College of Charleston, an almost exact contemporary of Washington and Lee, exemplified a high style rather than a provincial one. Of three colleges chartered by the South Carolina state legislature in 1785, only the one at Charleston attained full collegiate status. On land originally designated for a free school, instruction began in 1790 in a one-story brick structure which had been a Revolutionary War barracks, and six students were graduated at the first commencement in 1794. After that the college curriculum gradually disappeared, and for thirty years the institution functioned largely as a grammar school. In 1824 the Reverend Jasper Adams assumed the presidency and reintroduced collegiate studies. Observing that the college was "a mass of ruinous, ill-looking, and inconvenient buildings," he argued that "success was not to be expected without a new and handsome edifice."[13]

The trustees made an application "to W. Strickland in Philadelphia for a plan of a college building." The designer of the most important early Greek Revival building, the Second Bank of the United States, constructed while a Charlestonian, Langdon Cheves, was its president,

Strickland had also built a Philadelphia house for Cheves. That Cheves had been a trustee of the College of Charleston probably explains the choice of Strickland as architect for the college building. Robert Mills, who had been a student at the college when it was primarily a grammar school, also may have been involved; at any rate, he is known to have been in South Carolina during the time of its planning and construction (1826–1829). Strickland and Mills had both been assistants to Benjamin Latrobe, and Strickland's design bears a close resemblance to Mills's Fireproof Building in Charleston.

Throughout the 1840s plans were proposed to add a portico to the college building and to landscape the campus. In the words of one trustee:

> The finishing of the building according to the original plan, the improvement of the college square, the planting of it with ornamental trees, and the putting of an iron railing around it, in whole or in part, as may best comport with the plan of improvement, would add exceedingly to the appearance of the college, make it, as it ought to be, an ornament to our city, and aid much in arousing and attracting, the notice and patronage of our citizens to the institution, and in prompting its prosperity.[14]

William Strickland and Edward Brickell White. College of Charleston, Charleston, South Carolina: 1828–1829 and 1850–1852. High style came to the college when White added a monumental portico to Strickland's simple functional building.

A monumental Ionic portico was erected in 1850, transforming the college building from the rational design of Strickland to the conscious high style of a classical temple. The architect, Edward Brickell White,[15] also constructed a Porter's Lodge on the opposite side of the yard to give a sense of definition and axis to the campus. Modeled on a Roman triumphal arch, the Porter's Lodge symbolized the heroic virtue of classical education, and was an architectural gesture fitting for antebellum Charleston. It was originally ornamental in purpose; the college never hired a porter, but it did become the residence of a succession of college janitors who continually frustrated the faculty and trustees by filling the arches with their firewood and laundry, and by grazing their cows and chickens on the campus lawn.

Nevertheless, the architectural program had succeeded in adding to the prestige of the college. In 1852 a significant museum of natural history was inaugurated at the college, drawing in part from the collections of Louis Agassiz, the distinguished Harvard naturalist who had spent some time studying in the Low Country and who had occasionally lectured at the college. The next year a private library of 4,000 volumes was given to the college, and in 1854–1856 a library was constructed on one side of the campus. Even though the three nineteenth-century buildings are neither homogeneous nor part of a comprehensive plan, their warm reddish stucco surfaces, and the natural ceiling formed by the branches of live oaks, combine in an ambience of organic wholeness.

CHAPTER EIGHT

WESTWARD EXPANSION: SOUTHERN ARCHITECTURE ACROSS THE APPALACHIAN MOUNTAINS

The southern way of life emanating from the plantation system spread gradually through a large and diverse geographical area. The traditional pattern of large landholdings developed first in Virginia, Maryland, and Carolina, and then along the rest of the Atlantic coast. It was in the nature of plantations to extend the frontier, with settlements moving to new land as the old was exhausted by a rapacious agriculture. Cheap western land gave a yeoman farmer a chance to improve his economic status, and the frontier was also the place where rugged individualists could live in relative freedom from the restraints of conventional society. Neither the Appalachian Mountains nor the foreignness of Spanish Florida, or of French Louisiana, was an impediment to expansion. Up until the Civil War, as a consequence, the South and its characteristic culture were being continually re-created over an enormous area.

Although the North also experienced population migrations—first to northern New England, to upstate New York, and to western Pennsylvania, and later across the Appalachians—the process was far less uniform than in the South; the Midwest developed economically in a very different way from the Northeast. What made westward movement in the South distinctive is the way tradition was reinforced rather than diluted by geographical expansion.

LIBERTY HALL, FRANKFORT, KENTUCKY
(c. 1796)

The typically southern pattern of architectural patronage came to the trans-Appalachian area in the late 1790s, when John Brown built a fine house in Frankfort, Kentucky. Born in the Shenandoah Valley, he was a second-generation American of Scots-Irish ancestry. His father, a Presbyterian minister and teacher, had directed the grammar school that later evolved into Washington and Lee University. After attending his father's school, Brown went to Princeton, where his studies were interrupted by the British in 1776. Two years later he resumed his studies at William and Mary, where the revised curriculum included training in law. When the arrival of the British in Williamsburg once again interrupted his education, he returned to the Piedmont and made use of Jefferson's law library at Charlottesville to complete his studies.

After the Revolutionary War, Brown crossed the mountains to Kentucky, then still part of Virginia, and practiced law there. He soon became a champion of statehood for Kentucky, and following the Constitutional Convention of 1787 served as a member of the Virginia congressional delegation. His contacts with James Madison, who had drafted the federal constitution, helped Brown frame a constitution for Kentucky. In 1792, Kentucky having become a state, he was elected to the United States Senate, an office he held until 1805. A contemporary described him as "a connecting link between the statesmen of the days of Washington and Jefferson and of those of more modern date."[1]

In a life of mobility and change, Brown also fulfilled a desire for rootedness and continuity. In 1796, at a time when his official responsibilities kept him in Philadelphia for much of the year, he purchased land in Frankfort, the Kentucky state capital. His desire for a place of retirement after his public life ended (as well as to provide a home for his elderly parents, who died there in 1802 and 1803) was similar to that of both Washington and Jefferson. As a token of ancestral respect, he gave his house the name of Liberty Hall, after his father's grammar school. And to associate his taste with that of his esteemed counterpart in Virginia, he consulted Jefferson concerning a design. Brown might have argued for the separate political identity of Kentucky, but he conceived of his house within an entirely traditional framework—an anomaly that parallels the Englishness of the colonial plantation houses.

Brown asked Jefferson for suggestions, which arrived after he had begun work on his house in 1797: "Though you thought you had made such progress in your plan that it could not be altered, yet I send you the one I mentioned, as you may perhaps draw some hints from it for the improvement of yours."[2] Brown ignored Jefferson's recommendation of a design with the rooms arranged on one floor and chose a more conventional two-story one. It was nearing completion when he married Margaretta Mason of New York; they moved into it in 1801.

The building of an elegant house had not been an easy undertaking. Brick was made on the property and a variety of woods was generally available, but glass, metal hardware, and furniture had to be brought from the East, most likely via Pittsburgh and then along the Ohio and Kentucky rivers. The high style of Liberty Hall, with its cubical format and its slightly projecting central pedimented pavilion, is a somewhat old-fashioned Georgian, whose antecedents include (as well as several houses in Pennsylvania and Delaware) the Hammond House in Annapolis of 1773–1774—likewise a townhouse built by a lawyer in a state capital with rising cultural aspirations.

The architectural conservatism of Liberty Hall is such as to suggest that Brown moved to Kentucky prior to the American Revolution. As a family seat, it would eventually be inherited by his oldest son, Mason. In 1835–1836, after a second son, Orlando, returned to Frankfort as a lawyer and journalist, John Brown built him a house on the property. Even though Orlando had been a classical scholar at Princeton, and even though the architect, Gideon Shryock, was a Greek Revivalist, conservatism again prevailed against erecting a thoroughgoing example of that style; rather, it continued in reverse the plan and general shape of Liberty Hall. A few Greek details—the pediment across the entire façade, the Ionic portico, and the interior mantelpieces—offered a grudging concession to modern taste, but the overall character is still decidedly Georgian. Together the two houses stand as the statement of a man determined to put down roots.

Liberty Hall, Frankfort, Kentucky: c. 1796. The Georgian plan and detailing provide a remarkable example of the longevity of venerable forms in southern architecture. (The National Society of the Colonial Dames of America in the Commonwealth of Kentucky.)

Farmington, Louisville, Kentucky: 1808–1810. The low profile of a one-story house set on a high basement reveals the influence of Thomas Jefferson.

FARMINGTON, LOUISVILLE, KENTUCKY (1808–1810)

In 1807, ten years after proposing to John Brown that he build his house with rooms all on one floor, Jefferson offered virtually the same advice to John and Lucy Speed, who were planning to build a house on a 1,500-acre tract near Louisville. Lucy Speed had family connections with Jefferson, and he had recently planned an addition to Farmington, her aunt's home near Charlottesville. Jefferson's plan for the Speeds' new house—also called Farmington—featured, with a masterful interplay of shapes, two octagonal salons separated by a rectangular hallway, and with four square rooms at the corners. Some minor changes were made in the plan, construction began in 1808, and the house was finished in 1810.[3] A one-story house raised on a high basement, Farmington has a low, horizontal exterior which gently follows the contours of the land. The interior has 14-foot ceilings throughout; the rooms are simply ornamented, elegantly proportioned, and spacious.

The contrast between Farmington and Liberty Hall—the early attempts at high style in the first trans-Appalachian state—is instructive. Liberty Hall has the formality of an urban setting inhabited by a man reluctant to break with tradition. Although Farmington's geometry is more radical, the Jeffersonian pedigree gave it respectability; the way its one-story format blends with the landscape is generally characteristic of southern plantations. Both Liberty Hall and Farmington became family seats, where distinguished guests were entertained—President James Monroe and two future Presidents, Andrew Jackson and Zachary Taylor, in 1819, as well as Lafayette in 1825, at Liberty Hall, and Abraham Lincoln at Farmington. In 1841, as a close friend of the Speeds' son Joshua, Lincoln in fact spent three weeks there during a traumatic period in his courtship of Mary Todd.

ASHLAND, LEXINGTON, KENTUCKY (1805–1813)

The continuity of political leadership and architecture across the Appalachian Mountains is also exemplified by Henry Clay. Born in Virginia, Clay read law under the direction of George Wythe, one of Jefferson's mentors. In the late 1790s he moved to Kentucky, where he established a successful law practice specializing in land claims, and was elected to the state legislature. He then began the building of Ashland, a Georgian-inspired house modeled after Liberty Hall, on land outside Lexington.[4] The contract, dated 1805, was with a local builder, and mentions no architect. By 1813, Clay had become a congressional champion of western development. Broadening his architectural horizons, in that year he commissioned Benjamin Latrobe, as a nationally prominent architect, to design additional wings, such as would transform Ashland into a proper setting for its owner's expanding political ambitions. Latrobe was a Washington acquaintance of the Clays, and Clay was perhaps also conscious that he had received Jefferson's patronage for the completion of the White House. The wings at Ashland provided for the mundane functions of bringing up a growing family—bedchambers and a kitchen respectively—but the crisply articulated geometrical volumes of the enlargement gave the whole a more prepossessing silhouette.

Although Clay was repeatedly thwarted in his ambition to be President, his prestige as the "great compromiser" during the years of sectional strife gave Ashland the aura of a national shrine. After his death in 1852, his son did the unthinkable: he tore the house down to its foundations and rebuilt it, preserving the original plan but freely altering the details, "in a style suitable to my taste and not wholly unworthy of my father." In the process, however, the venerable house itself had been virtually lost.

View of Ashland, Lexington, Kentucky: 1843. This rare view of the Ashland of Henry Clay shows the house before his son thoroughly rebuilt it in the 1850s. ("Ashland. The Seat of the Hon. Henry Clay," Lexington, Kentucky, drawn by W. Lewis and engraved by A. L. Dick: 1843. Library of Congress.)

THE HERMITAGE,
DAVIDSON COUNTY, TENNESSEE
(1819–1836)

Tennessee, the second southern state to be organized in western lands (from territory ceded by North Carolina), was admitted to the Union in 1796. It was here, behind a barrier of mountains even more formidable than those between Virginia and Kentucky, that Tennessee's greatest pioneer, Andrew Jackson, rose to national prominence. Born in upcountry Carolina, Jackson enlisted at thirteen in the Revolutionary army; in 1788, after several years spent groping for stability, including a sojourn in Charleston, he arrived in Nashville, where he became a lawyer largely because so few lawyers were available. The unruliness of the frontier and his own activist personality inevitably led to controversy. He married a woman who had not yet received a final divorce from her first husband; he was forced to sell his property after an unwise financial transaction; and he nearly lost his life in a duel over a horse race. Nevertheless, he was elected to a series of political offices; and notwithstanding the scandals with which his political opponents sought to embarrass him, the Jackson who built the fittingly named Hermitage is revealed as one who valued rootedness and marital devotion.

The first buildings on the 420 acres east of Nashville which he and his wife, Rachel, purchased in 1804 were a group of rustic log houses, including a two-story central structure that became the Jacksons' home.[5] Prosperity from cotton farming allowed them to erect a more comfortable house in 1819, and a simple, two-story brick structure similar in plan to Liberty Hall was erected on a site chosen by Rachel Jackson. Of the attention lavished on the interior, a visitor from Charleston wrote in 1827:

> You enter a large and spacious hall or vestibule, the walls covered with a very splendid French paper, beautiful scenery, figures, etc. . . . To the right are two large and handsome rooms furnished in fashionable and genteel style as drawing rooms—rich hangings, carpets, etc. To the left is the dining room and their chamber. There was no splendor to dazzle the eye but everything elegant and neat.[6]

The French wallpaper may have depicted scenes of Telemachus on the Island of Calypso (an apocryphal embellishment to Homer's *Odyssey* had Telemachus visiting the island in search of his father). The present wallpaper in the hall representing that theme dates after the fire of 1834, but it could have been a replacement. In any event, the story was particularly relevant to Jackson, since it depicts the longing of a son for his father (Jackson never knew his own father). No less appropriately, the combination of pastoral and classical imagery symbolized the transformation of Tennessee from wilderness to a cultivated region. Although there is no evidence that Jackson was aware of the symbolism, a statement made in Washington during the mid-1820s does reveal his strong attachment to the Hermitage: "How often does my thoughts [sic] lead me back to the Hermitage. There in private life, surrounded by a few friends, would be a paradise compared to the best situation here; and if once more there it would take a writ of *habeas corpus* to remove me into public life again."

Washington and Jefferson had both voiced very similar sentiments before assuming the office of President, to which Jackson was elected in 1828. For him the triumph was no more than bittersweet, since his beloved Rachel died in the midst of preparing to leave for the inauguration at Washington. Jackson never fully recovered from the loss. In 1831, with a happy event to celebrate—the marriage of his adopted son, Andrew, Jr., to Sarah York of Philadelphia—he prepared the Hermitage for them by adding a one-story room on each side and a two-story columned portico on the front and back. The newly added rooms were a dining room on one side and an office-library on the other—precisely what Washington had added at Mount Vernon—and the back portico likewise recalled Mount Vernon; two-story porticos had also been added to the White House in the 1820s. Although the architectural changes made the Hermitage a proper President's house, the front portico was derived from Linden at Natchez, the town where Jackson had courted Rachel and where the couple had spent their honeymoon. At the time of these alterations, he erected a tomb for Rachel in the garden; it had the form of a

The Hermitage, Davidson County, Tennessee, hall: 1819–1836. The expansive hall with a graceful cantilevered stairway was decorated with French wallpaper of scenes of Telemachus on the Island of Calypso. (Ladies' Hermitage Association, photo: Dan Quest.)

View of the Hermitage: 1856. The approach to the monumental façade was defined by cedar trees which Jackson planted in a guitar-shaped configuration. The Jackson tomb is to the right of the house. ("The Hermitage, Jackson's Tomb, and Andrew J. Donelson's Residence," Davidson County, Tennessee, lithograph by Endicott & Company: 1856. Library of Congress.)

Greek colonnaded rotunda and resembled the small classical temples in the landscape of the Telemachus wallpaper.

After a fire gutted the house in 1834, the ceilings were made higher, the fire-damaged brick on the front was painted white, and a new monumental front portico was added, more in the character of Mount Vernon and of the typical antebellum plantation of the Deep South. But the twenty-fifth anniversary of Jackson's victory at the Battle of New Orleans saw a return to rusticity, when a chimneypiece of roughly carved hickory, the work of an army veteran, was installed in the dining room. Three years later, Amos Kendall, who had been a member of Jackson's cabinet, wrote following a visit:

> Everything at the Hermitage looks perennial, perpetual; . . . Nothing here bears the stamp of ostentation and fastidious taste. There is an easy elegance which impresses the feeling that nature had done everything, and art nothing; and that all the comfort and all the beauties that abound there were scattered by the profuse hand of the same benevolent power which created Paradise a wilderness of spontaneous bounty and beauty. The General complains himself that he has not cultivated a taste for rural elegance. Everything about him shows that he has not studied the art of landscape gardening; but his

farming is like his fighting—for, although not done by rule, it turns out well.[7]

Nor did the architecture adhere to any rules—at least not to those of pure Greek Revival. The façade, a colonnaded screen, remains relatively independent of the body of the house. The monumental effect of the entablature, which hides the roof, appears from the side to be an architectural pretension. The portico is less important structurally than as a symbol of Jackson's status as a planter, and still more his rise to the highest office in the country. Upon his death in 1845, his property went to Andrew, Jr., with the provision that if the Hermitage were ever to be put up for sale, it should be offered first to the state of Tennessee. After this in fact occurred, the Ladies' Hermitage Association, modeled on the Mount Vernon Ladies' Association, assumed responsibility for its preservation, once again linking the Hermitage to Washington's mansion, which Jackson had admired and emulated.

GAINESWOOD,
DEMOPOLIS, ALABAMA
(1843–1861)

As rugged individualists who survived and thrived on frontier conditions, the settlers of Kentucky and Tennessee exemplified the popular conception of westward expansion. The pioneer migrations to Alabama and Mississippi, even though they brought with them many distinctive elements of the plantation system, and even though slaves did most of the physical labor, were in fact unglamorous enterprises. An English traveler in 1835 wrote of a family who had settled near Montgomery:

> Our friends were from South Carolina; and the lady, at least, does not relish living in Alabama. They were about to build a good house; meantime, they were in one which I liked exceedingly: a log-house, with the usual open passage in the middle. Roses and honeysuckles, to which hummingbirds resort, grew before the door. Abundance of books, and handsome furniture and plate, were within the house, while daylight was to be seen through its walls.[8]

Another such Alabama pioneer was Nathan Bryan Whitfield, whose family had settled in Tidewater, North Carolina, early in the eighteenth century. Educated at the University of North Carolina, he had served as a state legislator in the 1820s. Notwithstanding his position in North Carolina society, the prospects of the frontier lured him to Florida and Alabama in search of land. In 1834, with twenty-eight slaves, he made the overland trek to Marengo County, Alabama, where he acquired 1,200 acres on the Tombigbee River south of Demopolis. In the following year he sold his property in North Carolina and brought to Alabama his wife and family, their possessions, and the slaves who had remained behind.

With frequent acquisitions of land, Whitfield's plantation grew so that by 1860 he owned over 7,000 acres. In 1842, after three of his children died, he concluded that the situation of his house was unhealthful, and in the following year he purchased a plantation on the outskirts of Demopolis. The house into which the family moved was a wood-frame, two-room structure similar in plan to the one described by the English traveler. By the outbreak of the Civil War, the idiosyncratic building program on which Whitfield had embarked had transformed a rude cabin into the most palatial mansion in Alabama.[9]

Since Whitfield was his own architect and builder, the chronology of the successive additions is not very well documented. A daughter was married in the house in 1847, and for the next two years Whitfield's correspondence reveals a concern for getting it "enclosed." By 1856 the plantation had been given the name Gaineswood—possibly signifying that a major phase of construction had been completed. But Whitfield's most detailed description of the house, in 1861, indicates that work was still in progress:

> I send you an engraving of the house and grounds of Gaines-wood. . . . You will perceive that there are many attractions since you went away. The new portico front on the north and the pond or lake which has been dug out and is now watered by the artesian well which is bored just north of the old pantrys which has been removed further and in their place is a family bedroom which has a circular gallery as seen in the engraving. I have the house nearly complete, having just got through with the painting and papering. The parlor and dining room are also changed in effect by adding some lights to the ceiling, which are very beautiful. The large drawing room is now completed and I think is the most splendid room in Alabama.

The statement hints at a quixotic personality. Rooms had been built and then significantly changed or redecorated, porticos had been added, and an artificial lake enhanced the grounds. The engraving mentioned in the description shows Gaineswood at its height; no trace of a rustic log cabin remained. The grounds were picturesquely landscaped with paths along the undulating contours of a pond. A variety of trees had been planted, offering vistas of a garden temple based on the Choragic Monument of Lysicrates, and of the house with its recently added Doric portico.

Whitfield's taste was bewilderingly eclectic. The precisely archaeological garden temple is in the spirit of Greek Revival, whereas the house has a complexity bordering on the Victorian, despite its Greek ornamental details. The landscaping is informal, natural, and romantic—the very qualities that Frederick Law Olmsted had popularized with his design for Central Park in New York. The engraving shows the house as it would have been seen by an arriving visitor, from an angle rather than along an axial perspective, thus emphasizing the rich interplay of forms.

Whitfield as architect was both ingenious and sophisticated. His taste seems to have been influenced by Minard Lafever's handbooks on Greek Revival, most notably in the projecting porticos, which scale down and domesticate the temple front, but also in the capitals of the interior—Ionic in the master bedroom and Corinthian in the ballroom. But the glorious eccentricities of the house are Whitfield's own—giving the domed and skylighted parlor and dining room, and the ballroom with its French mirrors on opposite walls, the illusion of a palatial space, such as might hold the entire gentry of Alabama. No less than a colonial Virginia or South Carolina plantation house, Gaineswood's style was one of established elegance amid the drab monotonous terrain of the cotton belt.

View of Gaineswood, Demopolis, Alabama: 1860. The highly personal combination of classical formality, extravagant interior ornamentation, and picturesque landscaping reveals the stylistic transition between Greek Revival and Victorian. ("Gaineswood, near Demopolis, Alabama. Residence of Gen. N. B. Whitfield," engraving by John Sartain: 1860. Alabama Historical Commission.)

Gaineswood, ballroom: 1843–1861. (Alabama Historical Commission.)

State Capitol, Frankfort, Kentucky (1827–1830)

Greek Revival was the style most appropriate for public buildings where monumentality was sought. In Kentucky and Tennessee, where the conditions of the frontier yielded to settlement just as the style was gaining ascendancy, and where there was no long-standing architectural tradition, it was readily adopted. Not only was it equated with the states' coming of age; the style also had national implications. Statehood for Kentucky and Tennessee was an early example of nationalism and a precursor to the idea of manifest destiny, which arose as the territorial United States expanded from the Atlantic to the Pacific. A similar idea led to the erection of Greek Revival statehouses in Frankfort and Nashville.

In 1827, three years after the Kentucky Capitol was destroyed by fire, a competition was held to select an architect for a new building. Since one of the commissioners was John Brown of Liberty Hall, a conservative or even old-fashioned statehouse might have been expected. But a bold Greek Revival design proposed by Gideon Shryock, a young Ken-

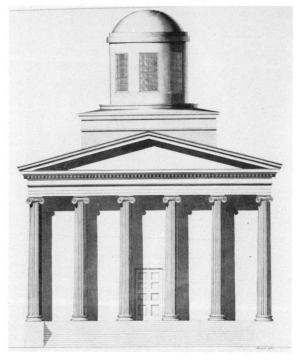

Gideon Shryock. Old Statehouse, Frankfort, Kentucky: 1827. The drawing presented to the competition commissioners promised an unequivocally Greek Revival building with a chaste cupola to light the stairway rotunda inside. (Drawing by the architect: 1827. Kentucky Historical Society.)

tuckian, won the competition. Shryock had trained with his father, a Lexington builder-architect, and had been sent to Philadelphia for a year to study under William Strickland. The building he produced was a stylistic innovation, not only for Kentucky but for the entire United States. Built of marble quarried near Frankfort, it was finished in 1830. As Shryock explained three years later, "The front elevation presents a hexastyle portico of the Ionic order the proportions of which are taken from the Temple of Minerva Polias at Priene in Ionia."[10] During the 1820s the Greeks had struggled for independence from the Turks; hence, Greek architecture expressed the desire for political freedom, along with cultural maturity, such as a western state might hope to display. The simple grandeur of the portico and the interior chambers, particularly the central rotunda, were thought to be capable of promoting political virtue, another aspect of classical culture that was admired in the antebellum South.

STATE CAPITOL, NASHVILLE, TENNESSEE (1845–1859)

In Tennessee, where Nashville had been designated the capital in 1843, Greek Revival taste also prevailed. The commanding site presented to the state was on an impressive hill near the city's center. The commissioners empowered to search for an architect selected William Strickland, who, in their words, "had displayed the utmost good taste in the buildings erected by him."[11] In 1845, as work began, Strickland freely identified the sources for his design: "The architecture of the building consists of a Doric basement, four Ionic porticos, surmounted by a Corinthian tower.... The porticos are after the order of the Erechtheum, and the tower from the Choragic Monument of Lysicrates at Athens." Since the elevated site suggested the Acropolis in Athens, Strickland chose the Ionic order of the Erechtheum, as Shryock had done at Frankfort, and as Jefferson had done at Richmond. The nineteenth-century Neoclassical aesthetic maintained a subtle distinction among the orders—the Doric as signifying strength; the Ionic, wisdom; and the Corinthian, beauty. Whereas the conventional format at the time combined a pedimented façade, a central dome, and flanking wings, Strickland designed a simple rectangular structure with pedimented porticos at both ends, and colonnades with entablatures but no pediments along the sides.

In Philadelphia, Strickland's Greek-inspired architecture had trans-

William Stickland. Tennessee Statehouse, Nashville, Tennessee: 1845–1859. While the Kentucky Statehouse was a simple imitation of a Greek building, the Tennessee Statehouse was a more eclectic combination of colonnades with and without pediments and a dominant cupola based on the Choragic Monument of Lysicrates. (Lithograph by P. S. Duval: 1845–1859. Tennessee State Library.)

formed a "city of brick" into one "of marble," to which newspapers often referred as the "Athens of America." Even before the Tennessee State Capitol was completed in 1859, Nashville was being described as the "Athens of the West"—a label (revised, with the coming of the Civil War, to "Athens of the South") that led ultimately, by a kind of self-fulfilling prophecy, to the building of the only full-scale replica of the Parthenon in the world.[12] In the 1890s Tennessee began to prepare for its centennial in 1897, an exposition modeled after the 1893 World's Columbian Exposition in Chicago. As its distinctive central structure, a building copied from the Parthenon at Athens was intended to promote Tennessee's industries and commerce, and at the same time to embody the city's historic epithet. The project was so tremendous a success that after 1897 there were public petitions to have it preserved. Early in the twentieth century, that part of the centennial grounds surrounding the Parthenon became a city park. Made of wood and plaster, the building had deteriorated by 1920. It was so greatly venerated, however, that it was reconstructed in concrete, with meticulous attention to authenticity, under the supervision of William Dinsmoor, an eminent archaeologist, and Russell Hart, a local architect. Finished in 1931, the Parthenon takes its place with the exactly contemporary restoration of Williamsburg in manifesting the respect of the South for traditional architecture.

MILLEDGEVILLE, GEORGIA

The shifting of capitals from the coast to a location nearer a colony's geographical center began as early as the founding of Annapolis and Williamsburg. It was, however, during and immediately following the American Revolution that this aspect of the general expansion westward reached its height. The movement provided a means of balancing the political power between Tidewater aristocrats and upcountry yeomen, and was a boon to interior settlement, with planned capitals emerging at Richmond, Raleigh, Columbia, Tallahassee, and Jackson.

In Georgia the first of several shifts occurred when the colonial seat of government was temporarily moved from Savannah during the British occupation. After the war, Augusta and then Louisville served briefly as capitals. In 1803, a statute authorized the creation of a town near the center of the state, to be named Milledgeville, after Governor John Milledge. The following year one of the commissioners reported to him the selection of a site on the Oconee River:

We have agreed on a plan and laid it out on the ground; made reserves of three squares, eighteen acres each, which I think are eligible and well chosen; say one for a statehouse, one for the governor's residence, and the other for a penitentiary, or such other public purposes as the legislature may please to apply to them. There will be two main streets of 120 feet width intended to front the statehouse; lots laid off in squares of four acres, which are to be checked into acre lots, the other streets to 100 feet wide.[13]

The plan's wide streets, large squares, and four-acre residential blocks were exceedingly ambitious. The squares, which may have been derived in theory from those of Savannah, were arranged in a cruciform manner which balanced the capitol, governor's mansion, penitentiary, and a fourth square for churches and a cemetery. The residential blocks were to be subdivided into one-acre squares with houses sited at the corners. The overall effect was of an expansive town with ample spaces on which distinguished architecture could be picturesquely landscaped. In 1827 a newspaper offered this somewhat pretentious account of the founders' motives:

> They were men, who had imbibed a love and taste for antiquity, whose brains had been soothed with the lore of the great "olden days," and that the resemblance of this site to that of classical Rome, determined their choice. The Oconee is about three times the size of the Tiber, and the infant Georgia Rome outstrips this day, in the number of her hills, her classical Italian mother. Considering the great advancement of the arts and sciences and the increase of the sources of wealth of modern times, it was no unreasonable calculation in the ancient selection of the site of this capital, that its hills would one day be covered with theaters, colosseums, temples, and superb private edifices.[14]

Milledgeville did not, however, develop into an American Rome. The statehouse into which the legislature moved in 1807 was Gothic in design. Little is known about the architects, Smart and Lane, or about why the style, an apparent anomaly like Benjamin Latrobe's Gothic design for the Baltimore Cathedral, was chosen. In fact, the regular plan was not very Gothic; only the pointed arches and the crenellated parapet were at all medieval.

The Governor's Mansion, built between 1836 and 1838, was far closer to the Neoclassical aspirations of Milledgeville's founders. Although not sited on the square reserved for it, the house was a monumental Greek Revival achievement. Two Georgia architects, John Pell and Charles B. Cluskey, were each paid $100 for the "best plan for the residence of the governor"; a northern architect, H. A. Norris of New York, also contributed to the design, however, and Timothy Porter of Connecticut supervised the construction. The exterior features a chaste and severe portico modeled after the Ionic Temple on the Ilissus in Athens. The plan is thoroughly Jeffersonian in its use of square, rectangular, circular, and octagonal rooms. The masterpiece of the interior is

Old Statehouse, Milledgeville, Georgia: 1805–1807, additions in 1828, 1836, and 1850. The Gothic style was an anomaly during a time when Neoclassical principles were at their height.

the central rotunda, rising 50 feet to a skylighted dome—a domesticated version of the Rotunda at the University of Virginia. Jefferson's designs for the executive mansions at Richmond and Washington also had central rotundas, and by retaining that feature the Georgia Governor's Mansion provides another example of the continuity in the South of conventional forms.

Milledgeville never attained the grandeur envisioned by its founders. After the main railroad bypassed it, a legislator in 1848 argued for the relocation of the capital in Macon; he described the Governor's Mansion as an "immense, half-finished, and already dilapidated monument of folly," the Capitol as "patched up" and "in ruins within." Milledgeville survived both this verbal attack and the arrival of General Sherman, who during the Civil War briefly used the Governor's Mansion as his headquarters. During Reconstruction, however, Atlanta became the administrative center of a federal military district, and in 1868 the state capital was moved there. The growth of Milledgeville stopped, and the sylvan ambience of the antebellum capital was preserved—the Capitol as part of Georgia Military College, and the Governor's Mansion as the president's house at Georgia College.

The rise of Atlanta had been meteoric since 1836—when, as the southern end of the railroad that was to run between the Tennessee and Chattahoochee rivers, it was called Terminus. In 1843 it was incorporated as Marthasville; the more auspicious name of Atlanta was given two years later. Its planning was entirely railroad-oriented: in the 1850s the city limits were defined by a perfect circle two miles in diameter, with the center at the zero milepost of the Western and Atlantic Railroad. In 1857 the Memphis and Charleston Railway was completed, making Atlanta, whose population still was under 10,000, the major inland transportation center of the entire region. Burned by Sherman in 1864, Atlanta was rebuilt and became the paramount urban creation of the New South.

Old Governor's Mansion, Milledgeville, Georgia: 1836–1838. Behind the chaste Greek Revival façade is a domed and skylighted rotunda of Palladian inspiration influenced by Thomas Jefferson's Rotunda at the University of Virginia.

CHAPTER NINE

TWO ANTEBELLUM CITIES: NEW ORLEANS AND CHARLESTON

New Orleans became part of the United States with the Louisiana Purchase of 1803, and thereupon began a period of spectacular growth. Not only was it a center for the trade in sugar and, eventually, in cotton as well; it was also the terminus for Mississippi River shipping, which linked the Midwest with the South. By 1815 a city plan showed significant changes. The fortifications that had surrounded the French and Spanish city were replaced by the broad streets which to this day define the Vieux Carré or French Quarter. That sector had been platted with regular square blocks which could not be easily extended because of the curve of the Mississippi River. Hence, faubourgs or suburbs were laid out on both sides of the French Quarter, with street systems connected to the old grid but altered where necessary to follow the riverbank. Each new section developed its own distinctive identity, with increasing competition between the old Creole establishment and the new American opportunism.

The American sector, immediately upriver from the French Quarter, underwent the most dramatic growth. The first speculative building there was without architectural elegance, in vivid contrast with the French Quarter's slumbering European ambience. When Benjamin Latrobe, the finest United States architect of his time, arrived in New Orleans in 1818, he praised the Old World character of Jackson Square as having "an admirable general effect," calling it "infinitely superior to anything in our Atlantic cities as a water view of the city."[1] He went on to add that "the square itself is neglected, the fences ragged, and in many places open. . . . Thus, a square, which might be made the handsomest in America, is really rather a nuisance than otherwise." Latrobe described the Cabildo, Cathedral, and Presbytère (on the north side of the square facing the river) as the finest buildings in the city, although his English background prevented him from praising specifically their architectural style—a free blending of French and Spanish features. In the vernacular Creole houses of the French Quarter, Latrobe recognized a style far more sensitive to the subtropical climate than the row houses erected by Americans:

> New Orleans, beyond Royal Street [in the French Quarter], . . . retains its old character without variation. The houses are, with hardly a dozen exceptions among many hundred, one-story houses. The roofs are high, covered with tiles or shingles, and project five feet over the footway. . . . However different this mode is from the American manner of building, it has very great advantages both with regard to the interior of the dwelling and to the street. In the summer the walls are perfectly shaded from the sun and the house kept cool. . . .

> The suburb St. Mary, the American suburb, already exhibits the flat, dull, dingy character of Market Street, in Philadelphia, or Baltimore Street, instead of the motley and picturesque effect of the stuccoed French buildings of the city. . . . The French stucco the fronts of their buildings and often color them; the Americans exhibit their red staring brickwork, imbibing heat through the whole unshaded substance of the wall. . . . I have no doubt that the American style will ultimately be that of the whole city, especially as carpenters from the eastern border of the union are the architects, and, of course work on in their old habits, for men accustomed to these sorts of houses. But although room may be thereby gained, the convenience of the houses will by no means be promoted—nor the health of the city improved.

He observed finally that New Orleans was changing: "It would be a safe wager that in one hundred years not a vestige will remain of the buildings as they now stand, excepting perhaps of a few public buildings and of houses built since the American acquisition of the country." The French Quarter, with its Cabildo, its Cathedral and Presbytère, and its Creole houses, had a sense of place similar to that of a southern plantation. The continual growth and change of the American sector, as a new type of city, endangered even the structures within the French Quarter. Progress meant that New Orleans would eventually be no different from cities on the eastern seaboard, such as New York, Philadelphia, and Baltimore.

In 1835 a newspaper published a long editorial on the condition of the city, stressing unrivaled opportunities resulting from increasing commerce and population (New Orleans, at that time, was the fourth-largest city in the United States), and arguing against the widely held belief that the city was an unhealthful place, particularly in summer. Architecture, however, was still "in a degraded state, . . . as proprietors of lots are usually their own architects; and erect as caprice may dictate or custom

James Gallier and Charles Dakin. View of the St. Charles Hotel, New Orleans, Louisiana: 1845. The monumentality of the hotel, related to that of the National Capitol, conveyed the idea that New Orleans had become a major metropolis in the United States. (Lithograph by Thayer: 1845. Louisiana State Museum.)

control."[2] But in that same year, work began on the St. Charles Hotel, a building in the American sector that differed from most previous New Orleans structures in being designed by a truly professional architect, James Gallier, Sr.[3] Irish-born and English-trained as a Neoclassicist, he had arrived in the United States in 1832. Two years in New York exposed him to the prominent practitioners of Greek Revival: James Dakin, who had worked with Ithiel Town and Alexander Jackson Davis, and Minard Lafever, who in 1833 published *The Modern Builders' Guide*, a standard Greek Revival handbook. Gallier's decision in 1834 to move to New Orleans was motivated by the glowing reports of building opportunities there.

To his design of the St. Charles Hotel, Gallier brought northern architectural taste, emulating the very latest in hotels—Tremont House in Boston and Astor House in New York, both designed by Isaiah Rogers. The St. Charles did not simply surpass them both, but was in fact the largest American hotel of its time, with a monumental portico and dome that made it far more pretentious than its predecessors. Patently intended to attract cotton and sugar brokers, the hotel epitomized the commercial importance of New Orleans. In its heroic Greek Revival style, the hotel assumed the appearance of a state capitol. It had, as its crowning feature, a dome that may have been designed by Dakin rather than Gallier. An

1845 guidebook described it as having a "circular colonnade [with] a beautiful gallery eleven feet wide, from whence can be seen the whole city, and all the windings of the river for several miles in each direction. The effect of the dome upon the sight of the visitor, as he approaches the city, is similar to that of St. Paul's, London."[4] A contemporary traveler declared: "The St. Charles . . . is not only the largest and handsomest hotel in the United States, but as it seemed to me, the largest and handsomest hotel in the world."[5]

The businessmen of the French Quarter, not to be outdone by the Americans, had meanwhile erected their own monumental hotel, the St. Louis. Not surprisingly, the stockholders commissioned a French architect, J. N. B. de Pouilly, who had arrived in New Orleans by 1833 after receiving his training at the Ecole des Beaux-Arts in Paris.[6] The first-story arcade of the St. Louis Hotel was modeled on the Paris buildings of Percier and Fontaine along the Rue de Rivoli, begun in 1802. In contrast to the dominant exterior dome of the St. Charles Hotel, the St. Louis Hotel had a magnificent skylighted space that rose from the ground floor to the full height of the building, but was not visible on the outside. A newspaper commented on the opening of the latter in 1838: "Our city possesses a monument worthy of the name, which, if not superior to anything among us, at least has no reason to fear a rival in grandeur and magnificence."[7]

A third great hotel of the 1830s, the Verandah, was designed by James Dakin, who followed Gallier to New Orleans because of the boom in building. A native of New York State, he had become a partner of the prominent New York firm of Town & Davis in 1832, when he was only twenty-six, and during that same year produced plans for his first work in New Orleans, a group of thirteen row houses on Julia Street.[8] Although fine in themselves, they were virtually indistinguishable from Philadelphia and Baltimore row houses of the type that Latrobe had criticized as poorly adapted to the New Orleans environment. After Dakin moved to New Orleans in 1835, the Verandah Hotel, diagonally opposite the St. Charles Hotel, was his first major commission. Although smaller in size and less monumental, it was enormously influential as a building prototype because of the iron balconies that ran along its entire length.

With the work of such architects as Dakin and Gallier, and the use of granite and iron as basic materials—in a city where buildings had generally been of brick, either exposed or stuccoed—high style had arrived in the American sector. St. Patrick's Church (1837–1840), designed by Dakin for the Irish Catholics in the American sector, was one of the earliest Gothic Revival churches in America. Two years before Richard Upjohn's influential Trinity Church was begun in New York, Dakin identified the sources for St. Patrick's:

The exterior is that of the Pointed Style of the Second Period of Ecclesiastical Architecture, and has been principally imitated from that unrivalled example of splendored majesty, York Minster Cathedral.... The ceiling of the interior is in imitation of the ceiling of Exeter Cathedral.[9]

The design was at the same time progressive in the use of iron in the truss roof over the nave. When problems emerged during the church's construction, Dakin was replaced by Gallier. Whereas Dakin had envisioned an open interior without supports, Gallier added iron columns which separated the nave and side aisles, and which were joined to the ceiling with elaborate fan vaulting. The Gothic ornamentation which Dakin had designed for the exterior of the tower was similarly not completed, although the remaining lancet windows and buttresses did have a Gothic verticality.

The architectural erudition shown by both Dakin and Gallier reflected a taste that had begun to differentiate among various styles in relation to the function of the building to be erected. For the hotels, as civic symbols, Greek Revival was deemed appropriate. For a church, on the other hand, as a postclassical institution, the Gothic style came to be viewed as uniquely suitable.

The Greek Revival inaugurated a new political era for New Orleans.

James Gallier. View of City Hall, New Orleans, Louisiana: 1848. The portico features a very pure Greek Revival style achieved by using granite and marble as the basic materials, and by imitating the Ionic details of the Erechtheum as closely as possible. (Drawn by T. K. Wharton and lithograph by F. Bedford: 1848. Historic New Orleans Collection.)

View of New Orleans, Louisiana: 1852. From the crenellated tower of St. Patrick's Church, the vista includes the primary buildings in the American sector—the City Hall and the St. Charles Hotel. (Drawn by J. W. Hill and Smith, lithograph by B. F. Smith, Jr. Library of Congress.)

During the 1830s antagonism between the American newcomers and the established French inhabitants had led to the division of the city into three autonomous municipalities—the French Quarter, the American sector, and the Faubourg Marigny. In 1845 Gallier was commissioned to design the building whose location in the American sector signaled the passing of the French Quarter as the governmental center. Gallier wrote of the new City Hall, which was completed in 1850, that the Greek Ionic portico "is considered as a very chaste and highly-refined example of that style."[10] In the direct study and borrowing of details from Greek architecture, the City Hall is, in fact, Gallier's most archaeological building. The capitals of the portico are modeled on those of the Erechtheum, and the entablature and pediment above are virtual compendiums of correct Ionic usage.

In 1849 an ambitious prophecy was made about the city's destiny:

The only rival New Orleans can have on the American continent is New York, and New York, although its commercial influences may be greater, will never have the same power over American civilization as New Orleans. . . . The Mississippi is the great center of the American confederacy . . . the band of steel that fastens together all the states of the Union. New Orleans . . . is the capital of the West. The influence of New Orleans over the western country is already perceptible, and is destined to be much greater. As Athens moulded Greece, and Greece Europe, so this city will influence the West, and through it, the whole American continent.[11]

An 1852 lithograph of the American sector reveals the new appearance of the city, as viewed from the tower of St. Patrick's Church. Of the independent buildings shown interspersed with the cityscape, the most prominent were the St. Charles Hotel and the City Hall. St. Patrick's itself, as an isolated building, was a masterpiece of Gothic Revival, but an unharmonious contrast with the classical townhouses and the Greek Revival civic buildings. As the awakening to "modern" architecture made New Orleans less distinctive, Latrobe's prophecy of 1818 was already proving correct.

Frederick Law Olmsted, who visited New Orleans in 1853, lamented the losses which speculative building had caused: "Among the houses, one occasionally sees a relic of ancient Spanish builders, while all the newer edifices have the characteristics of the unartistic and dollar pursuing Yankees." He noted, however, that Jackson Square still had much of its original character:

> I was delighted when I reached the old Place d'Armes, now a public garden. . . . Fronting upon it is the old Hôtel de Ville, still the city courthouse, a quaint old French structure, with scaly and vermiculated surface, and deep-worn door-sills, and smooth-rubbed corners; the most picturesque and historic-looking public building, except the highly-preserved, little old courthouse at Newport, that I can now think of in the United States.[12]

Olmsted may be New Orleans's first preservationist in his respect for historic buildings; at least he saw little distinction in the antebellum city, labeling the St. Charles Hotel, where he stayed, "stupendous, tasteless, ill-contrived, and inconvenient."

Before Olmsted's visit a shift in taste to the romantic and picturesque had become manifest in the upriver city of Baton Rouge, to which in 1845 the legislature had approved the moving of the state capital. Two years later Dakin submitted plans for a new capitol. As recently as 1840 he had produced a Greek Revival design for a new statehouse (which was never built) in New Orleans; of the style he chose in 1847 he wrote:

> I have used the Castellated Gothic style of architecture in the design because it is quite as appropriate as any other style or mode of building and because no style or order of architecture can be employed which would give suitable character to a building with so little cost as Castellated Gothic.

> Should a design be adopted on the Grecian or Roman order of architecture, we should accomplish only what would unavoidably appear to be a mere copy of some other edifice already erected and often repeated in every city and town of our country. Those orders have been so much employed for many years past that it is almost impossible to start an original conception with them.[13]

James Dakin. Old Statehouse, Baton Rouge, Louisiana: 1847–1852. Although Gothic appears contrary to the mainstream of southern architecture, the impulse behind the choice of style was a romanticism similar to that which had led to the picturesqueness of Oak Alley.

Believing that Greek Revival had lost its vitality, Dakin also redefined Gothic Revival. Unlike that of St. Patrick's Church, built ten years earlier, the style of the State Capitol was almost totally devoid of cultural associations. Rather, Dakin's primary objective was a distinctively original building. The only other Gothic state capitol in existence was the one in Milledgeville, Georgia; and as compared with Greek Revival, which had come to mean an inhibiting adherence to established models and rules, castellated Gothic offered the possibility of a freer conception, the visual equivalent of literary romanticism, to which the viewer was expected to respond subjectively. The difficulty here was that the associations of a state capitol were political rather than literary. One newspaper comment in 1852, when the building was finished, raised troublesome issues: "As a capitol for a republican state we can see neither justness of conception, propriety of taste, nor beauty of architecture in it. It is in the style of a castle of the dark ages—the age of tyranny, of baronial oppression, of monastic superstition."[14]

In 1862, during the Union occupation of Baton Rouge, fire destroyed the interior of the Capitol. The reconstruction of 1880–1882 included a magnificent cast-iron skylighted rotunda and the addition of a fourth story. On the exterior, however, the appearance remained much as it had been before the war. Mark Twain perhaps understood its underlying character more fully than anyone else, his unsympathetic northern bias notwithstanding:

> Sir Walter Scott is probably responsible for the Capitol building; for it is not conceivable that this little sham castle would ever have been built if he had not run the people mad a couple of generations ago, with his medieval romances. The South has not yet recovered from the debilitating influence of his books. . . .
>
> It is pathetic enough that a whitewashed castle, with turrets and things—materials all ungenuine within and without—should ever have been built in this otherwise honorable place; but it is much more pathetic to see this architectural falsehood undergoing restoration and perpetualization in our day, when it would have been so easy to let dynamite finish what a charitable fire began, and then devote this restoration money to the building of something genuine.[15]

ANTEBELLUM CHARLESTON

Charleston experienced little of the spectacular growth that characterized antebellum New Orleans. Throughout the first half of the nineteenth century, its population remained relatively static. From its position in 1820 as the South's second most populous city—with 24,780 as compared to New Orleans's 27,176—by 1860 it had grown to only 40,522, while slipping to third place (behind Louisville). Meanwhile New Orleans grew dramatically to a population of 168,675.

The ascendancy of New Orleans was one reason for Charleston's eclipse. As the eighteenth-century port for colonial Carolina, Charleston had been the South's primary city. As the balance of power shifted westward, the state capital was moved to Columbia in 1790. With the development of cotton as the new agricultural staple, Charleston still held on to the assumption that it would continue as a major port, but even the canal and railroad building of the 1820s and 1830s was insufficient to compete with the new urban centers. As the prospects of economic growth and prosperity proved more and more illusory, Charleston was left with a noble architectural heritage of Georgian and Federal churches, civic buildings, and townhouses, designed primarily by master builders and gentleman-amateur architects. It was the city that had produced Robert Mills, the "first native American who directed his studies to architecture as a profession."[16] Born in 1781 and educated at the College of Charleston, Mills had worked as a draftsman for James Hoban, architect of the White House. It was at this time that President Jefferson befriended Mills and offered him the use of his architectural library, where, as Mills later recalled, he had "found several works, all of Roman character, principally Palladio, of whom Mr. Jefferson was a great admirer." Later, Mills had worked for Benjamin Latrobe, under whom he completed his training:

> The talents of this gentleman were of the first order; his style was purely Greek. . . . The example and influence of Mr. Jefferson at first operated in favor of the introduction of the Roman style into the country, and it required all the talents and good taste of such a man as Mr. Latrobe to correct it by introducing a better. The natural good taste and the unprejudiced eye of our citizens required only a few examples of the Greek style to convince them of its superiority over the Roman.

Mills himself contributed to the shift in architectural taste with his Monumental Church (1812–1814) in Richmond, and the First Baptist Church in Charleston (1819–1822), which he proudly described as "the best specimen of correct taste in architecture of the modern buildings in this city . . . purely Greek in style, simply grand in its proportions, and beautiful in its detail."[17] Of greater importance as an example of professional architecture, however, was Mills's Fireproof Building (1822–1827), designed for state offices and the storage of documents.[18] Although a rendering shows it with a Greek Doric portico, the actual structure was so much simplified and stripped of ornament as to become one of the most powerful buildings of its time. A skillful integration of planning, structure, and massing, it is composed of cellular spaces, eight to a floor, each space defined by a brick groin or barrel vault that provides the fireproofing, with a central skylighted stairway and two corridors connecting the porticos. The units are also clearly apparent on the exterior, where the window and door openings articulate the parts as well as join in an indivisible whole.

The architectural excellence of the Fireproof Building consists in the way form is generated by function and structure rather than by style, as had generally been true of earlier Charleston buildings. Mills might be remembered simply as Charleston's premier antebellum architect had President Jackson not appointed him architect of public buildings in Washington. Instead, he became the preeminent architect in the nation: the Washington Monument, the Treasury Building, the Patent Office, and the Post Office were all built from his designs.

In Charleston, meanwhile, the Louisville, Cincinnati & Charleston Railroad (organized in 1836–1837) was promoted as a channel of trade through the port of Charleston. Although the railroad itself had failed by 1840, it stimulated a number of civic improvements: streets were opened or extended, marshes were drained, parks were established, and the general health of the population improved. In 1837 the College of Charleston was reorganized under municipal governance, and in 1839 the High

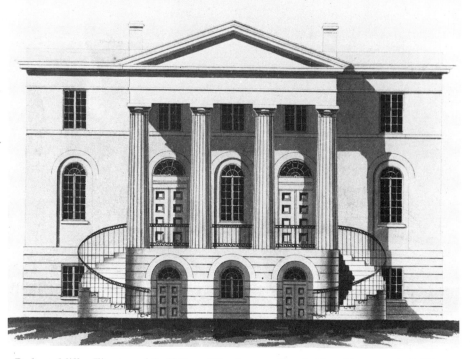

Robert Mills. Fireproof Building, Charleston, South Carolina: c. 1828. The architect's rendering shows a building much more specifically Greek Revival than the one erected, whose architectural excellence lies in its simplification of details and its emphasis on elemental architectural qualities—planning, structure, and form. (Drawing by the architect: c. 1828. South Carolina Historical Society.)

School of Charleston was established. All this activity notwithstanding, Charleston differed from such cities as New Orleans, Louisville, and Richmond in one major respect: the Nullification Controversy of 1832–1833 had made it the champion of states' rights and the spearhead of sectional strife between North and South. This is clear from a letter to a Charleston newspaper in 1837:

> In improving Charleston, an eye must be had to what the city is destined one day to become. In the revolution of states, Charleston will be to the South what New York is to the Union. Sooner or later the western railroad will be completed, and bring its great corresponding advantages. May I not look a little farther into futurity. Mr. [John Quincy] Adams has declared in his place in Congress, that the annexation of Texas to the South, will destroy the Union. . . . If the prediction of Mr. Adams comes to pass, Charleston will be the Queen of the South.[19]

The architectural symbol of the new city was the Charleston Hotel (1837–1839), designed by Charles F. Reichardt, whose credentials were no less impressive than those of Gallier, Dakin, and de Pouilly. A pupil of the German Neoclassical architect Karl Friedrich Schinkel, Reichardt arrived in Charleston late in 1836 from New York, where earlier in the same year he had been a founder of the American Institution of Architects. His having gone immediately to work on two prestigious city buildings—the hotel and also the New Theater—suggests that he had been invited to Charleston by civic leaders.[20] The hotel introduced to the city the archaeological Greek Revival which Gallier had recently used in the St. Charles Hotel in New Orleans. Its monumental colonnade of fourteen colossal Corinthian columns, with capitals modeled after the Choragic Monument of Lysicrates, was described in a local newspaper as "unsurpassed in taste and elegance by any similar building in the United States." As illustrious as the classical source of the colonnade were the nineteenth-century parallels—Schinkel's Altes Museum in Berlin; Town, Davis & Dakin's Lafayette Terrace in New York; and Mills's Treasury Building in Washington.

In 1838 stockholders and city leaders met in the nearly finished hotel to celebrate the accomplishment. A newspaper editor summarized the meaning of the occasion in his toast: "The Charleston Hotel and the great railway—our splendid and commodious palace is ready for the coming throng of western travellers."[21] One month later, the hotel was destroyed by a disastrous fire. Reconstructed on the same plans, the hotel was portrayed in 1839 as having been "raised, Phoenix-like, from its ashes," and according to a description of the interior, "among the decorations was a painting, executed by a Charleston artist, representing the harbor of

Charles F. Reichardt. View of the Charleston Hotel, Charleston, South Carolina: c. 1845. The hotel was promoted by civic leaders to project a more aggressive image of the city as the "Queen of the South." (Drawn by J. H. Bufford, lithograph by B. W. Thayer: c. 1845. Carolina Art Association.)

Charleston in 1850 [i.e., eleven years in the future], crowded with the noble steamships that are to bring the wealth of the world into the lap of the fair Queen of the South."[22]

Even after the campaign to adorn the city with classical buildings had been curtailed by the aftermath of the Panic of 1837, a Greek Revival monument was commissioned by the Hibernian Society. Another nationally prominent architect, Thomas Ustick Walter, designed their building, constructed between 1839 and 1841. According to the building committee, "the beautiful Ionic temple, consecrated to the Muses, on the banks of the Ilissus," was the chosen model.[23] Inside the portico was a three-story domed and skylighted rotunda with superimposed Greek orders—Doric, Ionic, and Corinthian—still one of Charleston's most impressive interior spaces.

An economic recovery in the 1840s saw a number of individual, unrelated commissions, which resulted from the growing pluralism of the city. Edward Brickell White, Carolina-born and trained in engineering at West Point, who emerged as the leading architect of the decade, responded with eclecticism to a diversity of clients and building types.[24] His Market Hall (1840–1841), built for the city government, is Roman, with bucrania (ox heads) and ram's heads along the metopes; in this the

Thomas Ustick Walter. Hibernian Hall, Charleston, South Carolina: 1839–1841. Modeled after the Ionic Temple on the Ilissus in Athens, the portico was badly damaged by the earthquake of 1886 and rebuilt with Victorian modillions and an Italianate window in the pediment.

Edward Brickell White. Huguenot Church, Charleston, South Carolina: 1844–1845. Ecclesiological Gothic was adapted to Low Country materials: pointed arches and buttresses of traditional brick masonry covered with stucco, finials of cast iron, and on the inside a vaulted ceiling simulated in lath and plaster.

Aemilian Basilica in the Roman Forum, which was also a market, had been the model. For the Second Baptist Church (1841–1842; now the Centenary Methodist Church), White designed as close a copy of a Greek Doric hexastyle temple as was ever built in Charleston. The temple format expressed the religious liberalism of the denomination; its style also may have been suggested by the First Baptist Church, which Mills, its architect, had described as "purely Greek."

White's next major commission was the Huguenot Church (1844–1845), designed for a group of Episcopalians of French ancestry who had decided to return to French Protestantism. In their own way they were following the ecclesiological movement, which had originated in the 1830s at Oxford and Cambridge, and which stressed historical correctness in the liturgy and ecclesiastical furnishings. White adopted Gothic as epitomizing pure Christian style. Whereas the Gothic of Dakin's and Gallier's St. Patrick's Church in New Orleans was derived from a knowledge of specific Gothic buildings, White evidently drew instead upon the English Gothic Revivalist Augustus Welby Pugin, whose *The True Principles of Pointed or Christian Architecture* (1841) contains illustrations of Gothic details very similar to those of the Huguenot

Church. A description of the church, after it was finished, as "the only specimen of pointed, or emphatically Christian architecture, which has ever been erected in our city," employs the crucial words of Pugin's title.[25]

Charleston's prestigious Episcopal churches—St. Michael's and St. Philip's—had been designed after eighteenth-century English prototypes, particularly James Gibbs's St. Martin's-in-the-Fields. Thus White's Gothic church for the Grace Episcopal congregation, erected in 1847–1848, boldly broke with local tradition. The architectural eclecticism of the 1840s, rather than implying a lack of aesthetic conviction, offered an architect the means for individualizing each commission. By the same token, it signified that the remarkable homogeneity of Georgian and Federal Charleston was waning. A letter to a newspaper in 1853 suggests a romanticized consciousness of the city's architectural destiny:

> We recollect . . . the feeling of disappointment with which we first beheld Charleston. We had been accustomed to consider her as the first of Southern cities . . . but we could only compare her to a decayed old woman: though we were obliged to admit that even in her decay, she was unmistakably a lady. . . . [The city] has aroused herself and . . . is about to put on garments worthy of her renewed and beautiful womanhood.[26]

Early Victorian architecture came to Charleston in a series of stylistically and structurally innovative buildings by Edward C. Jones and Francis D. Lee, who had formed a partnership in 1852.[27] For the State Bank (1853–1855) they used the Italianate style and Connecticut brownstone; the Farmers and Exchange Bank (1853–1854) employed the same material but was in the Moorish style. Buildings entirely of stone were a radical departure from the traditional Charleston use of brick, usually covered with stucco. Gone, too, were the heroic implications of Greek Revival and the religious rectitude implicit in Gothic Revival. A prominent South Carolina novelist, William Gilmore Simms, recognized the shift in taste:

> The American rage for Grecian models, some few years back, made its way to the Palmetto City, and several [buildings] were raised of this class, which consumed a great deal of money, without any adequate result in beauty. . . . The Grecian style is wholly inappropriate to such a dead level as that of Charleston. The skies, climate, and plain surface of the city considered, and the light, Moorish, Saracen, Italian—even the Gothic—are all in better propriety.[28]

The new Victorian attitude is best expressed by the Unitarians, who renovated their church in 1852–1854 with Jones & Lee the architects, and whose building program revealed some ambivalence concerning venerable structures. "A certain degree of reverence" caused the congregation to retain their 1774–1787 church's surrounding walls, which were nevertheless adapted "to a more pleasing structure" by a gothicizing of the interior after the fan and pendant vaulting of Henry VII's Chapel at Westminster Abbey.[29] The Unitarian denomination shared almost nothing with early Tudor England, and the squareness of the eighteenth-century meetinghouse virtually precluded an approximation of the Gothic style. With typical Victorian disregard for such apparent contradictions, however, Jones & Lee provided a remarkably faithful semblance of Perpendicular Gothic—even though the vaults were lath and plaster simulations. Though it may be heretical to suggest that a nineteenth-century imitation could be as distinguished as its sixteenth-century source, the Unitarian interior is a truly sublime congregational space.

Jones & Lee were pioneers in bringing to Charleston a new building type, the department store. Their Browning and Leman Building (1852) was a mercantile palace of exceptional beauty and functional efficiency. The interior's domed and skylighted spaces were supported by iron columns. Another Jones & Lee building, the New Fish Market (1853–1856), used iron even more extensively: a newspaper description proudly asserted that the iron was made locally. In 1853–1854 a rotunda domed with iron and glass, designed to serve as an exchange, was erected in the central courtyard of the Charleston Hotel; a newspaper described it as "a miniature Crystal Palace." Cast-iron fronts were constructed on commercial buildings in the mid-1850s, a progressive innovation: the prototypical structures—James Bogardus's first cast-iron building in New York of 1848, Joseph Paxton's Crystal Palace in London of 1851,

Edward C. Jones and Francis D. Lee. Unitarian Church, Charleston, South Carolina: 1852–1854. By emulating Tudor Gothic fan and pendant vaulting, the Unitarian congregation's architectural choice was based on aesthetics rather than ideology. (Carolina Art Association.)

and Victor Baltard's Les Halles in Paris of 1853—were only slightly earlier.

The buildings of the 1850s were unequivocally modern, reflecting an optimism based on renewed economic prosperity (which now included industrial development) and a rekindled awareness of the city's destiny. The architectural awakening, however, was largely restricted to new public buildings, leaving virtually unchanged the characteristic Charleston "single house" and the venerable monuments of the city's early history. In 1856 Frederick Law Olmsted wrote:

> Charleston . . . has the character of an old town, where careful government and the influence of social organization has [sic] been long in operation. It is much more metropolitan and convenient than any other southern town; and yet, it seems to have adopted the requirements of modern luxury with an ill-grace, and to be yielding to the demands of commerce and the increasing mobility of civilized men slowly and reluctantly.[30]

Antebellum New Orleans and Charleston were constantly in the process of becoming, in striking contrast to the southern plantation and to the early history of either city. The French Quarter, a place established by the first platting of New Orleans, has retained a distinctive quality down to the present. Georgian and Federal Charleston have, likewise, a timelessness that has resisted change. The urbanism of 1835–1860, on the other hand, had as its ultimate goal the transformation of both cities into modern metropolises. Success was increasingly measured by national standards, and southern cities were indeed triumphs—over the diseases prevalent in a subtropical climate, over the agrarian basis of the economy, and over the resistance to industrial development.

In New Orleans and Charleston similar buildings were actually erected, as they had not been one hundred years earlier. Often designed by professional architects from outside the South, these buildings compared favorably to those of the precedent-setting Northeast. The customhouses in New Orleans and Charleston manifest most fully the architectural dilemma of the antebellum city. The prominent New Orleans architects—Gallier, Dakin, and de Pouilly—all furnished plans in a competition of 1845.[31] But a lesser architect, Alexander Thompson Wood, received the commission through political influence. His design projected a dull granite exterior with vaguely Egyptian features, castigated by Dakin as fit only for a "mausoleum or tomb for an Egyptian king." The admixture of styles did not produce a masterpiece. The Custom House was enormous—the largest building in the United States with the exception of the Capitol in Washington—but massiveness had been achieved at the expense of effective interior planning and severely restricted the aesthetic possibilities.

The Charleston Custom House had a remarkably similar history. Jones provided a plan for a castellated Gothic building, which was ap-

Alexander Thompson Wood. Custom House, New Orleans, Louisiana:
1848–1881. As a federal building, the Custom House is large and amorphous,
with little sense for place. (Library of Congress.)

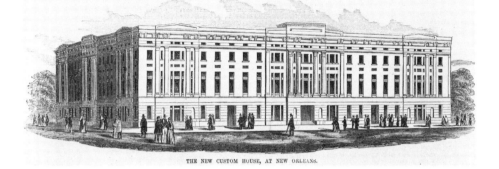

THE NEW CUSTOM HOUSE, AT NEW ORLEANS.

Ammi Burnham Young. Custom House, Charleston, South Carolina:
1850–1879. During the Civil War the unfinished building was described as a
curious anachronism, and when construction resumed in 1870 the dome was
eliminated from the plans. (Lithograph by P. S. Duval and Company: c.
1855. Library of Congress.)

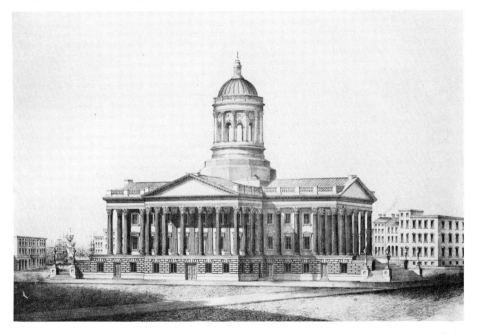

proved in 1850 by the local commissioners, only to be rejected by the
Secretary of the Treasury in Washington. A New England architect,
Ammi Burnham Young, was then given the commission, with White designated the supervisor of construction. Designed with porticos and a
dome in the manner of Neoclassical Washington, and faced with imported granite and marble, the building was not typical of Charleston architecture, but it did receive enthusiastic local praise:

This . . . is a noble structure, and one of which our Palmetto City need not be ashamed. It is of marble, lofty, and extensive. It is a costly work and will consume several millions of dollars. . . . More than one architect was connected in the original design: but we believe that their several plans were finally fused together by some presiding genius . . . at Washington.[32]

The three ingredients that led to this architectural excellence were stone construction, an extravagant budget, and an outside architect. Neither the New Orleans nor the Charleston customhouse was completed until after the Civil War. Federal buildings could scarcely have been meaningfully "southern" at a time when increasing sectional hostility was threatening to disrupt the Union.

CHAPTER TEN

THE NEW SOUTH: FROM PICTURESQUE RUINS TO PROGRESSIVE RESURGENCE

The destruction by federal troops during the Civil War, coupled with natural disasters, transformed many southern buildings into picturesque ruins, which endured as visible signs of the demise of an aristocratic society. Although historians today tend to minimize the so-called Cavalier interpretation of southern history, the physical damage resulting from the war was very real. In 1861 the heart of Charleston was devastated by a fire, not kindled by military action; four years later the city fell to Union troops, and the Low Country plantations were ravaged by detachments of Sherman's army. For years, the hardships of Reconstruction interfered with rebuilding. A writer in 1870 poignantly described the condition of the city:

> If the ruins of Charleston do not date back amid the dim vista of bygone centuries, nor furnish wild legends of romance, yet they belong to a time that revolution has made more distant than ages of peace, and tell of heroic deeds and noble suffering that all the centuries have never surpassed. . . . The crumbling walls, broken pillars, and fallen spires of Charleston, tell of the deeds of men who fought for liberty in vain, and whose memory is yet fresh in the hearts of our people.[1]

Laments for the passing of an aristocratic society occasionally appeared in northern journals:

> The Ashley River . . . was once the scene of great magnificence, the residences and the ways of living being modeled upon those of the English nobility, from whom, in many instances, the planters were descended. This style of living was even more liberal than its English prototype, owing to the warm climate—which almost necessar-

ily promoted indolence and consequent lavishness—to the rich lands, and especially to the number of slaves owned and employed, making each estate patriarchal in its administration, government, and system of supplies. . . . [Along the river] are the ruins of Middleton Place, once one of the most beautiful plantations in South Carolina. This was the home of Arthur Middleton, the signer of the Declaration of Independence. Here he lived and here he died. The old oaks, the hedges, the elaborate terraces and ponds, still remain, but the place is deserted, and the spirit of melancholy broods over it.[2]

The Louisiana Statehouse, burned in 1862 during the Union occupation of Baton Rouge, was portrayed in the same manner:

The Statehouse still stands, a melancholy shell, and looks much more like an ancient castle than it ever had any hope of doing while perfect. . . .

Nothing is left inside the Statehouse but the bare brick walls; even the debris seems to have been removed. The structure is a species of castellated Tudor Gothic, and our young country, I think, has no other ruin so fine.[3]

Because there was so little building in the South at the time, High Victorian architecture never swept the region as it did the rest of the country. This was in one sense a blessing, since the more homogeneous Georgian, Federal, and Greek Revival cityscapes that survived were largely spared the intrusion of Victorian irregularity, eccentricity, and polychromy, as well as the cheap construction and the shoddy materials and craftsmanship into which the style often degenerated. The burgeoning northern cities, enriched by the spoils of military victory as well as by rampant industrialization, were so extensively redeveloped that by the end of the nineteenth century relatively few pre–Civil War structures remained.

HENRY HOBSON RICHARDSON
AS A SOUTHERN ARCHITECT

The different architectural destinies of North and South are revealed by the career of Henry Hobson Richardson. Born in 1838 on a Louisiana sugar plantation, immediately downriver from Oak Alley, that belonged to his mother's family, he grew up in New Orleans, where his father was a cotton merchant. The Richardsons lived in one of the Julia Street row

houses that had been built in the 1830s. The combination of the aristocratic life of the plantation and the urbanity of New Orleans is reflected
in Richardson's early education, which consisted almost entirely of private tutoring. By the time he was in his teens he had shown proficiency
in mathematics and drawing; he played the flute, spoke French, and had
acquired a patrician elegance along with the skills of the rider and sports-
man. Expecting to pursue a career in the army, he received a nomination
to West Point through a family friend, but a speech impediment prevented him from matriculating at West Point, and consequently from
having to choose, as a commissioned officer, between the Union and the
Confederacy.

Instead, he spent a year at the University of Louisiana (located at
the time in New Orleans), and then enrolled at Harvard College for a
degree in civil engineering. It was during his convivial but academically
undistinguished years at Cambridge that he decided to become an architect. After his graduation in 1859, he traveled to England and France, in-
tending to return to New Orleans after a few months. But from what had
been conceived as a grand tour, he turned to the serious study of architecture at the Ecole des Beaux-Arts and then to employment with a French
architect, Théodore Labrouste. Behind the change in plans lay the grim
reality of the Civil War. In 1862, Richardson returned to Boston, hoping
to begin his architectural career; but no one would give him the work he
wanted, and having refused to swear allegiance to the Union, he went
back to Paris for the duration of the war. After learning that New Orleans had been occupied by the Union navy, Richardson wrote to his fiancée in Boston:

> New Orleans is taken—governed by strangers. . . . What a position
> to be placed in! . . . I have in vain reasoned about the right and
> wrong. . . . How I have suffered and do suffer, no one can ever know.
> To remain in Europe I think my best plan—in fact I *must*. But I
> burned with shame when I read of the capture of my city and I in
> Paris.[4]

The prolongation of Richardson's architectural study also entailed
his own striving for perfection, which he saw as a heroic struggle against
overwhelming odds. He added: "If I persevere I must succeed in the end,
and my profession will be much dearer to me from the very pain it has
caused me." Returning to the United States in 1865, he chose the Northeast as the location for his practice, and never again visited New Orleans.
But the personal qualities which in other circumstances might have allowed Richardson to remain "southern" in fact, as well as in sentiment,
did not disappear. Willfully defying the industrial spirit of his age, he
waged a lifelong protest against the mechanizing tendencies that had
cheapened the practice of architecture.

Equally "southern," notwithstanding his preference for medieval
over classical architecture, was Richardson's use of style to evoke roman-

tic associations. As a youth in Louisiana, he would have been familiar with the picturesque formality of Oak Alley and the heroic Greek Revival temple that housed the University of Louisiana. In the 1850s New Orleans architecture shifted to an eclecticism including Gothic Revival, Italianate, and Early Victorian. During his years in Boston and Paris, these styles had become more erudite, sophisticated, and international. Buildings were conceived of as conveying knowledge and emotion rather than logic—a principle that Richardson accepted, although he insisted on greater architectural integrity through honest use of materials, masterly craftsmanship, and concern with function.

Richardson's national reputation eventually became so great that "Richardsonian Romanesque" dominated the period after the building of his Trinity Church (1872–1877) in Boston. During the next decade he did less borrowing from historical sources. Among his commissions was a series of libraries, designed as powerfully articulated blocks in which the distinct interior areas were functionally efficient and visually clear, and in which he usually blended quarry-faced granite with darker sandstone. Nowhere, however, was the polychromy decorative; rather, it distinguished the parts and integrated them into a monumental and utilitarian whole.

Late in his career Richardson was asked by Charles T. Howard to design a public library in New Orleans, on a site just one block west of the Julia Street row house in which he had grown up. Howard and Richardson both died before the library could be built, but a newspaper fully describes their original intent:

> The conception of a public library suggested itself to [Charles T. Howard] as the best form in which he could embody this noble purpose [of] a donation to New Orleans of a character which would prove of general and enduring advantages to its people.... His sudden demise checked the execution of plans which had nearly been perfected, but Miss Annie T. Howard, aware of the wishes of her father, and believing that a public library would constitute the fittest monument to his memory, has been for some time past engaged in measures looking to the consummation of that design.... The edifice will be erected according to plans by the late Henry Hobson Richardson, of Boston, a native of New Orleans.... The design, which was not prepared in connection with this particular library, ... is characterized by the chaste beauty and the bold individuality which marked the conceptions of the great architect.[5]

The plans of the Howard Library were apparently derived from the Hoyt Library project (1886) for Saginaw, Michigan, and revised by Richardson's successors, Shepley, Rutan & Coolidge, for the New Orleans site.

The building, opened in 1889, is typical of Richardson's libraries in the bold color of its quarry-faced sandstone and its medievally derived corner turrets. But it is also "southern" in its rootedness, its memorial purpose, and its eleemosynary program. One newspaper praised it as exceeding "all institutions of a similar character in the South and [comparing] favorably with the most notable institutions of the North," and a library magazine noted that "especial attention will be paid to gathering books printed in the South, works of the Rebellion, southern newspapers, books by southern authors, and agricultural works treating of special southern products."[6] The building itself signified a return to high-style architecture in New Orleans after the difficulties of the Civil War and Reconstruction. One writer saw it also as a "memorial to Richardson," who ended his career as he had begun it, as a southerner.

Richardson's commissions throughout his career were for church, government, and university buildings. To each one he steadfastly gave a strong sense of place that may be traced to his own southern background. He was conservative to such a degree that one historian has described him as "the last traditional architect; a reformer and not an initiator."[7] His southern origins seem invariably to have led him to reinforce the authority of established institutions during a time of dramatic change.

BILTMORE,
ASHEVILLE, NORTH CAROLINA
(1889–1895)

The devastation of southern agriculture by military action during the Civil War, together with the emancipation of slaves, which made the plantation system unprofitable, led to the subdivision of plantations and subsistence farming by freed blacks, yeoman farmers, and even many former planters. Despite this radical upheaval, the manorial ideal of the plantation continued to be romanticized as a model for aristocratic living.

George Washington Vanderbilt, who came to Asheville, North Carolina, in the 1880s, gradually developed Biltmore as an estate analogous to a plantation. He apparently began with no predetermined use for his property. He had originally intended to build a large frame house, but after a trip to France with his architect, Richard Morris Hunt, he decided instead to erect a French Renaissance palace, based on the Loire Valley châteaux at Blois, Chambord, and Chenonceaux. The European sophistication of Hunt's architecture conformed to American taste after the Civil War. Having survived that conflict, the United States had acquired the status of a politically mature and powerful nation, and among American capitalists such as the Vanderbilts, there grew up a desire for worldliness and an embarrassment over the purely indigenous. The construction of a sumptuous château in poverty-stricken western North Carolina suggested this uneasiness in its dualism between European erudition and the

Richard Morris Hunt and Frederick Law Olmsted. Biltmore, Asheville,
North Carolina: 1889–1895. Biltmore was an erudite amalgamation of Old
World architectural sophistication and American picturesque landscaping,
amid an Appalachian wilderness of rugged beauty. (Sandak, Inc.)

natural landscape: the eastward-facing main front overlooks a formal
court characteristic of the Old World aristocracy, with a simpler and
more organic elevation facing westward onto a view of the Great Smoky
Mountains.

The interiors are decorated in baronial splendor, housing Vanderbilt's extensive collection of sculpture, paintings, prints, and tapestries, as
well as a library of 150,000 books. Such lavish taste allowed him to be as
comfortable at Biltmore as he was in his Fifth Avenue mansion in New
York. The circumstances are not entirely unlike those of William Byrd of
Westover, who found life in London more compatible to his personality
than that of a colonial planter, and who developed a library, an art collection, and an aristocratic manner in the rural South to compensate for its
cultural deprivations. Biltmore also was "southern" in its extravagant
high style, which transcended economic considerations. Vanderbilt had
inherited $10,000,000, but when he died in 1914 his assets totaled only
about $1,000,000; he had invested his fortune in his estate rather than in
the corporate enterprises that had produced his family's wealth.

By the time Vanderbilt had accumulated 125,000 acres, however, he
was able to make a cash crop of scientifically managed forestry. In this
endeavor he had relied heavily on the advice of Frederick Law Olmsted,
who suggested in 1891 a coherent plan based on English eighteenth- and
nineteenth-century manors:

Such land in Europe would be made a forest; partly, if it belonged to a gentleman of large means, as a hunting preserve for game, mainly with a view to crops of timber. That would be a suitable and dignified business for you to engage in; it would in the long run be of great value to the country to have a thoroughly well organized and systematically conducted attempt in forestry made on a large scale. My advice would be to make a small park into which to look from your house; make a small pleasure ground and garden, farm your river bottom chiefly to keep and fatten live stock with a view to manure; and make the rest a forest, improving the existing woods and planting the old fields.[8]

Olmsted also designed the landscaping of the grounds, including an approach road that winds picturesquely through gentle ravines shaded by a thick growth of trees, ascending after nearly three miles to the plateau that is the site of the house, and opening onto extensive views of the mountains. The gardens surrounding the house, with their formal landscaping, are a studied antithesis to the nearby wilderness, offering a sense of place as impressive as that of any antebellum plantation.

The combination of an affluent and impressionable client, a French-trained architect, and an American landscape gardener produced the equivalent of a European barony; even the idea of forest management was European. But thanks to Olmsted's own feeling for southern plantations, the character of Biltmore was also rooted in the topography of western North Carolina. The approach road may be seen as a late-nineteenth-century counterpart of the live-oak avenues Olmsted had described in the 1850s. Biltmore also proved to have a "southern" longevity; it is currently owned by two grandsons of George Washington Vanderbilt, who still carry on a forestry and dairy business. That certain contradictions were implicit, however—the same anomaly, in fact, as had existed between the main house and slave cabins of an antebellum plantation—is evident from the succinct comment of Vanderbilt's forester, Gifford Pinchot:

Biltmore House . . . was a magnificent château of Indiana limestone. Its setting was superb, the view from it breathtaking, and as a feudal castle it would have been beyond criticism, and perhaps beyond praise. But in the United States of the nineteenth century and among the one-room cabins of the Appalachian mountaineers, it did not belong. The contrast was a devastating commentary on the injustice of concentrated wealth.[9]

THE UNIVERSITY OF THE SOUTH, SEWANEE, TENNESSEE

Southern colleges fared no better than the plantations during the Civil War and its aftermath. Many closed at the outbreak of hostilities, and many endowments were either diverted to financing the war or devalued with the economic collapse of the South. The dramatic shift in the fortunes of antebellum idealism is suggested by the early history of the University of the South.[10] Founded at Sewanee, Tennessee, in the late 1850s by Episcopalians, it had an emphatically sectional orientation and an ambitious plan for Gothic Revival buildings, which was totally interrupted by the war. The site was abandoned, the endowment vanished, and the meager temporary structures were burned. The university's guiding spirit, Bishop Leonidas Polk of Louisiana, had been educated at West Point before attending the Virginia Theological Seminary; he became a Confederate general and died in battle in 1864. When a grammar school opened on the old site in 1868, it was housed in rustic log houses. Before a college curriculum was finally installed and Gothic Revival stone buildings erected, the University of the South reverted almost to a frontier existence, such as recalls the humble origins of Washington and Lee University a century earlier.

TUSKEGEE INSTITUTE TUSKEGEE, ALABAMA

Whereas the University of the South stressed continuity with the aristocratic past, a radical transformation was the intent of the Tuskegee Institute in Alabama. Established to uplift black people, the school in many ways, nevertheless, perpetuated the history of the agrarian South. Its charismatic founder and principal, Booker T. Washington, had been born a slave; having acquired an education, he made an awesome commitment to share his achievements through a comprehensive program such as Jefferson probably would have supported. His campus became hallowed ground because of its mission, and Tuskegee is as "southern" as the more traditional colleges—a plantation, in fact, to the extent that it became a self-sufficient agricultural community.

Washington's autobiographical writings reveal a philosophy favoring gradual advancement of southern blacks through familiar endeavors:

[The Negro's] home being permanently in the South, it is our duty to help him prepare himself to live there, an independent, educated citizen. . . . Our greatest danger is, that in the great leap from slavery to freedom we may overlook the fact that the masses of us are to live by the production of our hands, and fail to keep in mind that we shall prosper in proportion as we learn to dignify and glorify common labor, and put brains and skill into the common occupations of life; . . . No race can prosper till it learns that there is as much dignity in tilling a field as in writing a poem. . . . There is, then, a place and an increasing need for the Negro college as well as for the industrial institute, and the two classes of schools should and as a matter of fact do, cooperate in the common purpose of elevating the masses.[11]

Washington came to Tuskegee in 1881 to organize a normal school after an annual appropriation of $2,000 had been granted by the state legislature. Instruction began inauspiciously in a Methodist church and a nearby shanty. Washington then purchased a 100-acre farm, one mile from the town, which became the site of a permanent campus; by 1900 the school had acquired about 2,000 acres. That this land had once been part of several plantations and maintained by slave labor, or that the students would now be doing similar work, did not trouble Washington. It did, however, subject him to considerable criticism from other black leaders.

The building of Tuskegee followed no master plan, but made use of available materials and labor as the need arose and the money was forthcoming. Porter Hall, erected in 1882–1883, with classrooms on the first floor, assembly rooms on the second, and a dormitory on the third, was a wood-frame and clapboard structure. It had hardly any architectural distinction other than its mansard roof; but more important than style was the way it fit into Washington's educational program:

I was determined to have the students do not only the agricultural and domestic work, but to have them erect their own buildings. My plan was to have them, while performing this service, taught the latest and best methods of labor, so that the school would not only get the benefit of their efforts, but the students themselves would be taught to see not only utility in labor, but beauty and dignity.[12]

When the department of architectural drawing began to supervise the construction of further buildings, and the quality of the brick made at the institute improved, so did the architecture. Washington then began to think about an integral campus plan: in 1894 he visited Frederick Law Olmsted in Massachusetts and asked him "to help us lay out our grounds."[13]

The way the buildings were being designed and constructed proved persuasive to prospective donors such as Andrew Carnegie, to whom Washington wrote in 1900 concerning a proposed library:

Such a building as we need could be erected for about $20,000. All of the work for the building, such as brick-making, brick-masonry, carpentry, blacksmithing, etc., would be done by the students. The money which you would give would not only supply the building, but the erection of the building would give a large number of students an opportunity to learn the building trades, and the students would use the money paid to them to keep themselves in school. I do not believe that a similar amount of money often could be made to go so far in uplifting a whole race.[14]

The Carnegie Library was described by the institute as "a building of classic outline—a noble structure of artistic symmetry and beauty that must appeal to everyone who has any appreciation of architectural beauty."[15] Its antebellum classicism, derived from Jefferson, is as conservative and conventional as Washington's overall philosophy. Today the library stands at the head of a group of buildings which together constitute a mall reminiscent of the University of Virginia, with an ambience that is breathtakingly beautiful—a loose configuration of red brick buildings articulated by white columns or entablatures amid the shade of irregularly placed trees on gently sloping terrain. It differs, however, from the precise and erudite formality of Jefferson's university, in having grown organically to accommodate a primarily agrarian institution.

The chapel, an impressive building from the late 1890s, stood across

Carnegie Library, Tuskegee Institute, Tuskegee, Alabama: c. 1900. Conventionally southern classicism, similar to that inspired by Thomas Jefferson, expressed the conservative educational philosophy of Booker T. Washington.

R. R. Taylor. Chapel, Tuskegee Institute, Tuskegee, Alabama: late 1890s. The chapel's simplified Richardsonian Romanesque style gave the institute a sense of solid establishment. (Library of Congress.)

a ravine from the library. Destroyed by fire in 1957, it had been designed by R. R. Taylor, a member of the faculty who had been the first black graduate of the Massachusetts Institute of Technology. Built of brick in the style of simplified Richardsonian Romanesque, it had the plan of a Greek cross, with a vast interior seating 2,400 people. The pulpit area was an expanded platform capable of holding the entire faculty and choir, symbolically emphasizing the institute's commitment to education, religion, and music. Near the site is a simple graveyard where Washington was buried in 1915, and George Washington Carver, Tuskegee's greatest scientist, in 1943.

HOTEL PONCE DE LEÓN, ST. AUGUSTINE, FLORIDA (1885–1887)

Part of the New South phenomenon was the discovery of the region by northerners. Henry M. Flagler, a financier who formerly had been asso-

John Carrère and Thomas Hastings. Hotel Ponce de León, St. Augustine, Florida: 1885–1887. Victorian opulence exudes from the attempt to recapture the Spanish past, providing a capricious setting for aristocratic vacationers to discover Florida's future.

ciated with John D. Rockefeller, visited St. Augustine in 1883 and, captivated by the place, embarked on what would be for him a lifelong enterprise of developing Florida for vacationers.[16] To encourage travel there he built the Florida East Coast Railway, which brought the affluent, predominantly from the North, to a series of hotels which he also commissioned. The Ponce de León in St. Augustine, designed by New York architects John Carrère and Thomas Hastings and built between 1885 and 1887, is a high-style fantasy based loosely on a Spanish idiom of colonnaded loggias, terra-cotta ornament, and red roof tiles. The effect is an architectural *tour de force*, rich enough to satisfy even the most voracious of palates. Notwithstanding the aristocratic clientele, here was the beginning of the hedonistic attraction to Florida which has culminated in similar, but more populist, extravaganzas such as Disneyworld near Orlando.

Louis Sullivan
and Ocean Springs, Mississippi

When the Chicago architect Louis Sullivan traveled to the Mississippi Gulf Coast for a rest in 1890, he was enchanted by the tranquillity at Ocean Springs:

> With daylight there revealed itself an undulating village all in bloom in softest sunshine, the gentle sparkle of the waters of a bay land-locked by Deer Island; a village sleeping as it had slept for genera-tions with untroubled surface; a people soft-voiced, unconcerned, easy going, indolent; the general store, the post office, the barber shop, the meat market, on Main Street, sheltered by ancient live oaks; the saloon near the depot, the one-man jail in the midst of the street back of the depot; shell roads in the village, wagon trails lead-ing away into the hummock land; no "enterprise," no "progress," no booming for a "greater Ocean Springs," no factories, no anxious faces, no glare of the dollar hunter, no land agents, no hustlers, no drummers, no white-staked lonely subdivisions. Peace, peace, and the joy of comrades, the lovely nights of sea breeze, black pool of the sky oversprinkled with stars brilliant and uncountable.[17]

It was in this languorously picturesque environment undoubtedly characteristic of many small southern towns at the end of the century, that Sullivan chose to put down his own domestic roots. He had never really made a home for himself in Chicago, but had moved frequently from one apartment flat or hotel suite to another. He purchased land in a pine forest along Biloxi Bay; and before returning to Chicago he planned two bungalows with stables and hired a local carpenter to build them. Romantically situated amid a grove of trees, the cottages' organic plans, shingle siding, and sheltering roofs suggest that Sullivan had the assis-tance of his young draftsman, Frank Lloyd Wright—who indeed would later claim that the designs were his. There is a local tradition that Sulli-van also had some part in the building of St. John's Episcopal Church, a simple wood Gothic Revival structure dating to 1891–1892.

Following Sullivan's discovery of Ocean Springs, he went on to pro-duce one of his greatest designs, the Wainwright Building in St. Louis. Whereas the Chicago Auditorium, finished just before he traveled south, was still part of the conservative masonry tradition of Richardson, the Wainwright Building established the archetypal form for the twentieth-century skyscraper, and it is of such importance that modern architecture may be said to have arisen with it. For all the difference between the two buildings, the seed may have taken root at Ocean Springs. Sullivan ac-knowledged that he did his finest thinking at his vacation retreat, and al-though there is nothing specifically "southern" about the skyscraper,

Sullivan's organic theory of architecture, postulating that "all things in nature have a shape . . . that tells us what they are," and that by analogy a building's form must follow and reveal its function, may in some way have been inspired by his annual visits to the South.[18] A New York associate who visited Sullivan at Ocean Springs in 1905 described the natural ambience:

> Here there has been for some fifteen years or so a modest, comfortable cottage, reached only by the touch of the wind and the golden sun; and embowered among stately trees, growing shrubs, clinging vines, and in season, blooming roses cultivated with the greatest care and thought. Across the front of the building runs an ample and commodious "gallery" or piazza (for here one stays outdoors as much as possible). . . . How can we leave the place knowing in full measure how much it has done for our art; and go out again to where its influences have spread abroad, for from this little spot has emanated the results of reflection and communion with real things which has produced an invaluable contribution to our American architecture.[19]

This statement reveals the antithesis between city and country that had arisen in America—an antithesis concerning which Sullivan emphatically declared:

> For while the great cities are great *battle grounds*, they are not great *breeding grounds*. The great minds may go to the great cities but they are not . . . born and bred in the great cities. In the formation of a great mind . . . *solitude* is prerequisite; for such a mind is nurtured in *contemplation*, and strengthened in it.[20]

Even though the post–Civil War South was not a place where Sullivan's skyscrapers could be built, any more than Richardson's career could unfold there, the southern experience of both had in different ways a lasting influence on their work, and thus ultimately on the course of American architecture.

CHAPTER ELEVEN

FRANK LLOYD WRIGHT: THE ARCHITECTURE OF USONIA SOUTH

By the end of the nineteenth century, truly distinctive southern architecture was no longer being produced. Of those architects who worked in the South, most had received their professional training in the Northeast or Midwest, and were interpreters of the South rather than manifestations of it. Even vernacular builders had shed their indigenous character. A conflict was inevitable—between surviving Old South buildings and new "American" architecture, and between preservation and development.

The theoretical basis of the New South was a narrowing of economic differences between North and South, as large numbers of southern agricultural workers became industrial laborers. Real as the change was, many mills and factories had actually been in existence before the Civil War. Southern cities such as New Orleans and Charleston had begun to diversify their economies before 1860, and as a railroad center Atlanta was virtually indistinguishable from its counterparts in the North.

Traditional attitudes still prevailed—racial pride, a laissez-faire manner of living, and a tendency toward fixed values have been noted by one historian.[1] Still more important, for architecture in particular, was an intense veneration for historic culture. Plantation houses had been revered from the start as distinctive places, then romanticized as relics of a lost planter aristocracy. They continued to be lived in as ancestral homes long after any economic rationale for their maintenance remained. The retention of many architectural treasures was a quiet, sensitive, and almost introverted process in which individuals preserved isolated fragments of the southern heritage through respect for the past, and often because they were too poor to leave the family homes they inherited.

THE PRAIRIE HOUSES
OF FRANK LLOYD WRIGHT

Although the career of America's greatest architect, Frank Lloyd Wright, hardly exemplifies the southern sense of place, in his own way he too upheld traditional values. After his birth in 1867, his family moved restlessly from Wisconsin to Iowa, Massachusetts, and Rhode Island, and then back to Wisconsin.[2] The Wrights were not members of a social establishment, and their staunch puritanical beliefs dissociated them from an aristocratic culture. Wright's early political consciousness was formed in the Midwest, a section of the country with a strong bias against the South. Yet he was increasingly aware of an ideological bond with Thomas Jefferson, and in the end he in fact made a significant contribution to southern architecture. Wright apparently became ideologically conscious of the South only after he moved in 1911 from Chicago to Spring Green in rural Wisconsin, where he established his own sense of place along with a twentieth-century version of Jeffersonian agrarianism. Farming to produce his own food supply, quarrying for necessary building materials, and employing local labor, he achieved an economic self-sufficiency analogous to that of a southern plantation.

Monticello has been perceptively defined as a "struggle between the fixed European past and the mobile American future, between Palladio and Frank Lloyd Wright."[3] Derived from European architectural handbooks, but with unprecedented horizontal extensions into the landscape, Monticello crowns its site in a far more organic manner than any Palladian villa, and is fully one with its environment. When Wright built Taliesin, his home and architectural studio in Spring Green, he wrote of it in words that might be applied to Monticello: "No home should ever be *on* a hill or *on* anything. It should be *of* the hill. Belonging to it."[4]

Wright's progressivism, which had revolutionized domestic architecture in the first decade of the twentieth century, was thoroughly rooted in American experience. In the typical cross-axial plans of his prairie houses, the central chimney mass and the sheltering roofs express the security of the family, while the aggressive horizontals and fluid space reflect the freedom of the individual—polarities which to a considerable extent may also be seen in Monticello. Two conflicting American attitudes had been synthesized: on one hand the desire for rootedness, typical of the colonial settlements and frequently manifested in southern plantation houses; and on the other the urge for mobility, which was implicit in the westward expansion of settlements.

BROADACRE CITY
AND USONIAN HOUSES

The Crash of 1929 increased Wright's estrangement from the urban world. From then on, Taliesin became a citadel from which he could preach, design, and build a new America. The Depression signified to him that capitalism had failed. Once again a statement by Jefferson offers a parallel to Wright's new outlook:

> Those who labor in the earth are the chosen people of God, . . . whose breasts he has made his peculiar deposit for substantial and genuine virtue. . . . Corruption of morals in the mass of cultivators is a phenomenon of which no age nor nation has furnished as example. . . . The mobs of great cities add just so much to the support of pure government, as sores do to the strength of the human body.[5]

Louis Sullivan had expressed similar sentiments, but had continued to shuttle between architectural practice in Chicago and rural relaxation at Ocean Springs. Wright made Jeffersonianism the basis of his entire life.

As his solution for the problems of America, Wright proposed that every individual should be given one acre of land. The population was to be dispersed over the entire country, with families living on small farms of one to ten acres, where they would grow their own food and work part time in nearby small factories. Modern technology was to have one significant role: in the advanced transportation systems, consisting of high-speed trains and superhighways, that were made necessary by decentralization. At the local level automobiles would provide access to all basic needs, nowhere more than forty minutes from any individual's home. The utopian Broadacre City, designed to carry out this plan, was never realized, and following World War II the nation's long-standing antithesis between city and country became even more extreme.

The archetypal residence for Broadacre City was the Usonian house (Wright substituted his own designation "Usonia" for the "United States of America"). Whereas only one of his prairie houses was actually erected in the South—the Ziegler House (1909–1910) in Frankfort, Kentucky—two of the finest Usonian houses are in the South: the Pope-Leighey House (1939–1941) built at Falls Church, Virginia (now at Woodlawn Plantation), and the Rosenbaum House (1939–1940) in Florence, Alabama. In describing the house he had in mind, Loren Pope, a Washington journalist, wrote to Wright:

> There are certain things a man wants during life, and, of life. Material things and things of the spirit. The writer has one fervent wish that includes both. It is for a house created by you. Created is the proper word. Many another architect might be able to plan or design

a house. But only you can create one that will become for us a home. . . . A home, besides being a thing of beauty and a place for living, is to me, a spiritual concept, and a thing of the spirit isn't created by a plan and labor and materials of themselves. There must also go into it the creed and soul of the creator, if it is to be a home.[6]

Wright's response to this lyrical prose was straightforward and laconic: "Of course I am ready to give you a house." Construction began in the spring of 1940 with a Taliesin apprentice supervising the work—the usual practice with the building of a Usonian house. Delighted with its beauty, function, and economy, the Popes moved into the house in 1941.

The manner of living which the Popes sought and for which Wright designed the house can be read from the plan. The entrance under the

Frank Lloyd Wright. Pope-Leighey House, originally in Falls Church and now at Woodlawn Plantation, Fairfax County, Virginia: 1939–1941. Even at its new site, the house presents a humble yet assertive profile, and its organic brick and cypress convey an image of family integrity and domestic warmth. (National Trust for Historic Preservation, photo: Jack Boucher.)

Pope-Leighey House, interior. By combining the living and dining room in one integral space, Wright sought to bring the family together and to achieve a prototypical house for Depression-ridden America. (National Trust for Historic Preservation, photo: Jack Boucher.)

carport provides access to three discrete areas—Pope's study (later converted into a bedroom), a private wing with two bedrooms, and on axis the living quarters. Brick walls enclose the utilities and kitchen (which Wright preferred to call the work space); sandwich partitions of wood, liberally perforated with windows, surround the dining and living areas. There is no wasted space, either in room sizes or ceiling heights, which Wright masterfully varied to take the greatest possible advantage of the cubic footage and to preserve a domestic scale. The living room's greater height than the more functional or private areas was achieved naturally by siting the house on sloping terrain, with the floor five steps lower than the entry. The dining area is part of the living room but is distinguished from it by a lower ceiling, which gives a more enclosed and intimate setting for family meals. In placing the fireplace at the juncture of the living and dining areas, Wright manifested his strong conviction about the integrity of the family.

The technological features of the Usonian houses are analogous to Jefferson's quasi-scientific gadgets at Monticello. Concrete floor slabs were poured directly on the ground over hot water heating pipes in a rock ballast bed. Furniture was largely built in, with ornamental trim eliminated, and the wood exposed to reveal its natural beauty. The early Usonian houses were designed on a unit system (usually a two-by-four-foot grid), which standardized planning and construction without sacrificing the client's particular needs or compromising the nature of the site. The result was a house with individualized character, but also one with economies made possible by modular production—economies that are no longer possible, however, since the Usonian house was conceived before materials such as cypress and reliance on labor-intensive construction were ruled out by rising costs. After the end of World War II, the dream of building houses for Broadacre America vanished.

Wright had advised his Usonian clients to "go way out into the country—what you regard as 'too far'—and when others follow, as they will, move on." He foresaw the proliferation of residential subdivisions and commercial strip developments around metropolitan centers. Pope himself was restless; in 1946 he sold the house to the Robert Leigheys, and in the early 1960s it was nearly demolished for an interstate highway. In 1964–1965, after prolonged delay and much prodding, the National Trust for Historic Preservation moved the house from Falls Church to Woodlawn Plantation. The floor slab and the brick walls had to be reconstructed, but the cypress walls were retained. As a pioneer venture in the preservation of recent architecture, the house continues to be the home of Marjorie Leighey, who wrote of it:

> That [the house] could have feelings, as well as a feeling, arises from its real union of the outdoors with the inside, from the glorious, ever-changing play of patterned sunlight upon the walls and from three paradoxes intrinsic to its structure. Small, yet large because there is no point in the house where one feels spatially bound. Complex with a careful development of patterned and plain areas held together by imaginative and attentive design, yet simple in its forthright presentation of minimal living space. Proud almost to the point of arrogance in boldly declaring itself for what it is and standing thereon, yet humble in never pretending to be other than it is.[7]

The Stanley Rosenbaums of Florence, Alabama, also commissioned Wright to build them a house in 1939.[8] Wright gave it the name "Rhododendron" (a play on the family's name), in the manner of a southern plantation. The L-shaped plan is similar to that of the Pope-Leighey House, but the floor area was increased by almost one-third to accommodate a larger family. In 1948, when even that was no longer sufficient, Wright designed and built a major addition. Houses of historical or architectural distinction, particularly in the South, had often assumed sacrosanct status, precluding changes in structure, ornamentation, and furnishings. Wright, however, considered enlargement and modification part of the program: "A Usonian house, if built for a young couple, can, without deformity, be expanded, later, for the needs of a growing family." Just as Monticello and the Hermitage had both undergone significant revisions throughout the domestic lives of their owners, the principles of the Usonian house were rooted in experience both present and past.

AULDBRASS,
YEMASSEE, SOUTH CAROLINA
(1939–1950)

While he was still at work on the Usonian houses, Wright received a commission to design an entire plantation—Auldbrass, near Yemassee, South Carolina, the spelling of whose original name "Old Brass" Wright changed when he began work. In the eighteenth century the land had been developed as three rice plantations, and during the American Revolution part of this tract was owned by Arthur Middleton of Middleton Place. The Middleton family continued to grow rice there until after the Civil War. The present property, totaling about 4,000 acres, includes the site of what were once Yemassee Indian settlements, as well as a colonial fort; it was traversed by military routes used by the British during the Revolutionary War and by Sherman during the Civil War. More recently, the land had been owned by timber companies. It was acquired during the 1930s by C. Leigh Stevens, an energetic and versatile management consultant, who envisioned a modern plantation where he could farm, hunt, and entertain, and he called on Wright to transform his ideas into architecture.[9] A Charleston newspaperman with a conservative bias reported:

> The story is that Mr. Stevens, with a considerable amount of money, suddenly got the idea that he wanted a plantation in the South, but didn't want anything which even remotely resembled anything anybody else might have in any section of the country. He got the idea across to Frank Lloyd Wright, nationally known architect, who started to work.[10]

Although Auldbrass resembles a traditional plantation in its organic wholeness, its architecture is radically modern. Included in the early construction were two workers' cabins, hexagonal in plan, and an ingeniously complicated farm building of interconnected stables, kennels, and caretaker's quarters. This low structure is essentially a sheltering roof, retaining an informality by changing direction irregularly in response to the terrain, and so as to avoid the live oaks which tower over it. The same writer itemized its idiosyncrasies:

> The finished product, to cost about $200,000, will include beside the main house, two tenant houses, and a stable 200 yards long, and

without a sign of a right angle. The roofs of the buildings swoop down to the ground on one side, then point up to the sky on the other side. Each building is constructed entirely of the finest cypress and cedar, without a single nail. Each section of wood is attached to the next by screws. More startling still . . . is the fact that none of the buildings have any windows. The lighting will come through glass doors, which also are set at a madcap angle. The walls slant inward, and the doors slant with the walls, and are not rectangular but are parallelograms. . . . The livestock may become psychopathic cases before they manage to accustom themselves to their slanted and new-fangled fixtures.

While construction was under way, Stevens had in fact sponsored a contest among agricultural students at Clemson University and the University of Georgia for detailed plans of "a family-sized farm on sound management principles from the viewpoint of continuous profit."[11] One "Hypothetical Farm Plan," addressed condescendingly to "A. Newcomer," has survived; it recommended cotton and potatoes as the major cash crops, and the growing of corn, wheat, oats, and clover to feed cows, pigs, and chickens for market, as well as for family consumption. All of this reveals a Depression-influenced program aimed at self-sufficiency. Thus Auldbrass could hardly be a plantation in the antebellum sense, since the region's historic rice culture was to be replaced by a diversified agriculture. Stevens's concept coincided with Wright's work in the 1930s—the establishment of Taliesin as his home, office, and architectural school and the formulation of Broadacre City as a utopian reaction to the Depression. In Stevens, Wright found a client whose business background had led him independently to similar conclusions, at least concerning the development of his property.

In 1941, after the farm buildings were finished and the foundations had been laid for the main house, Wright summarized his thoughts on the regions of the United States.[12] He divided the country into three quasi-independent federations: New England (the urban and industrial Northeast including New York, New Jersey, Pennsylvania, Delaware, and Maryland), Usonia South (the traditional southern states plus Texas), and Usonia (the rest of the country). Wright conceived of Usonia South as different from Usonia largely because of its historic striving for a distinct identity. In thus reviving the idea of the Old Confederacy, he also contributed to the romanticization of the South, and carried on his campaign for a return to Jeffersonian agrarianism:

Thomas Jefferson prophesied the democratic aristoi. We his people must now not only meet the radical changes in our philosophy and social systems but face no less these changes in the basis of our culture. If integrity of spirit inheres in man, its natural countenance will be found in his architecture: the countenance of principle. Be-

Frank Lloyd Wright. Auldbrass, Yemassee, South Carolina: 1939–1950. Amid a cluster of live oaks, a "southern" picturesqueness is created by an informal design of natural materials, avoiding right angles, both in plan and in the walls. (S. D. Loring.)

Auldbrass, interior. The hexagonal plan directs all activity toward the central fireplace, a hallmark throughout Wright's career. (S. D. Loring.)

cause architecture presents man as he is, he will live anew in the free spirit of organic architecture of our own time.[13]

The house at Auldbrass (completed about 1950) exemplifies Wright's organic architecture in its sensitive synthesis between the natural setting and twentieth-century technology. It rests on a concrete slab, allowing the floors to continue the level of the surrounding land. The one-story height and the horizontality of the sheltering roof extend the structure into the landscape, and most of the hallmarks of traditional plantation houses are missing—formality, monumentality, and high style. In their place is a thoroughly casual, rooted, and indigenous structure that hugs the earth. Walls are not impenetrable barriers but thin screens, two cypress boards thick. To heighten the informality further, the boards are battered and slanted at an eighty-degree angle that reflects the tilt of nearby live oaks. Also individualizing the place are its symbolic overtones: specifications for *brass* screws and hardware, ornamental downspouts whose design suggests a pendulous clump of Spanish moss, and a clerestory of perforated boards with patterns of Indian arrows or feathers.

The fluid interior spaces generated by the hexagonal plan come to a masterful climax in the living room, whose materials are all organic—the natural wood, the floor slab dyed an earthy red, and the brick fireplace which gives focus to the room. Much of the furniture was designed by Wright, and the overall effect is simultaneously grand and comfortable. Large enough to accommodate a crowd yet scaled so that an individual is not overwhelmed, open to the outside through glass doors yet emphatically sheltered by the roof, the room is a sublime creation.

Auldbrass is not, in either its theory or its architecture, merely a nostalgic re-creation of an antebellum environment, but its functional similarities with the traditional southern plantation are undeniable. The farm was worked by laborers who lived in the outlying cabins, and the planning of the main house, with a kitchen separated from the living areas, required many servants. Another part of the complex (never built) was to be a twelve-room guest house. Other unrealized projects included a canal from the house to the river and the conversion of the swamp behind the house into a lake—both reminiscent of the legacy of rice cultivation and even of the water gardens at Middleton Place. And like a number of traditional plantations, the property soon acquired a historic aura. In 1976, after only a quarter of a century, it was placed on the National Register of Historic Places—the first twentieth-century building in South Carolina to be so designated.

Frank Lloyd Wright. Florida Southern College, Lakeland, Florida:
1938–1959. Wright's "democratic" architecture is seen in the individual
shapes of buildings, the non-right-angular intersections of the covered
walkways, and the unconventional design of the campus as a whole. (Florida
Southern College.)

FLORIDA SOUTHERN COLLEGE,
LAKELAND, FLORIDA
(1938–1959)

The new campus of Florida Southern College in Lakeland, begun late in
the 1930s, with seven major buildings comprises the largest collection of
Wright's buildings on one site. There is no evidence that he was familiar
with the architecture of Tuskegee Institute, but he would have respected
the work ethic of that institution, its agrarian orientation, and the construction of buildings with student labor and local materials—all features
which he incorporated into the Florida campus, creating another "southern" place, simultaneously traditional and innovative.

Founded by the Methodist Church in 1885, the college consisted of
five undistinguished Neo-Georgian buildings at the time its president,
Dr. Ludd M. Spivey, inspired with an idea for a new campus, flew to
Wisconsin to meet with Wright, whom he knew only by reputation as
the country's foremost architect. Notwithstanding a sardonic view of
higher education—"Were I . . . rich, I would buy up our leading universities—close them and hang out the sign—closed by the beneficence of
one, Frank Lloyd Wright"[14]—Wright was intrigued by Spivey's project

Florida Southern College, Annie Pfeiffer Chapel: 1938–1941. Through architectural elements, rather than familiar references to traditional churches, Wright shaped a religious space to uplift the spirit and emancipate it from bondage to the past. (Florida Southern College.)

of building an entire campus. He traveled to Florida to inspect the site—a hillside orange grove sloping down to a clear blue lake—and exclaimed: "Every building is out of the ground into the light—a child of the sun. Buildings should seem to grow from the earth and belong as a tree belongs."[15]

Together, Spivey and Wright conceived a master plan of eighteen buildings without the usual contract between architect and client (in the end most of the architectural fees were not paid until after both men were dead). The buildings were to be of concrete or concrete block to blend with the sandy soil, the blocks to be held in place by steel rods along their grooved edges, into which concrete was to be poured to stabilize the wall. The advantages were obvious: the blocks could be cast on the site, thereby eliminating much of the expense of skilled labor by drawing on student labor and locally made materials. A plan was devised for allowing students to divide the week into three days of construction work and three of academic study.

The first building to be erected was the chapel, the only building in the complex that is predominantly vertical. The hexagonal plan fused the congregation within the interior, and an open lantern rising from the center lifted the vista upward. Wright intended to have the balconies and lantern adorned with planters and trailing vines to create the image of a building planted in the ground and growing like a tree. For the library Wright designed a low circular space which was also skylighted, not for symbolic reasons but to admit natural light into the reading room. With his intense concern for making the building "a child of the sun" he made no provision for evening study. The circular plan recalls the Rotunda of the University of Virginia; and both reading rooms mold individual students into the spirit of collegiate education.

Wright connected the buildings with covered walkways that gave shelter from the rain and sun. These colonnades follow the paths that students inevitably would have made across the grounds from building to building. The colonnades and arcades of Jefferson's university were primarily formal; they joined the ranges along parallel axes, but did not reflect everyday pedestrian patterns. Wright's informal diagonals integrate the campus into an organic whole consisting of differentiated but interconnected units. And the varied building shapes—hexagonal, circular, and rectangular—express his idea of a democracy based on strong-willed individualism.

Although dramatically modern, Florida Southern College is analogous in its architecture and planning to historic southern institutions. The recurrence of certain themes is a result more of coincidence than of direct influence, but the conviction that a physical environment can affect the quality of education is constant throughout. During his visits to the college, Wright more than once spoke of this:

> [Dr. Spivey] has placed you in a position so that you can find out about [architecture]. . . . Here at Florida Southern College you will be educated in an atmosphere of truth. And if you can only see it you have a better chance of growing into something fine spiritually as you are being educated in a good atmosphere.
>
> I am sure that every student here has within him—or her—the stem of a truly American culture. Florida Southern College will be praised in history as notable because it has taken the first step . . . shown the way . . . to a culture of our own.[16]

CHAPTER TWELVE

MODERN ARCHITECTURE IN THE SOUTH: NEW BUILDINGS AND PRESERVED PLACES

The impact on the South, after World War II, of aggressively promoted modernism has been vividly described by C. Vann Woodward:

> The symbol of innovation is inescapable. The roar and groan and dust of it greet one on the outskirts of every southern city. That symbol is the bulldozer, and for lack of a better name this might be called the Bulldozer Revolution. The great machine with the lowered blade symbolizes the revolution in several respects: in its favorite area of operation, the area where city meets country; in its relentless speed; in its supreme disregard for obstacles, its heedless methods; in what it demolishes and in what it builds. It is the advance agent of the metropolis. It encroaches upon rural life to expand urban life. It demolishes the old to make way for the new.[1]

Architects are increasingly confronted by having to decide whether to preserve a historic place or join in the Bulldozer Revolution. The occasional sensitive accommodations between the two that have occurred deserve special recognition as the significant "southern" architecture of the present.

THE SOUTHERN ARCHITECTURE OF PAUL RUDOLPH

One such building is the Tuskegee Institute Chapel, designed by Paul Rudolph after a fire in 1957 destroyed its austere predecessor. Born in Kentucky, Rudolph began his training in architecture at Alabama Polytechnic Institute, but after studying at the Harvard Graduate School of Design he established his office in New York. In giving the commission to Rudolph, the board of advisers at Tuskegee abandoned their previous provincial attitude toward architecture. They were not prepared, however, for the asymmetrical sculptural design offered them by Rudolph in 1960. Intensely personal, "strong to the point, almost, of brutality—of rough concrete rather than brick," it related to Le Corbusier's spectacular church at Ronchamp in eastern France, and had little to link it with the humble institutional setting of Tuskegee.[2] After major revisions in the design, the chapel was completed in 1969.

Two black architects, Louis Edwin Fry and John A. Welch, both former heads of the institute's Department of Architecture, had supervised the construction. In place of the concrete, the structure was given a less expensive steel frame and encased in brick, the material used in the older buildings on the campus. The aggressive exterior features—covered walkways, terraces, and stairs—were largely eliminated, allowing the building to rest more comfortably on its site. Its dominant feature is the entrance, consisting of screen walls that form a partially enclosed loggia, with an exterior pulpit, preparing worshipers as they enter for what awaits them inside. The asymmetrical design of the interior, which was not drastically changed, is simply but powerfully integrated into one of the most moving religious spaces to be found in any modern church. It is similar to the earlier chapel in that a deep space for the choir is located behind the pulpit, allowing the new building also to function as a concert hall. The irregular brick surfaces of the walls serve an acoustical purpose, and skylights along their upper edges flood the interior with light. As a dramatic expression of the spiritual force underlying the history of the institution and the civil rights movement since World War II, the Tuskegee Chapel is a sublimely modern building, rooted in the culture which produced it.

Rudolph's extensive architectural practice in the South included a series of houses that established him as one of the first modernist champions of regionalism. The recognition that spatial fluidity was germane to a subtropical climate governed his plan for the John Wallace House (1961–1964) in Athens, Alabama. The exterior is articulated by brick columns, painted white, which at once define the various functional areas and constitute a modern version of the colonnaded plantation house, as Rudolph freely acknowledged: "My first impressions of architecture were of Greek Revival Architecture of the south. This attempted restatement has overlays of early twentieth-century European architecture and can be read on many different levels."[3]

For Burroughs Wellcome (1969–1972) in Research Triangle, North Carolina, Rudolph designed a building organically related to its natural environment:

This complex climbs up and down a beautiful ridge in the green hills of North Carolina and is architecturally an extension of its site.

An "A frame" allows the greatest volume to be housed on the lower floors and yet connected to the smaller mechanical system at the apex of the building. The diagonal movement and interior space open up magnificent opportunities. Anticipation of growth and change is implicit in the concept.[4]

Rudolph's description of the building as "not unlike a growing tree . . . a living organism rather than a box-like form," indicates his indebtedness to Frank Lloyd Wright. But whereas the latter always sought a harmonious rapport between building and site, Rudolph's forms are dynamically sculptural. His tendency to be willfully personal, in strong contrast to the ubiquitous steel and glass architecture in the style of Mies van der Rohe, may stem in some degree from his southern background—and is at any rate fully expressed in his southern buildings.

Paul Rudolph. Tuskegee Institute Chapel, Tuskegee, Alabama: 1960–1969. In contrast to the gentle quality of the rest of the campus, the chapel's dynamic forms signal a change from the conservative philosophy of Booker T. Washington to the more aggressive post–World War II civil rights movement. (Tuskegee Institute, photo: Walter Scott.)

Paul Rudolph. Burroughs Wellcome Company, Research Triangle, North Carolina: 1969–1972. Through its strong personal statement, the building attains the sense of place typical of southern architecture.

The Historicism of Edward Durell Stone

Edward Durell Stone, another architect born in the South and trained in the Northeast, began his career under the influence of the International Style of the 1930s. At Mepkin, a historic plantation in the South Carolina Low Country, he designed for the Henry R. Luces a crisply geometrical complex of buildings. Underlying its rational functionalism, however, was an almost mystical affinity with the site, which Stone described as a grove of "giant oak trees . . . dating back to the Norman Conquest. Hung with Spanish moss, these groves of great trees are unmatched in their eerie tranquil beauty."[5] Notwithstanding the Luces' insistence on modern design, Stone wrote of linking the buildings "to form a walled garden typical of the Charleston area, a bow to ante-bellum tradition. The fourth wall enclosing the garden was serpentine and perforated, a variation of Jefferson's solid wall."

As Stone's romantic and historicist attitudes grew more pronounced, he deplored the conformity that gave more and more modern buildings an overly functional and mechanical character. Arguing that emotion still had its place in architecture, he strove in his work for "a formality and dignity that one associates with historic monuments," maintaining that "the inspiration for a building should be in the accumulation of history."[6] Stone also defied those modernists who had banned ornament from architecture: "I believe too that people now yearn for fine materials and a quality of richness."

Stone's approach at its most effective can be seen in the Legislature

Building for North Carolina in Raleigh. The Greek Revival statehouse (1833–1840) designed by Ithiel Town and Alexander Jackson Davis had become too small for all the branches of state government. In 1959 plans were formulated to erect a separate building for the legislature—a significant decision in itself, since it meant that a historic building of architectural distinction was to be preserved. Stone's design was for a truly modern building, not the imitation of an earlier structure that is so often the outcome of such a project, particularly in the rebuilding of governors' mansions. Rejecting the purism of functional architecture, however, he surrounded the building with what amounted to a monumental colonnade, covering the square supports of reinforced concrete with gleaming white marble, and articulating the top with pedimented shapes and pyramidal roofs. Rather than an expression of structure, one of the pervasive dogmas of modern architecture, through a concentration on dazzling spatial and superficial effects Stone gave a contemporary building the classical formality of a plantation house. When the Legislature Building opened in 1963, it was described as "a restatement of [Stone's] present goals: permanence, refinement of materials, spatial drama, and, in plan, the elimination of corridors by the use of great interior courts."[7]

Even more specifically evocative of historic architecture, though less admirable, is what began in 1958 as the National Cultural Center and in 1963 was renamed the John Fitzgerald Kennedy Cultural Center—a building which in Stone's words "should represent twenty-five hundred years of Western culture rather than twenty-five years of modern architecture."[8] Three functionally different auditoriums—for opera, concerts, and theater—are enclosed in a templelike structure, thus adding another

Edward Durell Stone. Legislature Building, Raleigh, North Carolina: 1959–1963. Through ornament and historical allusions, the building manifests continuity with the past.

Edward Durell Stone. John Fitzgerald Kennedy Cultural Center, Washington, D.C.: 1965–1971. By emulating in modern guise the Neoclassical ideals of L'Enfant and Jefferson, the building raises the question of how an architect should venerate a historic environment.

Neoclassical building to the federal capital of Washington, Jefferson, L'Enfant, and Mills. Kennedy Center has been described by a critic as "enclosed with bland marble with two Babylonian entrance openings and adorned by the ephemeral columns supporting the flat lid, . . . without this gift wrapping . . . nothing but a colossal white box."[9] Another critic has written of the exterior and the grandiose foyer with its gaudy decoration and enormous chandeliers, "This is architectural populism. [Stone] has produced a conventional crowd pleaser. It is a genuine people's palace."[10] While intentionally rejecting the idiom of modern architecture, Stone may be accused of failing to live up to the lofty cultural aspirations which the building was intended to express. The classical mode becomes, in the circumstances, a meaningless gesture, lacking in the heroic overtones of traditional southern architecture.

THE GLASS BOXES OF ODELL ASSOCIATES

Of recent buildings in the South, many of the finest are only minimally related to historic styles or materials. The work of Odell Associates, with headquarters in Charlotte, North Carolina, in the contemporary mode of steel and glass, with affinities to the architecture of Skidmore, Owings, and Merrill, has progressed beyond the pure structuralism of Mies van der Rohe. For the corporate headquarters of Burlington Industries in Greensboro (finished in 1971), Odell designed a six-story tower and a lower office facility surrounding it on three sides. The exposed steel structure and reflective glass walls respond to the client's desire to project a national rather than a regional image.[11]

Odell's North Carolina Blue Cross and Blue Shield Headquarters outside Chapel Hill is a radically transformed steel and glass box, with the structure enclosed so as to allow the exterior surface to become a virtually unbroken plane of reflective glass.[12] Instead of a rectangular prism, the building is a three-dimensional rhomboid, dramatically juxtaposed to the nearby highways. The slope of the walls tends to conserve energy by reducing the amount of summer heat absorbed from the sun, while the angle of the glass surface allows solar radiation to enter in winter, when the sun is low in the sky.

For the world headquarters of R. J. Reynolds Industries (1976–1977) in Winston-Salem—a company concerned with another long-standing southern staple crop—Odell Associates have continued their experimentation with the glass box. Joining the corners of eight cubical units has produced a dynamically expressive exterior for a building whose plan in fact is essentially a simple rectangle with large open interior spaces. Again the building is sheathed in reflective glass to reduce solar heat gain and to lighten the visual impression of an enormous building—one whose imaginative design transcends the ordinariness of the tobacco warehouses and factories near the site. By exploiting the po-

Odell Associates. North Carolina Blue Cross and Blue Shield, Chapel Hill, North Carolina: 1971–1974. The unusual shape was in part determined by energy conservation (a consideration related to earlier vernacular buildings in the South), and the walls of glass reflect images of the surrounding landscape.

tential of thoroughly modern materials and forms, the Odell buildings sparkle with a beauty arising from economy and function.

JOHN PORTMAN & ASSOCIATES— THE ARCHITECT AS DEVELOPER

John Portman of Atlanta typifies the architect-developer whose primary concern is with the economic vitality and growth of urban centers. But instead of producing standard, conservative, and dull commercial buildings such as abound in major southern cities, he has shown the exuberant flair of a virtuoso. The simple reinforced concrete exterior of the Atlanta Hyatt Regency (1964–1967) in no way prepares a visitor for the spatial drama of the interior. The center of the hotel is an open lobby-atrium, 120 feet square and twenty-two stories high. The public functions (registration, lounges, and services for visitors) are placed in the open amid fountains, sculpture, and large planters. Vine-covered balconies surrounding the atrium provide access to the rooms that are arranged along the peripheral walls of the hotel. Elevators designed as glass-enclosed

Odell Associates. R. J. Reynolds Industries, Winston-Salem, North Carolina: 1976–1977. Dramatic form and dazzling surfaces combine with functional planning in a building that is simultaneously monumental and respectful of its environment.

*John Portman & Associates. Hyatt Regency Hotel, Atlanta, Georgia:
1964–1967. The open atrium with its eye-catching effects was conceived to
gain a competitive edge over conventionally designed hotels. (John Portman
& Associates.)*

space capsules ascend in full view of the atrium. The overall experience is
a pluralistic combination of European street cafés, landscaped parks, the
attractions of Disneyworld, and the spatial drama of Baroque architecture. Portman justified the captivating effects by sound commercial rea-
soning:

> I wanted to explode the hotel; to open it up; to create a grandeur of
> space, almost a resort, in the center of the city. The whole idea was

to open everything up; take the hotel from its closed, tight position and explode it; take the elevators and literally pull them out of the walls and let them become an experience within themselves, let them become a giant kinetic sculpture.[13]

In expressing urban diversity, movement, and change, Portman's architecture is not particularly "southern"—in fact, a rapid succession of his spectacular hotels has gone up in Chicago, San Francisco, Los Angeles, and Detroit. His Peachtree Center Plaza Hotel, finished in 1976, is an even more grandiose addition to the Atlanta skyline.[14] Seventy stories high, and thus the South's tallest building, it is a shimmering cylindrical tower sheathed in reflective glass. The lobby is a seven-story space of reflecting pools, bridges, and landscaping, and the elevators ascend on the outside of the building, giving a breathtaking view of the city. All of this dynamism is placed on a massive podium of reinforced concrete, which encloses a parking garage, meeting rooms, ballrooms, and a swimming pool. No significant contribution is made to the Atlanta streetscape; visitors are expected to drive into the complex and experience the urbanity of the whole from within. In this respect Portman's exhilarating spaces differ from those of antebellum cities where pedestrians were given sensitive consideration. Moreover, the means to these extravagant superblocks is the bulldozing of all existing structures on the site.

PIAZZA D'ITALIA, NEW ORLEANS, LOUISIANA

Piazza d'Italia in New Orleans, on the other hand, is a recent project that respects both the pedestrian and the preservation of older buildings. At a time when buildings in New Orleans were being demolished at an alarming rate, a decaying block was replanned to celebrate Italian achievements in a city where French and Spanish ancestry was more often venerated. The nineteenth-century commercial buildings on the site were to be restored as meeting rooms, offices, restaurants, and stores for the nearby community.

The renovation of the existing buildings was planned by a firm of local architects, August Perez & Associates, but a nationally known architect, Charles Moore, received the commission to design a fountain for the open space at the center of the block.[15] In 1975, with funds still lacking, work was begun on the fountain as a tangible impetus for completing the entire project. Moore's St. Joseph's Fountain, a bravura performance, is essentially a circular configuration with paved walkways to the streets surrounding the block. Concentric, multicolored colonnades give it the shape of a Roman amphitheater, with water flowing over an 80-foot-long

Charles Moore. St. Joseph's Fountain, Piazza d'Italia, New Orleans, Louisiana: 1975–1978. The fountain provides compelling evidence that architecture can still be a delightful experience of sensitive meanings, human-scaled elements, and unforgettable places.

map of Italy worked into the stone of the pavement, and with screen walls presenting the Italian orders of architecture—Etruscan to Renaissance, Doric to Composite. The overall effect is one of pleasure and delight, heightened by the repeated surprises as the spectator moves along the walkways. Whereas architecture is too often all seriousness or merely dull, the liveliness of the Piazza d'Italia startles one into joyous smiles.

Moore's conception of architecture not as pure form, pure structure, pure function, or pure anything, but rather as erudite amalgamation of history, visual sensations, and human experiences, has been given the label of "postmodern architecture." Philip Johnson, who began his career as an International Style purist, has become a convert to this way of thinking, and recently astounded the architectural profession by declaring, "If you were building in Virginia you wouldn't think of not paying attention to the architecture of Thomas Jefferson."[16] Moore with his fountain—a marvelously inventive recapitulation of the classical orders to extol the Italian heritage—has produced a masterpiece that pleads for the restoration of the surrounding buildings.

PROPOSED HOTEL-CONVENTION CENTER, CHARLESTON, SOUTH CAROLINA

Not all city blocks have experienced even the potential good fortune of the Piazza d'Italia. In Charleston, the city and a Washington developer have been planning since 1977 a hotel-convention center for the heart of the commercial district, with a hotel and retail stores on a half-block space which for several years has been a surface parking lot. The rest of the block presently includes a historic church and graveyard and mid-nineteenth-century commercial structures. The church would remain unchanged, while several buildings would be demolished, and along one street only the façades and the interiors to a depth of forty feet would be retained. The resulting space on the interior of the block would be used for convention facilities and a parking garage. From the beginning controversy has arisen concerning economic feasibility, and the implications for historic preservation, and the environmental impact of the project on the "Old and Historic District," in which the block is located.[17] What has not yet been seriously enough addressed is the architectural quality of the design. As this is written, the working drawings have not been completed; but judging from the present plans, architectural distinction has not been a high priority of the promoters. The projected hotel is a twelve-story, brick-covered mass of overwhelming bulk and inarticulate scale, with little visual interest. Although the lower perimeter buildings are intended to be in harmony with the historic, three-story scale of the area, they are shown as eighteenth-century Neo-Palladian pavilions in a context that is entirely of the nineteenth century.

The contrast with the Charleston Hotel, erected almost one hundred and fifty years earlier, is significant. The hotel's heroic Greek Revival style had been deliberately chosen to proclaim civic destiny. The proposed hotel–convention center expresses no similar aspirations, but neither does it offer anything to capture the imagination in the manner of a Portman hotel interior, or any of the felicitous ingenuity of the Piazza d'Italia. In a city that prides itself on its architectural heritage, the proposed buildings are neither sensitive evocations of the past nor creative examples of modern architecture.

THE RECONSTRUCTION OF WILLIAMSBURG, VIRGINIA

A survey of modern architecture in the South indicates how difficult it is to combine high quality and historic "southernness." Although the notion of regionalism is increasingly popular among contemporary architects, no easy formula exists for transferring the principles of historic architecture to new buildings. Jefferson himself would no doubt be puzzled by the problem. He planned the Virginia State Capitol and the University of Virginia as exemplary of both the great architecture of Western civilization and the new American republic. But as one who believed in rational change and who thoroughly rebuilt Monticello in his own lifetime, he would be shocked by the crass and superficial present-day imitations of his work. Nor would he enjoy seeing Monticello as it is today—a house museum where lines of people are continually ushered through a relatively fixed series of exhibits.

Given the obstacles to the creation of a modern "southern" architecture, preservation may be the South's major contribution in the twentieth century. The most compelling reason for preserving historic buildings is to provide a tangible means of establishing contact with the past. The successes of historic preservation can be measured in terms of humanely livable houses and neighborhoods, appreciating real estate values, income from tourism, and—most important of all for architecture—the sense of place and time, which has been blurred by American mobility and change.

Williamsburg, the South's most famous preservation project, had its beginnings in the mid-1920s, when the former rector of Bruton Parish Church, the Reverend William A. R. Goodwin, convinced John D. Rockefeller, Jr., that the re-creation of the colonial capital of Virginia would be a worthy endeavor. Each of the main buildings presented a different problem. Bruton Parish Church had already undergone restoration in 1905. The post–Civil War building of the College of William and Mary was thoroughly rebuilt to the design of the second college building (1709–1716), as portrayed on the Bodleian plate of about 1737. That document also provided illustrations of the Capitol and Governor's Palace, of which only the foundations were extant. Beginning with meticulous archival and archaeological research, by 1935 sixty-six colonial buildings had been restored, eighty-four others reconstructed—and 440 later buildings either torn down or moved outside the colonial area.[18] The ideals of the program notwithstanding, such wholesale demolition and rebuilding are somewhat analogous to the razing of an urban block for purely commercial purposes.

The enormous success of Colonial Williamsburg has inevitably led to criticism. Scholars have pointed out inconsistencies in the historical re-creations, and preservationists have questioned the theoretical basis of presenting the capital at a specific point in time, rather than as an accretive process of growth and change. As Frank Lloyd Wright summarized it, "The restoration *is* a fine museum piece and as such valuable to Americans if they would only let it be a museum piece and not an *illusion*, and would study it for what significance it has where our life is concerned, and not attempting to live in it still."[19]

But Williamsburg was to a considerable degree an "illusion" even during the period when it was the colonial capital. By an act of will, a colonial governor and a group of prominent planters envisioned and built Williamsburg as the setting for urbane living amid a rural and sparsely populated landscape. Accordingly, it ought not to be disconcerting nowadays to see guides and craftsmen in eighteenth-century dress entertaining visitors to this most skillfully presented of tourist attractions. Ironically, just outside Colonial Williamsburg's specially designed ambience is a commercial highway strip whose motels and fast-food franchises rival the best of that preeminently American medium; and on the other side of town, the Busch Gardens amusement park features Old World scenes, including a French outdoor café and a German beer hall. Williamsburg is a place for all people to enjoy, from the serious antiquarian to the ordinary citizen. And since some of its reconstructions are now fifty years old, the distinction between reality and illusion has already begun to blur under a veneer of age.

The Restoration of Old Salem, North Carolina

The Moravian town of Salem, in North Carolina, is an example of a historic community which though restored continues as a living environment. It was founded in 1766 according to instructions and a model sent from Bethlehem, Pennsylvania, stressing communal virtues, although each family had its own house, yard, and garden.[20] A major street ran through the town, and near the center was an open square, around which what there was in the way of public buildings were erected. The community was not primarily agricultural, but consisted mainly of craftsmen whose earnings allowed the Moravians to continue their missionary work in the Piedmont.

Salem was nearly swallowed up in the twentieth century by greater Winston-Salem. In 1950, when a supermarket threatened to destroy what remained of the community, Old Salem was incorporated in order to preserve and restore the area. The work proceeded sensitively, with a recognition of the historic use of the buildings as well as the diversity which had grown up over the years. The Home Moravian Church (not part of the Old Salem Restoration) continues to serve its congregation at the northeast corner of the square. Immediately to the south is Salem College, which had developed in the nineteenth century out of a Moravian girls' school on the site. Across the square is the Single Brothers House, originally built as living quarters for young unmarried men while they learned a trade, in which Moravian crafts are now demonstrated.

The Museum of Early Southern Decorative Arts is housed in part in a recycled building that had previously been a grocery store. Five other restored buildings open to the public serve as museum houses, shops, and a tavern. Most of the remaining structures are private residences, assuring Old Salem a modern life amid its historic ambience.

Whereas Williamsburg is a display of architectural homogeneity, the Moravian buildings, evolved over a period of time, are in a variety of materials—wood-frame, stone, brick, and half-timber construction. As vernacular structures, they were erected simply and solidly, and with a masterful sense of proportions and human scale. The high style of the coastal establishment was assiduously avoided, and the tranquil setting of shade trees, green yards, and gardens conveys both a historic and a contemporary image of men living in harmony with nature and at peace—the literal meaning of "Salem."

The Preservation of Beaufort, South Carolina

Before the American Revolution, Beaufort, South Carolina, was a relatively prosperous shipbuilding center. Later it developed into a fashionable retreat, where planters from the Sea Islands and the Low Country congregated during the hot, humid summer months. As an English visitor described the antebellum town, "Beaufort [is] a picturesque town composed of villas, the summer residences of numerous planters who retire here during the hot season, when the interior of South Carolina is unhealthy. . . . Each villa is shaded by a verandah, surrounded by beautiful live oaks and orange trees laden with fruit."[21]

Among the elegant houses amid a veritable paradise of vegetation, one typical villa is characterized by a simple cubical volume, with an integrating hipped roof and a two-story portico of Palladian derivation, with the nearby Drayton Hall and Miles Brewton House in Charleston as intermediary influences. Another plan features a veranda across the façade to shade the living areas from the intense heat of the sun. Inside most Beaufort houses, high-style mantelpieces and ornate moldings convey the aristocratic aspirations of the planters—a manner of living which suddenly ended with the Civil War:

> The lovely town of Beaufort, embowered in groves of orange and magnolia trees . . . has for a century or more been the seat of a wealthy and aristocratic population, and evidences of their taste and love for the beautiful and the sumptuous are yet perceptible in the town, which though partially dismantled and greatly come to grief, yet shows in its half-ruined and neglected gardens, costly and gen-

erously large houses, and arbored streets and squares, what manner of people formerly occupied the place.[22]

After the war, poverty led to the subdivision of many of the large houses, which fell into disrepair, although usually no irrevocable damage was done. The town also survived, but was too poor either to tear down its old houses or to expand its commercial district. During the twentieth century, the region's slow progress toward economic recovery led to the saving of the villas, not as incorporated campaigns like Colonial Williamsburg or Old Salem, but as individual projects based on the same respect for historic architecture that had produced the houses in the first place. Beaufort's special ambience, as a series of picturesque mansions on large landscaped lots, is preservation in its fullest sense, with only minimal alterations to the historic structures and their context.

Primarily because of the preservation movement, southern buildings and cities have never looked better than they do today. Yet the fruits of this commendable activity are increasingly under attack as a result of the ever-present thrust of urban development, and even of the attraction they have for tourists. Preserved environments are extremely fragile, since to survive at all they have to withstand the erosion caused by the prevalent mobility and change. The challenge today is to achieve a harmony between respect for the past and the promise of the future. An architecture capable of meeting that challenge can still leave behind meaningful statements, that subsequent generations in their turn will deem worthy of preservation.

NOTES

CHAPTER TWO:
FROM FRONTIER SETTLEMENTS
TO URBANE CITIES

Pages 9 through 27

1. For Jamestown, see John W. Reps, *Tidewater Towns: City Planning in Colonial Virginia and Maryland* (Charlottesville, 1972), pp. 31–45. In 1893, to prevent further erosion of the site, the Association for the Preservation of Virginia Antiquities purchased 23 acres on Jamestown Island. The same organization, together with the National Park Service, currently administers the historic area as part of the Colonial National Historical Park.

2. This and the following quotations are taken from the Shaftesbury Papers (Sir Anthony Ashley Cooper), published as Vol. V of the *Collections of the South Carolina Historical Society* (Richmond, 1897), pp. 323, 343, and 361. Additional information on the planning of Charleston can be found in Frederick R. Stevenson and Carl Feiss, "Charleston and Savannah," *Journal of the Society of Architectural Historians*, X (Dec. 1951), 3–6; and John W. Reps, *The Making of Urban America* (Princeton, 1965), pp. 175–179.

3. Alexander Hewatt, *An Historical Account of the Rise and Progress of the Colonies of South Carolina and Georgia*, II (London, 1779), 290.

4. Duc de la Rochefoucauld-Liancourt, *Travels through the United States of North America, the Country of the Iroquois, and Upper Canada*, I (London, 1799), 556.

5. For Annapolis, see Reps, *Tidewater Towns*, pp. 117–140; and Russell J. Wright, "The Town Plan of Annapolis," *Antiques*, CXI (Jan. 1977), 148–151.

6. William Eddis, *Letters from America* (London, 1792), pp. 18–19.

7. "Speeches of Students of the College of William and Mary, Delivered May 1, 1699," *William and Mary Quarterly*, X (1930), 329–333.

8. The ideological significance of Williamsburg is perceptively analyzed by Sylvia Doughty Fries, *The Urban Idea in Colonial America* (Philadelphia, 1977), pp. 108–131.

9. Reps, *Tidewater Towns*, pp. 143–146.

10. *Ibid.*, pp. 156–170.

11. Hugh Jones, *The Present State of Virginia* (London, 1724), pp. 25–32. For the ar-

chitecture of Williamsburg, see Marcus Whiffen, *The Public Buildings of Williamsburg* (Williamsburg, 1958).

12. For Savannah, see Stevenson and Feiss, "Charleston and Savannah," 6–9; Reps, *The Making of Urban America*, pp. 185–192; and Fries, *The Urban Idea in Colonial America*, pp. 136–162.

13. Frederick Law Olmsted, *A Journey in the Seaboard Slave States* (New York, 1856), p. 404.

14. For the planning of Spanish and French colonial cities, see Reps, *The Making of Urban America*, pp. 26–87.

CHAPTER THREE:

PLANTATIONS:

THE ROOTS OF SOUTHERN LIFE

Pages 28 through 47

1. For the Adam Thoroughgood House, see Hugh Morrison, *Early American Architecture from the First Colonial Settlements to the National Period* (New York, 1952), pp. 143–145; and William H. Pierson, Jr., *The Colonial and Neo-Classical Styles* (Garden City, 1970), pp. 23–29. Restored in the twentieth century, the house is owned by the Chrysler Museum of Norfolk and is open to the public.

2. For Middleburg, see Samuel Gaillard Stoney, *Plantations of the Carolina Low Country* (Charleston, 1938), pp. 48–49. With the exception of an addition on the north end and redecoration of the main rooms about 1800, the house is remarkably unaltered; it presently is in the possession of descendants of the original builder.

3. For Mulberry, see *ibid.*, pp. 51–52; and Morrison, *Early American Architecture*, pp. 172–174. About 1800 the principal rooms were redecorated in the Federal style, in the early twentieth century the house was restored, and today it remains a private residence.

4. For Stratford Hall, see Thomas Tileston Waterman, *The Mansions of Virginia, 1706–1776* (Chapel Hill, 1945), pp. 92–102; Morrison, *Early American Architecture*, pp. 335–339; and Connie H. Wyrick, "Stratford and the Lees," *Journal of the Society of Architectural Historians*, XXX (March 1971), 71–78. In 1929 the house was purchased and restored by the Robert E. Lee Memorial Association, and it is open to the public.

5. *Ibid.*, p. 75.

6. For Westover, see Waterman, *The Mansions of Virginia*, pp. 148–163; Morrison, *Early American Architecture*, pp. 339–343; and Pierson, *The Colonial and Neo-Classical Styles*, pp. 73–78. The house remains a private residence, but the grounds are open to the public.

7. For Drayton Hall, see Stoney, *Plantations of the Carolina Low Country*, p. 61; Morrison, *Early American Architecture*, pp. 401–404; Frederick D. Nichols, "Drayton Hall, Plantation House of the Drayton Family," *Antiques*, XCVII (April 1970), 576–578; John Cornforth, "The Future of Drayton Hall," *Country Life*, CLVI (Aug. 1, 1974), 290–293; and Marian Page, *Historic Houses Restored and Preserved* (New York, 1976), pp. 33–40. Since 1974 Drayton Hall has been jointly owned by the National Trust for Historic Preservation and the state of South Carolina; it is open to the public.

8. Duc de la Rochefoucauld-Liancourt, *Travels through the United States of North America, the Country of the Iroquois, and Upper Canada*, I (London, 1799), 591. For Middleton Place, see Stoney, *Plantations of the Carolina Low Country*, pp. 64–65; and Sarah Lytle, "Middleton Place," *Antiques*, CXV (April 1979), 779–793. The Middleton Place Foundation has opened the gardens to the public, as well as the restored south wing of the plantation house (burned during the Civil War).

9. For Arlington House, see Murray Nelligan, "The Building of Arlington House,"

Journal of the Society of Architectural Historians, X (May 1951), 11–15. Restored after 1925, the house is currently administered by the National Park Service and is open to the public.

10. Frederick Law Olmsted, *A Journey in the Seaboard Slave States* (New York, 1856), p. 417. Olmsted does not identify the plantation, but from the context of his narrative it seems to have been located in coastal Georgia.

11. For Oak Alley, see J. Frazer Smith, *White Pillars: Early Life and Architecture of the Lower Mississippi Valley Country* (New York, 1941), pp. 191–193; W. Darrell Overdyke, *Louisiana Plantation Homes* (New York, 1965), pp. 138–141; and Pierson, *The Colonial and Neo-Classical Styles*, pp. 456–458. In 1925 the house was saved from rampant deterioration, restored, and is open to the public.

12. For the John Thomas Grant House, see Frederick D. Nichols, *The Architecture of Georgia* (Savannah, 1976), pp. 306–307. The house is the official residence of the president of the University of Georgia.

13. For Longwood, see Samuel Sloan, *The Model Architect*, II (Philadelphia, 1852), 55–56 and 71–72; *Samuel Sloan's Homestead Architecture* (Philadelphia, 1861), pp. 57–62; and William L. Whitwell, *The Heritage of Longwood* (Jackson, 1975). In 1970 the house was given to the Pilgrimage Garden Club of Natchez, restored, and opened to the public.

CHAPTER FOUR:
SOUTHERN CHURCHES:
FROM ESTABLISHED CONVENTIONS
TO STYLISTIC ECLECTICISM

Pages 48 through 64

1. For St. Luke's Church, Smithfield, see James Grote Van Derpool, "The Restoration of St. Luke's, Smithfield, Virginia," *Journal of the Society of Architectural Historians*, XVII (March 1958), 12–18; and William H. Pierson, Jr., *The Colonial and Neo-Classical Styles* (Garden City, 1970), pp. 34–45. In 1832 the church closed for services and began to deteriorate; it was restored in the 1890s and the 1950s, and now serves an Episcopal parish.

2. For St. James' Church, Goose Creek, see Samuel Gaillard Stoney, *Plantations of the Carolina Low Country* (Charleston, 1938), pp. 50–51. References to the construction of the church are included in Frank J. Klingberg, ed., *The Carolina Chronicle of Dr. Francis LeJau, 1706–1717* (Berkeley, 1956). LeJau, a missionary sent to Carolina by the Society for the Propagation of the Gospel, became the church's first rector. Regular services stopped in the early nineteenth century, and the church was severely damaged by the earthquake of 1886. Restoration occurred in the late 1950s and early 1960s, but the church, situated in a sparsely populated and picturesquely overgrown Low Country setting, still is only infrequently used.

3. For Christ Church, Lancaster County, see Thomas Tileston Waterman, *The Mansions of Virginia, 1706–1776* (Chapel Hill, 1945), pp. 123–130; and Hugh Morrison, *Early American Architecture from the First Colonial Settlements to the National Period* (New York, 1952), pp. 349–350. The church was restored in the 1960s by the Foundation for Historic Christ Church and is open to the public.

4. For St. Michael's Church, Charleston, see Carl Bridenbaugh, *Peter Harrison: First American Architect* (Chapel Hill, 1949), pp. 63–67; George Walton Williams, *St. Michael's, Charleston, 1751–1951* (Columbia, 1951); and Beatrice St. Julien Ravenel, *Architects of Charleston* (Charleston, 1964), pp. 29–35.

5. For St. Philip's Church, Charleston, see *ibid.*, pp. 163–165.

6. For the Baltimore Cathedral, see Fiske Kimball, "Latrobe's Designs for the Cathedral of Baltimore," *Architectural Record*, XLIII (Jan. 1918), 37–45; Walter Knight Sturgis, "A Bishop and His Architect: The Story of the Building of Baltimore

Cathedral," *Liturgical Arts*, XVII (Feb. 1949), 53–54 and 63–64; Talbot Hamlin, *Benjamin Henry Latrobe* (New York, 1955), pp. 233–252; and Pierson, *The Colonial and Neo-Classical Styles*, pp. 360–372.

7. For the Government Street Presbyterian Church, Mobile, see Arthur Scully, Jr., *James Dakin, Architect: His Career in New York and the South* (Baton Rouge, 1973), pp. 68–72.

8. James Silk Buckingham, *The Slave States of America*, I (London, 1842), 282–283.

9. For the First Presbyterian Church, Nashville, see Jesse E. Wills, "An Echo from Egypt: A History of the Building Occupied by the First Presbyterian Church, Nashville, Tennessee," *Tennessee Historical Quarterly*, XI (1952), 63–77; Agnes Addison Gilchrist, *William Strickland, Architect and Engineer, 1788–1854* (New York, 1969), pp. 17 and 114–115; and Thomas B. Brumbaugh, *Architecture of Middle Tennessee* (Nashville, 1974), pp. 64–66.

10. *Nashville Gazette*, April 23, 1851.

11. For information on the Church of the Nativity, I am indebted to Mr. and Mrs. Henry B. Richardson of Union, South Carolina. In addition, a manuscript, "Recollections of England by Mary Poulton Dawkins in 1902" (now in the Caroliniana Library at the University of South Carolina), provides biographical material on the Poulton sisters.

12. *Southern Episcopalian*, IV (1856), 151; and VI (1859), 226 and 383.

CHAPTER FIVE:

PATRONS AND ARCHITECTS:

THE SHAPING OF SOUTHERN LIFE

Pages 65 through 79

1. R. T. Gunther, ed., *The Architecture of Sir Roger Pratt* (London, 1928), pp. 60–61 and 64. Additional background on the architecture of English country houses is found in John Wilton-Ely, "The Rise of the Professional Architect in England," in Spiro Kostof, ed., *The Architect: Chapters in the History of the Profession* (New York, 1977), pp. 180–208; and Mark Girouard, *Life in the English Country House: A Social and Architectural History* (New Haven and London, 1978).

2. *South Carolina Gazette & Country Journal*, Aug. 22, 1769. For the Miles Brewton House, see Beatrice St. Julien Ravenel, *Architects of Charleston* (Charleston, 1964), pp. 49–53. The house remains a private residence owned by direct descendants of the builder.

3. For William Buckland and Gunston Hall, see Rosamond Randall Beirne and John Henry Scarff, *William Buckland, 1734–1774: Architect of Virginia and Maryland* (Baltimore, 1958), pp. 1–33 and 141–154; Thomas Tileston Waterman, *The Mansions of Virginia, 1706–1776* (Chapel Hill, 1945), pp. 223–230; and Helen Hill Miller, *George Mason: Gentleman Revolutionary* (Chapel Hill, 1975), pp. 44–62. Gunston Hall is now owned by the Commonwealth of Virginia, administered by the National Society of the Colonial Dames of America, and open to the public.

4. For the Matthias Hammond House, see Beirne and Scarff, *William Buckland, 1734–1774*, pp. 90–95; and William H. Pierson, Jr., *The Colonial and Neo-Classical Styles* (Garden City, 1970), pp. 150–156. According to local legend, the house was built to please Hammond's fiancée, who, upon observing his preoccupation with the house, refused to marry him. In the nineteenth century the house passed into the hands of the Harwood family; it is presently owned by the Hammond-Harwood Home Association, which has opened it to the public.

5. Robert Oresko, ed., *Works in Architecture of Robert and James Adam* (London, 1975), pp. 45–46.

6. For Gabriel Manigault and the Joseph Manigault House, see "The Manigault Family of South Carolina from 1685 to 1886," *Transactions of the Huguenot Society of*

South Carolina, IV (1897), 81–83; and Ravenel, *Architects of Charleston*, pp. 55–66. The house is owned by the Charleston Museum and is open to the public.

7. Mills Lane, *Savannah Revisited: A Pictorial History* (Savannah, 1977), p. 57.

8. For William Jay and the Richard Richardson House, see James Vernon McDonough, "William Jay—Regency Architect in Georgia and South Carolina" (unpublished Ph.D. dissertation, Princeton University, 1950); and Frederick D. Nichols, *The Architecture of Georgia* (Savannah, 1976), pp. 45–49. The house is open to the public, administered by the Telfair Museum of Art, which refers to it as the Owens-Thomas House in deference to the family who lived in it from 1830 to 1951.

9. For the William Scarbrough House, see Marian Page, *Historic Houses Restored and Preserved* (New York, 1976), pp. 139–143. The house has been recently restored by the Historic Savannah Foundation and is open to the public.

10. Tyrone Power, *Impressions of America during the Years 1833, 1834, and 1835*, II (London, 1836), 117–118.

CHAPTER SIX:

WASHINGTON AND JEFFERSON:

ARCHITECTS OF THE AMERICAN REPUBLIC

Pages 80 through 96

1. This and the following statements of Washington concerning Mount Vernon are taken from *Mount Vernon: An Illustrated Handbook* (Mount Vernon, 1974). See also Thomas Tileston Waterman, *The Mansions of Virginia, 1706–1776* (Chapel Hill, 1945), pp. 268–298; and Hugh Morrison, *Early American Architecture from the First Colonial Settlements to the National Period* (New York, 1952), pp. 355–367. The mansion and the surrounding 500 acres are administered by the Mount Vernon Ladies' Association, the first major preservation organization in America.

2. Worth Bailey, "General Washington's New Room," *Journal of the Society of Architectural Historians*, X (May 1951), 16–18; and Alan Gowans, *Images of American Living* (Philadelphia, 1964), pp. 165–166.

3. The letter was written in May 1780 from Paris, where John Adams was minister to France; it is published in Page Smith, *John Adams*, I (Garden City, 1962), 468–469.

4. Letter to James Madison, Sept. 20, 1785, in Merrill D. Peterson, ed., *The Portable Thomas Jefferson* (New York, 1975), p. 390.

5. Letters to James Madison, Jan. 30, 1787, in *ibid.*, p. 147; and to William S. Smith, Nov. 13, 1787, in Bernard Mayo, ed., *Jefferson Himself* (Boston, 1942), p. 145.

6. Thomas Jefferson, *Notes on the State of Virginia* (New York, 1964), pp. 146–147.

7. Marquis de Chastellux, *Travels in North America in the Years 1781, 1782, and 1783* (New York, 1827), p. 227. For Jefferson's architecture, see William H. Pierson, Jr., *The Colonial and Neo-Classical Styles* (Garden City, 1970), pp. 286–334; Desmond Guinness and Julius Trousdale Sadler, Jr., *Mr. Jefferson Architect* (New York, 1973); William Howard Adams, ed., *The Eye of Thomas Jefferson* (Washington, 1976); and Frederick D. Nichols, "Jefferson: The Making of an Architect," in William Howard Adams, ed., *Jefferson and the Arts: An Extended View* (Washington, 1976), pp. 159–185.

8. Letter to the Comtesse de Tessé, March 20, 1787, in Peterson, *The Portable Thomas Jefferson*, p. 418.

9. Letter to James Madison, Sept. 20, 1785, in *ibid.*, p. 389.

10. Letter to the Comtesse de Tessé, March 20, 1787, in *ibid.*, p. 418.

11. Letter to William B. Giles, March 19, 1796, in Adams, *The Eye of Thomas Jefferson*, p. 272.

12. Letter to William Hamilton, July 1806, in Peterson, *The Portable Thomas Jefferson*, pp. 502–503. The Thomas Jefferson Memorial Foundation purchased Monticello in 1923, and the house is open to the public.

13. For the planning of Washington, see Saul K. Padover, ed., *Thomas Jefferson and the National Capital* (Washington, 1946); John W. Reps, *Monumental Washington: The Planning and Development of the Capital Center* (Princeton, 1967); and Paul F. Norton, "Thomas Jefferson and the Planning of the National Capital," in Adams, *Jefferson and the Arts*, pp. 187–232.

CHAPTER SEVEN:
SOUTHERN COLLEGES:
PLANTED CAMPUSES

Pages 97 through 108

1. Hugh Jones, *The Present State of Virginia* (London, 1724), pp. 83–94.
2. Thomas Jefferson, *Notes on the State of Virginia* (New York, 1964), p. 144; and Edgar W. Knight, ed., *A Documentary History of Education in the South before 1860*, I (Chapel Hill, 1949), 550–551.
3. *Ibid.*, III, 5–9.
4. John Morrill Bryan, *An Architectural History of the South Carolina College, 1801–1855* (Columbia, 1976), pp. 6–7 *et passim*.
5. Paul Venable Turner, review of Bryan, *An Architectural History of the South Carolina College, 1801–1855*, in the *Journal of the Society of Architectural Historians*, XXXVII (May 1978), 112–113.
6. Letter to George Wythe, Aug. 13, 1786, in Merrill D. Peterson, ed., *The Portable Thomas Jefferson* (New York, 1975), p. 399.
7. Letter to L. W. Tazewell, Jan. 5, 1805, published in the *New York Times*, April 26, 1931, sec. 8, p. 20. Jefferson proposed a similar "academical village" to the trustees of East Tennessee College in a letter dated May 6, 1810, published in Don Gifford, ed., *The Literature of Architecture* (New York, 1966), pp. 78–79.
8. For the architecture of the University of Virginia and its sources, see William B. O'Neal, *Jefferson's Buildings at the University of Virginia: The Rotunda* (Charlottesville, 1960); William H. Pierson, Jr., *The Colonial and Neo-Classical Styles* (Garden City, 1970), pp. 316–334; and William Howard Adams, ed., *The Eye of Thomas Jefferson* (Washington, 1976), pp. 284–304.
9. Gérard Le Coat, "Thomas Jefferson et l'architecture métaphorique: le 'Village Académique' à l'Université de Virginie," *Revue d'art canadienne*, III (No. 2, 1976), 8–34.
10. For Jefferson's letter and the responses of William Thornton and Benjamin Latrobe, see Fiske Kimball, *Thomas Jefferson Architect* (Boston, 1916), pp. 75–77; and Desmond Guinness and Julius Trousdale Sadler, Jr., *Mr. Jefferson Architect* (New York, 1973), pp. 120–125.
11. Letter to Augustus B. Woodward, April 3, 1825, in Guinness and Sadler, *Mr. Jefferson Architect*, pp. 148–149.
12. For Washington and Lee University, see Jerry Donovan, "John Jordan, Virginia Builder," *Journal of the Society of Architectural Historians*, IX (Oct. 1950), 17–19; Parke Rouse, Jr., "The Buildings of Washington and Lee University," *Antiques*, CIV (Oct. 1973), 651–656; and Royster Lyle, Jr., and Pamela Hemenway Simpson, *The Architecture of Historic Lexington* (Charlottesville, 1977), pp. 145–167.
13. [Jasper Adams], "A Historical Sketch of the College of Charleston, South Carolina," *American Quarterly Register*, XII (Nov. 1839), 164–177; and J. H. Easterby, *A History of the College of Charleston* (New York, 1935), pp. 67–118.
14. *Charleston Courier*, March 19, 1847.
15. For the buildings of the College of Charleston, see Beatrice St. Julien Ravenel, *Architects of Charleston* (Charleston, 1964), pp. 172–173, 195–198, and 245.

CHAPTER EIGHT:
WESTWARD EXPANSION:
SOUTHERN ARCHITECTURE
ACROSS THE APPALACHIAN MOUNTAINS

Pages 109 through 127

1. Rebecca K. Pruett, "The Browns of Liberty Hall" (published by the National Society of Colonial Dames of America in the Commonwealth of Kentucky, 1966), p. 17.

2. Fiske Kimball, "Jefferson's Designs for Two Kentucky Houses," *Journal of the Society of Architectural Historians*, IX (Oct. 1950), 14. See also "Liberty Hall," *Register of the Kentucky State Historical Society*, XXXIV (Oct. 1936), 392–394; and Rexford Newcomb, *Architecture in Old Kentucky* (Urbana, 1953), pp. 44–46. Liberty Hall and the Orlando Brown House are owned by the National Society of the Colonial Dames of America in the Commonwealth of Kentucky. Liberty Hall is presently undergoing major restoration, but it will eventually reopen to the public.

3. For Farmington, see Dorothy Park Clark and Melville O. Briney, "History in Houses: Farmington, in Louisville, Kentucky," *Antiques*, XCIII (Feb. 1968), 224–229; and Desmond Guinness and Julius Trousdale Sadler, Jr., *Mr. Jefferson Architect* (New York, 1973), pp. 99–102. Farmington has been restored by the Historic Homes Foundation of Louisville and is open to the public.

4. For Ashland, see Newcomb, *Architecture in Old Kentucky*, pp. 54–56; Talbot Hamlin, *Benjamin Henry Latrobe* (New York, 1955), pp. 381–382; James F. Hopkins, ed., *The Papers of Henry Clay*, I (Lexington, 1959), 169–170, 791–792, 818–819, 823, and 851–852; and Thomas D. Clark, "Ashland," *Antiques*, CXIV (Oct. 1978), 803–807. The Ashland rebuilt by James Clay between 1853 and 1857 is administered by the Henry Clay Memorial Foundation and is open to the public.

5. For the Hermitage, see Stanley F. Horn, "The Hermitage: Home of Andrew Jackson," reprinted from the *Tennessee Historical Quarterly*, XX (March 1961); *idem*, "The Hermitage, Home of Andrew Jackson," *Antiques*, C (Sept. 1971), 413–417; and Thomas B. Brumbaugh, *Architecture of Middle Tennessee* (Nashville, 1974), pp. 122–124. Since 1889 the Ladies' Hermitage Association has owned the house and the surrounding property. Not only is the Hermitage a house museum open to the public, but on the grounds is a research center and archive.

6. Julia Ann M. Conner, "Diary of a Trip from Charleston to Tennessee in 1827" (manuscript at the South Carolina Historical Society in Charleston).

7. *Charleston Courier*, May 31, 1843.

8. Harriet Martineau, *Society in America*, I (New York, 1837), 220–221.

9. For Gaineswood, see Jesse G. Whitfield, "Gaineswood and Other Memories" (Demopolis, n.d.); and Walter S. Patton, "General Nathan Bryan Whitfield and Gaineswood" (unpublished study, 1972). The house has been recently restored by the Alabama Historical Commission and is open to the public.

10. For the Old Kentucky Statehouse, see Bayless E. Hardin, "The Capitols of Kentucky," *Register of the Kentucky State Historical Society*, XLIII (July 1945), 180–185; Newcomb, *Architecture in Old Kentucky*, pp. 110–113; and William Barrow Floyd, "The Restored Old Capitol, Frankfort, Kentucky," *Antiques*, CXIV (July 1978), 108–116. In 1909 the state government moved to a new building; since 1920 the Old Statehouse has been the home of the Kentucky Historical Society, and in the past decade the interior was restored to its original appearance.

11. For the Tennessee Statehouse, see Nell Savage Mahoney, "William Strickland and the Building of Tennessee's Capitol, 1845–1854," *Tennessee Historical Quarterly*, IV (1945), 99–111; Clayton B. Dekle, "The Tennessee State Capitol," *ibid.*, XXV (Fall 1966), 213–238; Agnes Addison Gilchrist, *William Strickland, Architect and Engineer, 1788–1854* (New York, 1969), pp. 15–19 and 106–112; and Brumbaugh, *Architecture of Middle Tennessee*, pp. 2–9.

12. "The 'Parthenon,' Nashville," *Architectural Forum*, XLVI (May 1927), 433–436; and Louise Littleton Davis, "The Parthenon and the Tennessee Centennial: The Greek Temple That Sparked a Birthday Party," in Robert M. McBride, ed., *More Landmarks of Tennessee History* (Nashville, 1969), pp. 209–227.

13. For the planning and architecture of Milledgeville, see James C. Bonner, *Milledgeville, Georgia's Antebellum Capital* (Athens, 1978); John Linley, *The Architecture of Middle Georgia: The Oconee Area* (Athens, 1972), pp. 93–94 and 86–87; Frederick D. Nichols, *The Architecture of Georgia* (Savannah, 1976), pp. 57–58; and Henry D. Green, "Georgia's Early Governor's Mansion," *Antiques*, XCIV (Dec. 1968), 864–867.

14. *Georgia Statesman* (Milledgeville), April 16, 1827.

CHAPTER NINE:

TWO ANTEBELLUM CITIES:

NEW ORLEANS AND CHARLESTON

Pages 128 through 146

1. Benjamin Henry Boneval Latrobe, *Impressions Respecting New Orleans: Diaries and Sketches, 1818–1820*, ed. by Samuel Wilson, Jr. (New York, 1951), pp. 23–24 40–42, and 105–107.

2. *New Orleans Bee*, Oct. 2, 1835.

3. For James Gallier and the St. Charles Hotel, see *The Autobiography of James Gallier, Architect* (New York, 1973), pp. 23–24; James Robert Bienvenu, "Two Greek Revival Hotels in New Orleans: The St. Charles by James Gallier, Sr., and the St. Louis by J. N. B. de Pouilly" (unpublished M.A. thesis, Tulane University, 1961); Mary Louise Christovich, Roulhac Toledano, Betsy Swanson, and Pat Holden, *New Orleans Architecture, II: The American Sector* (Gretna, 1972), pp. 200–201; and Arthur Scully, Jr., *James Dakin, Architect: His Career in New York and the South* (Baton Rouge, 1973), pp. 44–50. The St. Charles Hotel was rebuilt without its dome after a fire in 1851, only to be destroyed again by fire in 1894, when an entirely different building was erected.

4. *Norman's New Orleans* (New Orleans, 1845), p. 141.

5. James Silk Buckingham, *The Slave States of America*, I (London, 1842), 331.

6. For the St. Louis Hotel, see Bienvenu, "Two Greek Revival Hotels in New Orleans," and Edith Elliott Long, "Jacques Nicolas Bussiere de Pouilly," in Christovich et al., *New Orleans Architecture, III: The Cemeteries* (Gretna, 1972), pp. 135–137. The St. Louis Hotel was severely damaged by fire in 1841, rebuilt shortly afterward, and demolished by the end of the century.

7. *New Orleans Courier*, Jan. 9, 1838.

8. For the Julia Street row of houses, see Christovich et al., *New Orleans Architecture, II: The American Sector*, pp. 80 and 174–177; and Scully, *James Dakin, Architect*, pp. 13–15. The row houses (often called the "Thirteen Sisters") were fashionable residences throughout the nineteenth century, but neglect and deterioration in this century had subjected them to an unpromising fate until recent work began to restore them.

9. For St. Patrick's Church, see Christovich et al., *New Orleans Architecture, II: The American Sector*, pp. 27 and 121–123; and Scully, *James Dakin, Architect*, pp. 88–97. St. Patrick's Church still serves its congregation.

10. For the City Hall, see *The Autobiography of James Gallier, Architect*, pp. 40–41; and Christovich et al., *New Orleans Architecture, II: The American Sector*, pp. 204–205. After restoration in the early 1970s, the building houses municipal offices, although it no longer is the city hall.

11. *New Orleans Daily Crescent*, Nov. 26, 1849.

12. Frederick Law Olmsted, *A Journey in the Seaboard Slave States* (New York, 1856), pp. 581–582.

13. For the Old Louisiana Statehouse, see Scully, *James Dakin, Architect*, pp. 126–161. In 1932 the building ceased being the Capitol, and it now houses the state Department of Art, Historical, and Cultural Preservation.

14. *New Orleans Daily Delta*, Feb. 29, 1852.

15. Mark Twain, *Life on the Mississippi River* (New York, 1957), p. 216.

16. For Robert Mills's writings on architecture, see H. M. Pierce Gallagher, *Robert Mills: Architect of the Washington Monument, 1771–1855* (New York, 1935), pp. 153–171.

17. Robert Mills, *Statistics of South Carolina* (Charleston, 1826), p. 411. For Mills's work in Charleston, see Beatrice St. Julien Ravenel, *Architects of Charleston* (Charleston, 1964), pp. 116–135.

18. For the Fireproof Building, see William H. Pierson, Jr., *The Colonial and Neo-Classical Styles* (Garden City, 1970), pp. 386–394; and Gene Waddell, "Robert Mills's Fireproof Building," *South Carolina Historical Magazine*, LXXX (April 1979), 105–135. The Fireproof Building now serves as the archive and library of the South Carolina Historical Society.

19. *Charleston Mercury*, Oct. 3, 1837.

20. For Charles F. Reichardt, see Ravenel, *Architects of Charleston*, pp. 177–181.

21. *Charleston Courier*, March 28, 1838.

22. *Ibid.*, April 19, 1839. In 1960 the Charleston Hotel was demolished to make way for a motel, built on the same foundations.

23. For the Hibernian Hall, see Augustine T. Smythe, "Centennial Address Delivered before the Hibernian Society of Charleston, S.C." (Charleston, 1902), p. 45; and Ravenel, *Architects of Charleston*, pp. 173–174. Although damaged by the earthquake of 1886 and rebuilt with a somewhat altered pediment, the Hibernian Hall still serves its original purpose.

24. For Edward Brickell White, see *ibid.*, pp. 183–202.

25. *Charleston Courier*, Aug. 5, 1845. The Huguenot Church has survived without major changes, and twice a year is still a place of worship for Huguenot descendants.

26. *Ibid.*, June 30, 1853.

27. For Jones & Lee, see Ravenel, *Architects of Charleston*, pp. 203–230.

28. [William Gilmore Simms], "Charleston, the Palmetto City," *Harper's New Monthly Magazine*, XV (June 1857), 13.

29. For the Unitarian Church, see "The Old and the New: or, Discourses and Proceedings at the Dedication of the Re-Modeled Unitarian Church, April 2, 1854" (Charleston, 1854). The Unitarian Church still serves its congregation.

30. Olmsted, *A Journey in the Seaboard Slave States*, p. 404.

31. For the New Orleans Custom House, see Christovich et al., *New Orleans Architecture, II: The American Sector*, pp. 131–133; and Scully, *James Dakin, Architect*, pp. 163–189. The Custom House was not finished until 1881, and now houses federal government offices.

32. [Simms], "Charleston, the Palmetto City," 8–9. For the Charleston Custom House, see also Ravenel, *Architects of Charleston*, pp. 237–238; and Lois Craig, *The Federal Presence: Architecture, Politics, and Symbols in United States Government Building* (Cambridge, 1978), pp. 106–108. The Custom House was not finished until 1879, and now houses federal government offices.

CHAPTER TEN:
THE NEW SOUTH:
FROM PICTURESQUE RUINS
TO PROGRESSIVE RESURGENCE

Pages 147 through 160

1. "A Sketch of Charleston," *South Carolina Institute Premium List* (Charleston, 1870), p. 38.
2. Constance Fenimore Woolson, "Up the Ashley and Cooper," *Harper's New Monthly Magazine*, LII (Dec. 1875), 4 and 9.
3. *Harper's Weekly*, Sept. 8, 1866, p. 556; and *Every Saturday*, Aug. 5, 1871, pp. 140–142.
4. For Richardson's letters, see Mariana Griswold Van Rensselaer, *Henry Hobson Richardson and His Works* (Boston and New York, 1888), pp. 11–12. See also Henry-Russell Hitchcock, *The Architecture of H. H. Richardson and His Times* (New York, 1936); Lewis Mumford, "The Regionalism of H. H. Richardson," in *The South in Architecture* (New York, 1941), pp. 79–110; and James F. O'Gorman, *Henry Hobson Richardson and His Office* (Cambridge, 1974).
5. *New Orleans Daily Picayune*, Jan. 30, 1887. For the Howard Library, see also O'Gorman, *Henry Hobson Richardson and His Office*, pp. 171–174.
6. *Library Journal*, XIII (Dec. 1888), 384. The Howard Library served its original purpose until 1941, when its collections were moved to Tulane University. After functioning as a radio station and an oil company office, the building now houses a law firm.
7. Hitchcock, *The Architecture of H. H. Richardson and His Times*, p. 299.
8. For Biltmore, see Albert Fein, *Frederick Law Olmsted and the American Environmental Tradition* (New York, 1972), pp. 13–14 and 55–57; Laura Wood Roper, *FLO: A Biography of Frederick Law Olmsted* (Baltimore, 1973), pp. 415–416; and Paul R. Baker, *Richard Morris Hunt* (Cambridge, 1980), pp. 412–432. In a manner typical of a southern plantation, Biltmore was given a distinguishing name, by combining "Bildt," the ancestral Dutch town of the Vanderbilts, and "more," an English term for rolling upcountry terrain. Today, it remains virtually as Vanderbilt left it, and it is open to the public.
9. Fein, *Frederick Law Olmsted and the American Environmental Tradition*, p. 13.
10. George R. Fairbanks, *History of the University of the South* (Jacksonville, 1905).
11. Louis R. Harlan, ed., *The Booker T. Washington Papers*, I (Urbana, Chicago, and London, 1972), 45 and 74; and Booker T. Washington, *Tuskegee and Its People: Their Ideals and Achievements* (New York, 1971), p. 9.
12. Harlan, *The Booker T. Washington Papers*, I, 294.
13. *Ibid.*, III, 469–470. In 1894 Olmsted began to reduce the amount of his professional work, and apparently never went to Tuskegee or furnished plans.
14. *Ibid.*, I, 316–317.
15. Washington, *Tuskegee and Its People*, p. 25.
16. Wayne Andrews, *Pride of the South: A Social History of Southern Architecture* (New York, 1979), pp. 151–152. The Hotel Ponce de León is now Flagler College.
17. Louis H. Sullivan, *The Autobiography of an Idea* (New York, 1924), pp. 294–298. For Sullivan's architectural career, see Hugh Morrison, *Louis Sullivan: Prophet of Modern Architecture* (New York, 1935).
18. Louis H. Sullivan, "The Tall Office Building Artistically Considered," in *Kindergarten Chats and Other Writings* (New York, 1947), pp. 207–208.
19. Lyndon P. Smith, "The House of an Artist-Architect: Louis H. Sullivan's Place at Ocean Springs, Mississippi," *Architectural Record*, XVII (June 1905), 471–490; and Mary Wallace Crocker, *Historic Architecture in Mississippi* (Jackson, 1973), pp. 96–99. With the eclipse of his career, Sullivan was forced to sell his Ocean

Springs property in 1910. The cottages have been considerably altered, and they remain private residences.

20. Sullivan, *Kindergarten Chats and Other Writings*, p. 112.

CHAPTER ELEVEN:

FRANK LLOYD WRIGHT:

THE ARCHITECTURE OF USONIA SOUTH

Pages 161 through 173

1. Robert S. Cotterill, "The Old South to the New," *Journal of Southern History*, XV
(Feb. 1949), 3–8; and republished in Patrick Gerster and Nicholas Cords, eds., *Myth
and Southern History*, II (Chicago, 1974), 33–38.

2. For the life and career of Frank Lloyd Wright, see Robert C. Twombly, *Frank Lloyd
Wright: An Interpretive Biography* (New York, 1973).

3. Vincent Scully, *American Architecture and Urbanism* (New York, 1969), pp.
51–56; and "American Houses: Thomas Jefferson to Frank Lloyd Wright," in Edgar
Kaufmann, Jr., ed., *The Rise of an American Architecture* (New York, 1970), pp.
165–168.

4. Frank Lloyd Wright, *An Autobiography* (New York, 1943), p. 168.

5. Thomas Jefferson, *Notes on the State of Virginia* (New York, 1964), pp. 157–158.

6. *The Pope-Leighey House* (Washington, 1969), pp. 12–15. For Broadacre City and
the Usonian House, see Frank Lloyd Wright, *The Living City* (New York, 1958),
and *The Natural House* (New York, 1954); John Sergeant, *Frank Lloyd Wright's
Usonian Houses: The Case for Organic Architecture* (New York, 1976).

7. Marjorie F. Leighey, "A Testimony to Beauty," in *The Pope-Leighey House*, pp.
59–62. Although the house remains a private residence, the National Trust for Historic Preservation opens it to the public on weekends from March to November.

8. For the Rosenbaum House, see Wright, *The Natural House*, pp. 110–113; and Sergeant, *Frank Lloyd Wright's Usonian Houses*, pp. 42–45. The house still is the private residence of the Stanley Rosenbaums.

9. For the background on Auldbrass, I am indebted to the Stanton D. Lorings (Stevens's daughter and son-in-law) for family material and architectural documents in
their possession. See also *Architectural Forum*, LXXXVIII (Jan. 1948), 95–96.
Until 1979 the Lorings farmed Auldbrass in the spirit of the original plans; it is now
owned by Westvaco Corporation, a timber and paper company.

10. *Charleston News and Courier*, Dec. 21, 1941, sec. ii, p. 14; and *Charlotte Sunday
Observer*, Jan. 4, 1942, sec. iv, p. 1.

11. Stevens's Farm Plan Contest and J. W. Harwell's Hypothetical Farm Plan are type-
written manuscripts in the Lorings's possession.

12. Frank Lloyd Wright, "Usonia, Usonia South, and New England: A Declaration of
Independence . . . 1941," *Taliesin Square Paper*, VI (Oct. 1941), 1–4.

13. Frank Lloyd Wright, *A Testament* (New York, 1957), pp. 62–63.

14. Wright, *An Autobiography*, p. 331.

15. The statement by Wright was remembered by Donna M. Stoddard, then a student at
the college and now head of the art department. Wright considered his work at Florida Southern College to be of national significance, since he frequently included it in
publications of his architecture: *Architectural Forum*, LXXXVIII (Jan. 1948),
127–135; *ibid.*, XCIV (Jan. 1951), 102–103; and *ibid.*, XCVII (Sept. 1952), 120.

16. Wright made the statements at a chapel service on October 25, 1951, and during his
last visit to the campus in March 1957. Today the campus is a National Historic
Landmark and Florida Southern College thrives as a coeducational liberal arts college
for 1,600 students.

CHAPTER TWELVE:
MODERN ARCHITECTURE IN THE SOUTH:
NEW BUILDINGS AND PRESERVED PLACES

Pages 174 through 189

1. C. Vann Woodward, *The Burden of Southern History* (Baton Rouge, 1960), p. 6.

2. For the Tuskegee Institute Chapel, see "Sanctuary of Sculptured Concrete," *Architectural Forum*, CXIII (Sept. 1960), 103–105; and "A Chapel for Tuskegee by Rudolph," *Architectural Record*, CXLVI (Nov. 1969), 117–126.

3. For the John Wallace House, see Sibyl Maholy-Nagy and Gerhard Schwab, *The Architecture of Paul Rudolph* (New York, 1970), pp. 72–75.

4. "Corporate Headquarters and Research Laboratories for Burroughs Wellcome & Co., Inc.," *Architectural Record*, CXLVIII (Nov. 1970), 92–100; and "Sculptural Forms for Pharmaceutical Research," *ibid.*, CLI (June 1972), 95–100.

5. "Mepkin Plantation," *Architectural Forum*, LXVI (June 1937), 515–522; and Edward Durell Stone, *Evolution of an Architect* (New York, 1962), pp. 33–34 and 48–51. In 1949 the Luces gave Mepkin to the Roman Catholic Diocese of Charleston, and the plantation is now a small Cistercian monastery. The main house designed by Stone has been thoroughly rebuilt.

6. Paul Heyer, *Architects on Architecture: New Directions in America* (New York, 1966), pp. 177–178.

7. "New Statehouse for North Carolina," *Architectural Forum*, CXIX (Dec. 1963), 86–92.

8. Heyer, *Architects on Architecture*, p. 182.

9. Wolf Von Eckardt, *A Place to Live: The Crisis of the Cities* (New York, 1967), pp. 217–218.

10. Ada Louise Huxtable, "Architecture: A Look at the Kennedy Center," *New York Times*, Sept. 7, 1961, sec. i, pp. 1 and 46.

11. For the Burlington Corporate Headquarters, see *Architectural Record*, CLI (Feb. 1972), 118–121.

12. "Blue Cross and Blue Shield," *ibid.*, CLV (May 1974), 134–135.

13. For the Atlanta Hyatt Regency, see John Portman and Jonathan Barnett, *The Architect as Developer* (New York, 1976), pp. 28–32; and "The Rise of Atlanta," *Progressive Architecture*, XLVIII (July 1967), 160–162.

14. For Peachtree Center Plaza Hotel, see Portman and Barnett, *The Architect as Developer*, pp. 36–39 and 148–191; and Jonathan Barnett, "What to Do for an Encore," *Architectural Record*, CLIX (June 1976), 103–110.

15. For the Piazza d'Italia, see *Progressive Architecture*, LVII (Jan. 1976), 82–83; "The Magic Fountain," *ibid.*, LIX (Nov. 1978), 81–87; and *ibid.*, LXI (Jan. 1980), 27. Charles Moore included a chapter, "Southernness: A Regional Dimension," in his and Gerald Allen's book, *Dimensions: Space, Shape & Scale in Architecture* (New York, 1976), pp. 143–156.

16. Philip Johnson made the remark at the 1978 convention of the American Institute of Architects in Dallas, and it was published in the *New York Times*, Dec. 28, 1978, sec. i, p. 17.

17. For an objective account of the controversy concerning the proposed hotel-convention center, see Tom Huth, "Should Charleston Go New South?" *Historic Preservation*, XXXI (July/Aug. 1979), 32–38.

18. The entire issue of the *Architectural Record*, LXXVIII (Dec. 1935), was devoted to the restoration of Williamsburg. See also Carlisle H. Humelsine, "Fifty Years of Colonial Williamsburg," *Antiques*, CX (Dec. 1976), 1267–1291.

19. Frederick Gutheim, ed., *Frank Lloyd Wright on Architecture* (New York, 1941), p. 241.

20. For Old Salem, see Chester Davis, "The Moravians of Salem," *Antiques*,

LXXXVIII (July 1965), 60–64; William J. Murtagh, "The Architecture of Salem," *ibid.*, pp. 69–76; and Ralph P. Hanes, "Old Salem," *ibid.*, p. 99.

21. Sir Charles Lyell, *A Second Visit to the United States of North America*, I (New York, 1849), 231; and Thomas D. Clark, ed., *South Carolina: The Grand Tour, 1780–1865* (Columbia, 1973), pp. 227–228.

22. P. J. Staudenraus, ed., "Occupied Beaufort, 1863: A War Correspondent's View," *South Carolina Historical Magazine*, LXIV (July 1963), 136.

INDEX